Risk and Resilience?

A Qualitative Study in County Wexford of Risk Factors for Young People

Wexford Area Partnership

Research Team
Dr. Niall McElwee, Research Consultant
Sheila McArdle B.Soc.Sc (Hons)
Dave O'Grady BA (Hons)

Wexford Area Partnership Ltd
9 Mallin Street
Cornmarket
Wexford
Ireland

© **Wexford Area Partnership Ltd. 2002**

Printed in Wexford by Impression Print
Cover design by Karen Nolan Design

The paper used in this book is made from wood pulp of managed forests

All rights reserved

No part of this publication may be reproduced, copied or transmitted in any form
or by any means without written permission of the publisher or else under the terms
of any licence permitting limited copying issued by the Copyright Licensing Agency,
The Irish Writer's Centre, Parnell Square, Dublin 1.

ISBN 0-9544698-0-1
A catalogue record for this book is available from the British Library

 in association with
Wexford Community Care, SEHB

 South Eastern Health Board

Acknowledgements

The authors wish to thank the following for their assistance, advice and support in the preparation of this document:

the Project Steering Committee, Wexford Area Partnership (especially Catriona and Sarah-Jane), the SEHB, the CWYARF, the many local committees, organisations and individuals in Wexford, Gorey, Bunclody and Campile, who regrettably we cannot name in order to protect the anonymity of their clients, and, most of all, the young people of County Wexford themselves, to whom this book is dedicated.

We would also like to acknowledge the contribution of Conor Dervan (B.Soc.Sc) to the research.

Sheila McArdle
Dave O'Grady

Risk and Resilience

LIST OF CONTENTS

CHAPTER ONE 9
1.1 Introduction 9
1.2 Aims 10
1.3 Background and Rationale 10
1.4 Contents of Report 12
CHAPTER TWO: YOUTH IN FOCUS – A QUANTITATIVE SPOTLIGHT ON COUNTY WEXFORD 15
2.1 Introduction 15
2.2 Demographics 15
2.2.1 Population Distribution and Dependency in County Wexford 16
2.3 Population Age Breakdown in Research Sample Areas 17
2.3.1 North Region Smaller Urban Area - Gorey 18
2.3.2 South West Region Smaller Rural Area – Campile 18
2.3.3 South Region Larger Urban Area - Wexford Urban 19
2.3.4 North West Region Larger Rural Area - Bunclody 19
2.4 Changes in County Wexford 1991 Census – 1996 Census 20
2.5 Provision of Health Services in County Wexford 20
2.5.1 Age Breakdown in S.E.H.B region 21
2.6 Breakdown of Service Provision in S.E.H.B region 22
2.6.1 Community Care Services 22
2.6.2 General Hospital Service 22
2.6.3 Special Hospitals 22
2.6.4 Health Promotion 23
2.7 Traveller Community in Ireland 23
2.7.1 National Distribution 23
2.7.2 Age Structure of Traveller Community 24
2.7.3 Traveller Health 25
2.8 Other Cultural Minorities in County Wexford 25
2.9 Parenting Alone 26
2.9.1 Lone Parent Household Structure 1996 26
2.9.2 One Parent Family Allowance 28
2.9.3 Births to Teenage Parents 28
2.10 Children in Care 28
2.10.1 Residential Care 29
2.10.2 Foster Care 30
2.11 Disabilities 30

2.12 Substance Misuse 31
2.12.1 Socio-demographic Characteristics and First Treatment 31
2.12.2 Example of Service Provision... 32
2.13. Education and Training 34
2.13.1 Early School Leavers 34
2.13.2 Retention and Attainment Levels 34
2.13.3 Specific Educational Initiatives in County Wexford 36
2.13.4 FÁS Initiatives in County Wexford 37
2.13.5 Community Response 37
2.13.6 Comment on Traveller Education Provision Nationally
        and in County Wexford 38
2.14 Youth Services.. 40
2.14.1 County Wexford Youth Service Provision 40
2.15 Juvenile Crime 41
2.15.1 Types of Offences committed by Juveniles 42
2.15.2 Regional comparisons 42
2.15.3 JLO Participation – Age/Sex... 43
2.15.4 Probation and Welfare Statistics 45
2.15.5 Example of Specific Justice Service Provision in County Wexford 46
2.16 Economics... 46
2.16.1 Unemployment among Young People 47
2.16.2 Long-term Unemployment.. 49
2.16.3 GMS 49
2.16.4 Family Income Supplement 50
2.17 Housing And Accommodation 50
2.17.1 Local Authority Housing... 51
2.17.2 Homelessness 51
2.17.3 Traveller Accommodation 52
2.18 Domestic Violence 54
2.19 Concluding Comment 55

CHAPTER THREE: LITERATURE REVIEW 58
3 Introduction... 58
3.1 Adolescence... 59
3.1.1. Theories of Adolescence 60
3.2 The Risk Society 66
3.3 Young People and Risk 68
3.3.1 Social Influences 71
3.3.2 Health Issues 73
3.3.3 Active Risk Taking... 77

3.4 Resilience 78
3.4.1 The Individual 79
3.4.2 The Family 79
3.4.3 The Wider Community 80
3.5 Irish Legislation on Child Care 83
3.5.1 The Voluntary Sector...83
3.5.2 The Statutory Sector 85
3.6. Inclusion and Participation 87
3.7 Conclusion 89

CHAPTER FOUR: RESEARCH DESIGN AND METHODOLOGY 90
4. Introduction 90
4.1 Research Families 91
4.1.1 Organic Growth of the Project..91
4.2 Ethical Framework 92
4.2.1 Consent...92
4.2.2 Confidentiality..93
4.2.3 Illegality 93
4.2.4 Storage of Information..93
4.2.5 Respect 94
4.2.6 Working with young people under the influence of alcohol, drugs
 or other substances 94
4.2.7 Prevention of Harm..94
4.2.8 Equality Proofing 94
4.3 Boundaries of the Study..94
4.3.1 Application of Markers 95
4.3.2 Engagement Methods...96
4.4 Sampling of Respondents 98
4.4.1 Number of Respondents by Detached Work and Area 99
4.4.2. Number of Respondents by Thematic Entry Points and Area 99
4.5 Data Collection and Design 99
4.5.1 Engagement Strategies...99
4.5.2 Youth Perceptions and Needs..101
4.5.3 Data Collection Tools..102
4.6 Data Management 107
4.6.1 Initial Stage of Data Collection 108
4.6.2 Focus Groups 109
4.7 Bias Proofing...112
4.8 Delimitations 112
4.8.1 Pilot Project..113
4.8.2 Pilot Taped Interview 113
4.8.3 Questionnaires..113

4.8.4 Focus Groups 113
4.8.5 Time Constraints 114
4.8.6 Scale Constraints 114
4.9 Study Trips 114
4.10 Conclusion..115
CHAPTER FIVE: RESEARCH FINDINGS..116
5. Introduction 116
Focus Group Profiles..117
5.1 Risk and Resilience 118
5.1.1 Introduction 118
5.1.2 Risk Findings 118
5.1.3 Resilience Findings 119
5.2 Health Findings 120
5.2.1 Introduction 120
5.2.2 Associated Behaviours 120
5.2.3 Other Health Issues 128
5.2.4 Current Health Services Identified 130
5.2.5 Perceptions of Identified Health Services..131
5.2.6 Development of Health Services 133
5.3 Education..134
5.3.1 Introduction 134
5.3.2 Attitudes to School 134
5.3.3 Social Interaction 134
5.3.4 Examination Year and Non-Examination Year 137
5.3.5 Transition Year, Leaving Certificate Applied and Leaving Certificate
       Vocational Programmes..137
5.3.6 School Size and Identity 138
5.3.7 Extra Curricular Activities and Services with School 139
5.3.8 Future Plans...140
5.3.9 Alternative Education...141
5.4 Youth Services..142
5.4.1 Introduction 142
5.4.2 Awareness...142
5.4.3 Appropriateness of Services...144
5.4.4 Development of Youth Services...147
5.5 Justice 148
5.5.1 Introduction 148
5.5.2 Perceptions of Illegal Activity 148
5.5.3 Knowledge of the Justice System 150
5.5.4 Court Sentences..151
5.5.5 Identified Services..152

5.6 Independence 152
5.6.1 Introduction 152
5.6.2 Family 153
5.6.3 Peer groups 157
5.6.4 Relationships 158
5.6.5 Employment 161
5.7 Culture 163
5.7.1 Introduction 163
5.7.2 Information and Communications Technologies 163
5.7.3 Media 164
5.7.4 Community 166
5.7.5 Different Backgrounds 167
5.7.6 Arts and Leisure Activities 168
5.7.7 Religion 169
5.8 Political Involvement 169
5.8.1 Introduction 169
5.8.2 Perceptions of Current Involvement in Decision-making 169
5.8.3 Decision Making and the Development of Services 171
5.9 Engagement Strategies 172
5.9.1 Introduction 172
5.9.2 Detached Method 172
5.9.3 Thematic Entry Points 176
5.9.4 Informing Practice 178
5.9.5 Researchers' Perspective 179
5. 10 Summary of Findings 180
5.10.1 Risk and Resilience 180
5.10.2 Health 180
5.10.3 Education 181
5.10.4 Youth Services 181
5.10.5 Justice 182
5.10.6 Independence 182
5.10.7 Culture 183
5.10.8 Political Involvement 184
CHAPTER SIX: RESEARCH ANALYSIS 185
6. Introduction 185
6.1 Risk and Resilience Analysis 186
6.1.1 Introduction 186
6.1.2 Risk 186
6.1.3 Young People's Perceptions of Risk 186
6.1.4 Resilience 188
6.2 Health 189

6.2.1 Introduction 189
6.2.2 Associated Behaviours 189
6.2 3 Other Health Issues 193
6.2.5 Perceptions of Current Health Services 194
6.2.6 Awareness of Current Health Services 195
6.2.7 Access 195
6.2.8 Services Suggested by Young People 196
6.3 Education 198
6.3.1 Introduction 198
6.3.2 Attitudes to school 198
6.3.3 Transition Year and Leaving Certificate Vocational Programmes 199
6.3.4 Alternative Education Programmes 199
6.3.5 Third Level Education and Future Plans 200
6.3.6 Extra Curricular Activities 201
6.4 Youth Services 201
6.4.1 Introduction 201
6.4.2 Private Sector Services 201
6.4.3 Community and Voluntary Sector Services 202
6.4.4 Development of services 205
6.4.5 Self-organised activities 205
6.5 Justice 206
6.5.1 Introduction 206
6.5.2 Perceptions of Illegal Activities 206
6.5.3 Knowledge of the Justice System 207
6.6 Independence 209
6.6.1 Introduction 209
6.6.2 Family 209
6.6.3 Peer Groups 210
6.6.4 Relationships 211
6.6.5 Employment 212
6.7 Cultural Needs 213
6.7.1 Introduction 213
6.7.2 Information & Communications Technologies (ICTs) 213
6.7.3 Media 214
6.7.4 Community 215
6.7.5 Different Backgrounds 216
6.7.6 Creative and Leisure Activities 217
6.8 Political Involvement- Participation and Decision Making 218
6.8.1 Introduction 218
6.8.2 Perception of Involvement in Decision-Making 218
6.8.3 Political Parties and Elections 219

6.8.4 Development of Participation Strategies to Involve Young People 219
6.9 Engagement Strategies..220
CHAPTER SEVEN: RESEARCH CONCLUSIONS..222
7. Introduction..222
7.1 Risk and Resilience..222
7.2 Health 224
7.3 Education...227
7.4 Youth Services...229
7.5 Justice..230
7.6 Independence...231
7.7 Culture...233
7.8 Political Involvement...234
7.9 Engagement Strategies...235
7.10 Overall Conclusion 236
CHAPTER EIGHT: RECOMMENDATIONS 239
8 Introduction...239
8.1 Risk and Resilience..239
8.2 Health 239
8.2.1 Organisation 239
8.2.2 Information...239
8.2.3 Support Services Identified by Young People 240
8.3 Education...240
8.4 Youth Services...241
8. 5 Justice...241
8.6 Independence...241
8.7 Culture...242
8.7.1 Technologies...242
8.7.2 Critical Analysis...242
8.7.3 Creative Activities..242
8.8 Political Involvement...242
8.9 Engagement Strategies...242
CHAPTER NINE: PILOT PROJECT...243
9. Introduction..243
9.1 The Youth Connector Model..243
9.1.1 Aims 243
9.1.2 Objectives...244
9.1.3 Ethical Considerations 245
9.1.4 Structure of the Youth Connector Model...245
9.1.5 The Integration Team 247
9.1.6 Underpinning Principles 250

9.2 Mobile Youth Unit 251
9.2.1 Mobile Unit 251
9.2.2 Meeting Identified Needs...252
9.2.3 Aims 255
9.2.4 Objectives..255
9.2.5 Local Area Management Team 255
9.2.6 Structure of Integration Team 255
9.2.7 Mobile Unit Youth Workers..255
9.3 The Triune Youth Model 257
9.3.1 The Vision 257
9.3.2 The Approach 257
9.3.3 The Youth Connectors (3 workers)..257
9.3.4 Youth Workers – Mobile Unit (3 workers) 258
9.3.5 Youth Mentor with Specific Skills (1 worker)..................................259
9.3.6 The Team 260
9.4 Conclusions...262

Appendix One	Project Steering Group members 263
Appendix Two	CWYARF members..264
Appendix Three	Map of Co.Wexford...265
Appendix Four	Letter of Introduction 266
Appendix Five	Extract from Field Notes 267
Appendix Six	Data Matrix Risk 268
Appendix Seven	Data Matrix Health 269
Appendix Eight	Data Matrix Education 276
Appendix Nine	Data Matrix Youth Services 279
Appendix Ten	Data Matrix Justice...284
Appendix Eleven	Data Matrix Independence 287
Appendix Twelve	Data Matrix Culture..294
Appendix Thirteen	Data Matrix Political Involvement......................................297
Appendix Fourteen	Focus Group Questions 299
BIBLIOGRAPHY	300

Chapter One
Introduction and Rationale

1.1 Introduction

This report is the result of a twelve month research project that involved two researchers contacting a total of 290 young people aged between 9 and 18 from across County Wexford, and recording their views on services and supports relevant to them. The purpose of the research was fourfold;

- to ascertain young people's perceptions of the supports available to them within their environment;
- to facilitate them in exploring the issues they considered relevant to their lives;
- to identify their needs;
- to recommend to Service Providers how best to respond to those needs.

Simultaneously, the researchers were to investigate what engagement strategies were most useful when working with young people 'at risk'. But to be 'at risk' can mean different things to different people. Service providers, when working with young people 'at risk', often tend to prioritise a single characteristic or specific risk factor; for example, the Juvenile Justice System focuses on Crime Diversion Programmes involving juvenile offenders, while the Education System concentrates on Stay-in-School initiatives. Although Service Providers acknowledge that some young people are more 'at risk' than others, rarely do agencies or organisations appear to adopt an array of interventions in attempting to meet the wide range of possible needs of vulnerable young people, and even more rarely do they embrace a resiliency perspective.

The recent government report *Youth as a Resource – Promoting the Health of Young People at Risk* (Department of Health and Children, 1999) offers a list of key characteristics generally recognised by agencies and youth organisations as identifying a young person who may be 'at risk'. These include:

- Being involved in criminal behaviour
- Being "in care"
- Living in poverty and/or poor quality housing
- Having a history of family problems or abuse
- Having a learning or physical disability
- Having psychological or behavioural problems
- Working in prostitution
- Having academic problems and/or bad experiences of school

- Having mental health problems
- Being out of home
- Having a crisis pregnancy at an early age
- Experiencing discrimination due to sexual orientation, race or ethnicity
- Being from a family with a history of substance misuse
- Living in a geographically isolated area (ibid.)

After considerable discussion, the Steering Committee of this project (see Appendix 2) agreed to the following definition of being 'at risk' for the purpose of the study:

> *"Youth are seen as being at risk when there is a significant mismatch between their needs and the supports currently available to them in their environments."*

But young people themselves may not acknowledge or recognise 'risk' in the same way that adults, agencies and organisations do. Differences in perspective between young people and service providers on what actually constitutes 'risk' may result in just such a mismatch of needs and available supports. So from the outset, principles of equality and participation were applied to the research process to ensure that the participants should be facilitated to identify risk from their own perspective at every stage.

The research question was therefore expressed as follows:

> *"An investigation of the perception by young people variously defined as 'at risk' of how their needs are to be best met, and the development of appropriate engagement strategies and model(s) of practice".*

From this formula, the following aims were established:

1.2 Aims

- To provide quantitative data regarding youth populations and current statutory and voluntary services available to them;
- To investigate what strategies are useful when attempting to engage with youth 'at risk';
- To gain an in-depth qualitative understanding of young people's perceptions of current supports available to them within their environment;
- To provide information to develop models of practice to best meet the needs of young people 'at risk'.

1.3 Background and Rationale

In May 2000, a conference organised by Youth New Ross and New Ross Travellers' Youth Club focused on groups of young people who the organisers felt were currently being excluded from current services. The groups surveyed by the conference included gay, lesbian and bi-sexual youth, young asylum seekers and refugees, young Travellers and young people whose behaviours presented problems to the organisations working with them.

Subsequent to the conference, a meeting was convened of Youth and Community groups, facilitated by the South Eastern Health Board (SEHB). This forum evolved into the Collaborative Group (see Appendix 1). The purpose of this first meeting was to identify young people from Co. Wexford who the participants considered to be 'at risk', and to outline possible responses to meet their needs.

The Collaborative Group, later renamed the County Wexford Youth At Risk Forum (CWYARF) (see Appendix 1), identified the target group for the research as displaying the following characteristics:

- Those most excluded with few or no resources to support them;
- Those who were emotionally disturbed;
- Those with a history of family distress (e.g. domestic violence, abuse, alcoholism);
- Those involved in illegal activity (e.g. petty larceny, drugs, prostitution);
- The homeless or semi-homeless;
- Those with a poor school attendance record;
- Those exhibiting behavioural problems (e.g. depression, self-mutilation, self-destructive behaviours, attempts at suicide);
- Those aged between 9 and 18 years.

The CWYARF decided to first conduct research into the target group, as representatives of both the voluntary and statutory service providers acknowledged that there was a perceived lack of accurate information among their organisations on the young people they considered to be "at risk".

The CWYARF entered discussion with the Wexford Community Care Section of the SEHB which had funds available both to conduct similar research and to establish a pilot project in this area. The administration of the proposed project was discussed with the Wexford Area Partnership (WAP) and the County Wexford Partnership (CWP). The Wexford Area Partnership agreed to manage the project, and a contract was drawn up and agreed between the SEHB and WAP on the 9th of March, 2001.

WAP convened a Research Steering Group (see Appendix 2) that included representatives of the CWYARF and service providers, in order that the research would proceed on a genuinely collaborative basis. The remit of the Steering Group was to function as a primary filter, to monitor the progress of the research, and to resolve ethical issues that might arise during the project.

From the beginning, the service providers acknowledged that many young people who could be regarded as 'at risk' according to a variety of accepted criteria, did not avail of their services. In order to consider ways of more effectively meeting the needs of these young people, it would first be necessary to consult with them, to gain an understanding of their perceptions and attitudes regarding current services, and to identify their needs. In addition such a process could provide information on the types of service that these young people themselves would prefer to use.

This proposed approach contrasts with the more conventional method which tends to rely on inputs from 'experts', and on research conducted with adults rather than with young people themselves. Its justification was that any identification of a possible "mismatch" between identified needs and current support provision could lead to the development and delivery of services more appropriate to the needs of those most 'at risk'.

This approach is also in keeping with The National Children's Strategy (Irish Government, 2000: p30) which advocates participation by young people in structures and processes that affect them. Its Three National Goals reflect the basic rationale of this project:

- "Children will have a voice in matters that affect them and their views will be given due weight in accordance with their age and maturity.
- "Children's lives will be better understood; their lives will benefit from evaluation, research and information on their needs, rights and the effectiveness of services.
- "Children will receive quality supports and services to promote all aspects of their development."

1.4 Contents of Report

The remaining chapters are presented under the following headings

- Chapter Two   –   Quantitative Spotlight on Wexford
- Chapter Three   –   Literature Review
- Chapter Four   –   Research Methodology
- Chapter Five   –   Research Findings
- Chapter Six   –   Research Analysis
- Chapter Seven   –   Conclusions
- Chapter Eight   –   Recommendations
- Chapter Nine   –   Pilot Project

Chapter Two – Quantitative Spotlight on Wexford

This section of the report views the demographic characteristics of County Wexford, with particular emphasis on social indicators that influence the environment of young people living within the county. It is intended that this statistical analysis will provide a context for the qualitative fieldwork and subsequent analysis of the report proper. In general, national statistics are first presented, followed by figures specific to County Wexford. Selected examples of service provision and associated client uptake are also discussed.

Chapter Three – Literature Review

This chapter is presented in six sections. Initially it traces the evolution of a holistic and ecological view of adolescence, linking individual, family, community and environmental factors. The second and third sections consider the concept of risk as applied to (post)modern society and to the lives of young people respectively. Risk behaviours associated with adolescent culture in Ireland are identified and explored. The fourth section provides a brief outline of the theory of resilience which identifies characteristics that appear to enable some young people to overcome adversity. This theory is developed to incorporate the idea of building resilient qualities within families and local communities. The fifth section outlines the development of Irish legislation on Child Care from the beginning of the twentieth century to the present day. The final section argues for inclusion and participation as key principles in working with young people in order to empower them to take charge of their own lives.

Chapter Four – Research Methodology

This chapter first outlines various research approaches, and explains the method adopted by the Steering Group to reflect the underpinning principles of participation and equality. The agreed ethical and good practice guidelines are detailed, together with the defined study boundaries and procedures for the collection, management and analysis of the research data.

An initial pilot project and pilot interview were undertaken prior to commencing full data collection. A description of these is followed by an analysis of issues of time-scale, budget, resources and generalisability of the research findings. Study visits which occurred throughout the research process are also explained. These were seen as a method of gaining local knowledge and information to assist in planning and supporting the research.

The chapter concludes with a description of the Bias-Proofing exercise undertaken when the field work was completed, which involved both young people and representatives of the service providers. Its purpose was primarily to validate the researchers' findings and to ensure that the participants' opinions and perceptions had not been lost or distorted in the subsequent analysis. Any significant gaps in the findings could also be highlighted. The exercise concluded with an exchange of ideas on the development and delivery of new services as suggested in the findings and analysis. This discussion assisted in the subsequent drafting of the Recommendations section of the overall report.

Chapter Five – Findings

The data collected through the research process was organised and arranged using a thematic framework incorporating nine interconnecting subsections. This chapter is arranged

as follows:
- Risk and Resilience
- Health
- Education
- Youth Services
- Justice
- Independence
- Culture
- Political Involvement
- Engagement Strategies

Chapter Six – Analysis

The research Analysis reflects on the implications of the Findings presented in Chapter Five, and under the same headings.

Chapter Seven – Conclusion

The key concepts of the Findings and Analysis of each section are drawn together, to provide a basis for the development of the Recommendations. The overall conclusion emphasises the need to avoid viewing sections in isolation, but rather in a holistic framework that reflects the interconnectedness of those issues and circumstances that influence the lives of young people 'at risk'.

Chapter Eight – Recommendations

Recommendations are offered for each of the sections provided in Chapter Five for consideration by the various Service Providers.

Chapter Nine – Pilot Project

Three pilot projects are presented for consideration. These proposed services reflect the research findings that models of practice need to incorporate a range of different sectors in a flexible form to best meet the needs of young people at risk.

Appendices and Bibliography

Chapter Two

Youth in Focus – A Quantitative Spotlight on County Wexford

Ashling Duggan Jackson, M.A.
Niall C. McElwee, PhD.
SocSci Consultancy

2.1 Introduction

This section of the report views aspects of demographic data considered as a backdrop to the qualitative fieldwork and subsequent analysis discussed in this report. It assesses characteristics of County Wexford with a particular emphasis on social indicators affecting youth living within the county. Where available, national statistics are first presented, followed by those specific to County Wexford. Selected examples of service provision and associated client uptake are also discussed.

Historically Wexford has been economically successful and prosperous. The recent decision by PFPC to establish in Wexford is evidence of Wexford's continuing attractiveness as a business location, and complements the existing industrial base throughout the county. However, statistics indicate that it is the poorest county in Ireland in terms of income per head, is home to just 14 of the country's 1,000 largest firms, and relies heavily on businesses located in "old economy" areas. Farming in Wexford, meanwhile, is relatively strong with large farms producing milk, crops and meat. However, farm incomes are small and increasingly have to be supplemented from elsewhere. International agreements both constrain the potential for increased production and are likely to reduce prices. And above all, farming is failing to attract and/or retain young people. With regard to tourism Wexford attracts less than 5% of Ireland's overseas visitors, and generates less than 2% of the country's overseas tourism revenue.

2.2 Demographics

Table 2.1 Comparison of Population Changes in County Wexford and Ireland

Year	Wexford	Ireland
1961	83,259	2,814,703
1971	86,351	2,978,248
1981	99,081	3,443,405
1991	102,069	3,525,719
1996	104,371	3,626,087
% Change 61-96	25.4	28.8
% Change 81-96	5.3	5.3

The table above shows that national changes in population in the years 1961-1996 have been very similar to County Wexford's, and exactly the same in the shorter time span 1981-1996. However, significant differences are present in the age structure of the population of County Wexford when compared to national trends. These are looked at in more detail in the section below.

2.2.1 Population Distribution and Dependency in County Wexford

2.2.1.1. Age Profile

In order to ascertain population distribution in Ireland, and specifically in County Wexford, 1996 Census figures are used as more recent Census figures are not yet available.

Table 2.2 Population of Ireland and Age Distribution

Age Group	Males	Females	Total	Percent
0-14	441,452	417,972	859,424	23.7%
15-19	173,950	165,586	339,536	9.4%
20-24	149,143	144,211	293,354	8.1%
25-44	503,302	512,789	1,016,091	28.1%
45-54	208,634	203,413	412,047	11.3%
55-59	77,809	75,998	153,807	4.2%
60-64	68,690	69,256	137,946	3.8%
65 years and over	177,252	236,630	413,882	11.4%
Total	1,800,232	1,825,855	3,626,087	100%

The above table shows that some 41.2% of the Irish population are 24 years or under, according to the 1996 Census, with 23.7% of the population being 0-14 years, 9.4% of the population being 15-19 years and 8.1% of the population being 20-24 years. Although children aged from 0 to 14 currently make up nearly 24% of the population in the State, this is down from 29% in 1986. In urban areas the figure in 1996 was 23%, and 25% for rural areas.

The young dependency ratio, which is derived by expressing the population aged 0-14 as a percentage of the population of those of working age (15-64 years), peaked at over 50% in the 1970s. However, it has since been in decline, reaching a low of 37% in 1996.

The total population of County Wexford in 1996 was 104,371 persons. This represents an increase of 2.3% between 1991 and 1996, and reflects national trends for that period. However differences in age structure are revealed when compared with the rest of the country, as demonstrated in Table 2.3.

Table 2.3 Population of Wexford and Age Distribution

Age Group	Males	Females	Total	Percent
0-14	13,224	12,660	25,884	24.7%
15-19	5,030	4,814	9,844	9.4%
20-24	3,885	3,382	7,267	6.9%
25-44	14,250	14,009	28,259	27%
45-54	6,209	5,897	1,2106	11.5%
55-59	2,400	2,279	4,679	4.4%
60-64	2,135	2,119	4,254	4%
65 years and over	5,299	6,779	12,078	11.5%
Total	52,432	51,939	104,371	100%

(1996 Census, CSO)

There is a higher dependency in Wexford in the 0-14 year age group and the 65+ age group than in the national averages. Some 23.7% of the national population are 0-14 years, whereas in County Wexford 24.7% of the county population are in the 0-14 year age group. With this rate of dependency being greater that the national average, one can assume a higher dependency on relevant social services than one might find nationally.

2.3 Population Age Breakdown in Research Sample Areas

Having established that age dependency in the under 15 years age group in County Wexford is higher than the national average, it is also necessary to look specifically at spatial distribution of youth in the sample research areas selected for this study, in order to assess similarities/differences with county/national averages.

2.3.1 North Region Smaller Urban Area - Gorey

Figure 2.1 Population Age Breakdown in Gorey Area

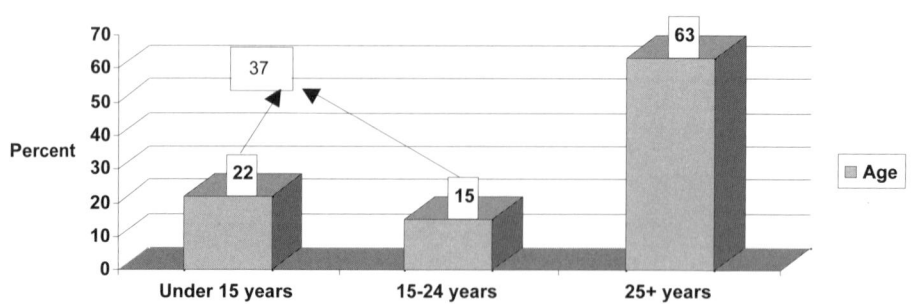

(Adapted from 1996 Census, CSO)

The above bar-chart (Figure 2.1) shows that some 37% of people living in the Gorey area are 24 years or under, with some 22% being under 15 years. In this designated research area, the latter figure is lower than the county and national average.

2.3.2. South West Region Smaller Rural Area – Campile

Figure 2.2 Population Age Breakdown in Campile Area

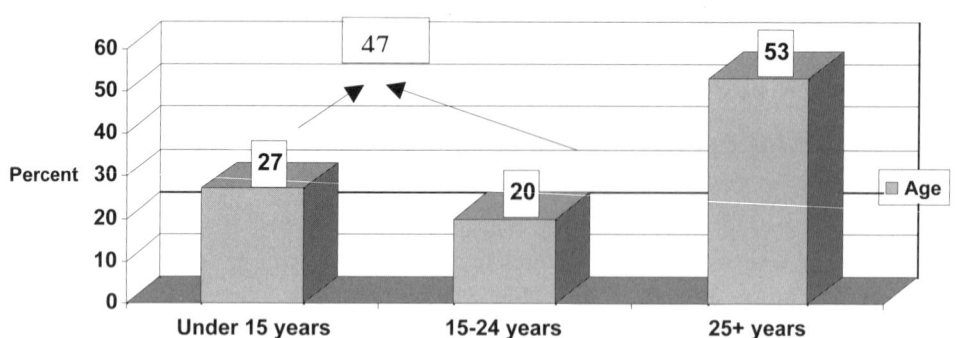

(Adapted from 1996 Census, CSO)

It can seen from the above bar-chart (Figure 2.2) that nearly half of the local population in Campile, i.e. 47%, are 24 years or younger with 27% being under 15 years. In this instance the population aged under 15 years is higher than the county and national average.

2.3.3. South Region Larger Urban Area - Wexford Urban

Figure 2.3 Population Age Breakdown in Wexford Urban Area

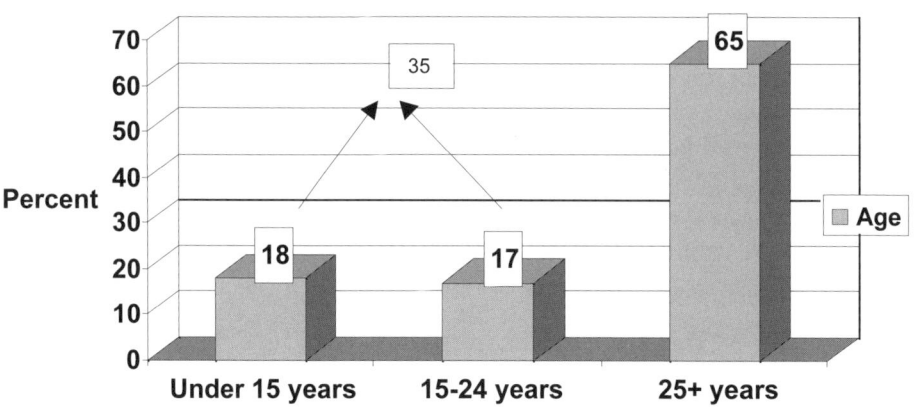

(Adapted from 1996 Census, CSO)

In the large urban area of Wexford (Figure 2.3), 65% of people are 25 years and over, while 18% are under 15 years and 17% are aged 15-24 years. The county and national population figures for the under 15 year age group (25% and 24%) are higher than the corresponding figure in Wexford Urban.

2.3.4. North West Region Larger Rural Area - Bunclody

Figure 2.4 Population Age Breakdown in Bunclody Area

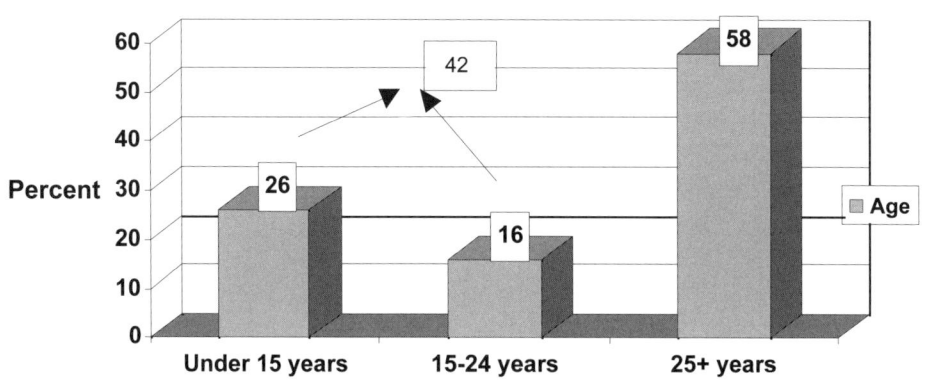

(Adapted from 1996 Census, CSO)

Interestingly, 42% of the population in this area (Figure 2.4) is 24 years or younger, with 58% of the local population being 25 old or more. In Bunclody the local population aged under 15 years is higher than the county and national averages of 25% and 24% respectively.

2.4 Changes in County Wexford 1991 Census – 1996 Census

While the total population of County Wexford increased in the period 1991-1996, parts of the county experienced population decline. Growth was predominantly concentrated in eastern and south-eastern areas, in coastal areas and in proximity to the main towns, particularly Wexford and Gorey. In 1996, 68% of the population lived in rural areas, i.e. outside Aggregate Town Areas. During the period from 1991 to 1996, the rate of population increase was greater in rural areas than in urban centres. The share of population accounted for by urban centres fell, while that of the environs of the towns of Wexford, Enniscorthy, New Ross and Gorey continued to rise. The main urban centres within the county are Wexford, New Ross, Gorey and Enniscorthy. Wexford is the largest, accounting for 31 % of the population. Wexford town has a population of some 15,400, just over twice the size of Enniscorthy, the next largest town within the County.

2.5 Provision of Health Services in County Wexford

The South Eastern Health Board is responsible for provision of health services in County Wexford. The Board's remit includes service provision to counties Carlow, Kilkenny, Tipperary South, Waterford and Wexford.

However when one looks at population distribution in the South Eastern Health Board area, it is evident that the largest population concentration is in County Wexford, i.e. 104,314 persons (Table 2.4).

Table 2.4 Population for the South Eastern Health Board Region

County	Population
Carlow	41,616
Kilkenny	75,155
Wexford	104,314
Waterford	94,597
South Tipperary	75,364
TOTAL	391,046

(Adapted from 1996 Census, CSO)

The South Eastern Health Board also has a relatively large number of urban centres within its region. The five major urban centres, all with populations of over 10,000 people, are Carlow, Clonmel, Kilkenny, Waterford and Wexford.

2.5.1 Age Breakdown in S.E.H.B region

Approximately 44% of the population is under 25 years of age, 28% is under 15 years and 12% is over 64 years. This is very similar to the national population profile. (1996 Census, CSO).

Figure 2.5 Trends in Population aged 0 – 14 years in each county of S.E.H.B. region

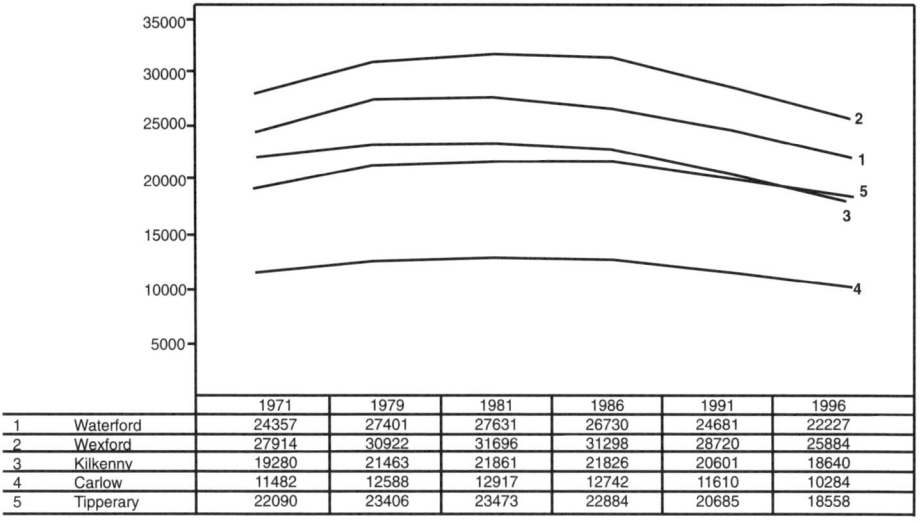

		1971	1979	1981	1986	1991	1996
1	Waterford	24357	27401	27631	26730	24681	22227
2	Wexford	27914	30922	31696	31298	28720	25884
3	Kilkenny	19280	21463	21861	21826	20601	18640
4	Carlow	11482	12588	12917	12742	11610	10284
5	Tipperary	22090	23406	23473	22884	20685	18558

(http://www.sehb.ie/publications/health/demo.html)

Despite an increase in the 1980's, the population of 0-14 year olds in the south east has fallen in the 25 years from 1971 to 1996 by 9%. This fall is greatest in South Tipperary (16%) and least in Kilkenny and Wexford (3% and 7% respectively).

Growth in population of the 14 – 44 year age group in the south east has increased by 46% over the past 25 years. The percentage increase is greatest in Carlow (54%) and least in South Tipperary (35%).

Figure 2.6 Trends in Population aged 14-44 years in each county of S.E.H.B. region

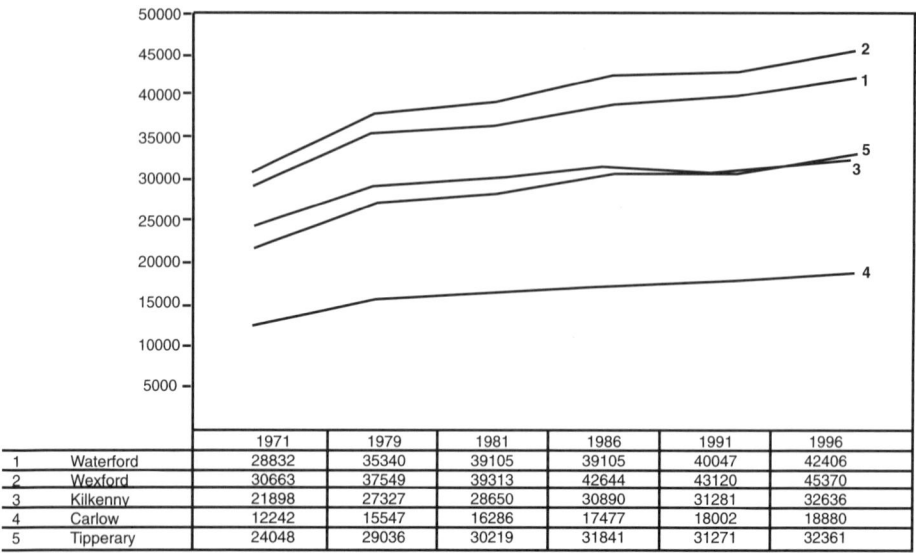

		1971	1979	1981	1986	1991	1996
1	Waterford	28832	35340	39105	39105	40047	42406
2	Wexford	30663	37549	39313	42644	43120	45370
3	Kilkenny	21898	27327	28650	30890	31281	32636
4	Carlow	12242	15547	16286	17477	18002	18880
5	Tipperary	24048	29036	30219	31841	31271	32361

http://www.sehb.ie/publications/health/demo.html

2.6 Breakdown of Service Provision in S.E.H.B region

Health Service provision is catered for under four types of Services:

2.6.1 Community Care Services

This covers the preventive health services, general practitioner services, public health nursing, health inspection, welfare and social work services, care of the aged, welfare homes, and services for the disabled. Community care services are divided into four geographical areas. These are Wexford, Waterford, South Tipperary and the combined counties of Carlow and Kilkenny. Each area has its own administrative headquarters. These are based in Clonmel, Kilkenny, Waterford City and Wexford.

2.6.2 General Hospital Service

The Board has a regional hospital at Waterford city and acute hospitals at Wexford and Kilkenny. The Acute Hospital service in South Tipperary, at present based in Cashel and Clonmel, is to be amalgamated on one site in Clonmel. There is a regional orthopaedic hospital based at Kilcreene in Kilkenny city. Six district hospitals are managed under the General Hospital Services, as is the regional ambulance service.

2.6.3 Special Hospitals

Special Hospital Services are responsible for the provision of psychiatric and geriatric services in the region. The psychiatric service is delivered at community level by sector teams, and at hospital level by five county-based hospitals. Hospital services for the elderly are provided for by special hospitals, as are services for persons with disabilities. There are seven geriatric hospitals in the South East region. The Board's three welfare homes are also managed within the Special Hospital Services.

2.6.4 Health Promotion

Health Promotion is an integral part of the services provided by the South Eastern Health Board, and the Health Education Unit was established in 1987 with an initial remit to implement health education in schools. The expansion to a regional Health Promotion Centre in 1993 broadened the service to include health services, and community and workplace initiatives.

Its functions include:

- Co-ordination of Health Promotion initiatives in the SEHB.
- Identification of health promotion priorities and the planning of appropriate interventions.
- Provision of training for professionals and community groups on health topics and skills development.
- Provision of advice and consultancy to professional and community groups in the development of health promotion initiatives.
- Dissemination of health information and resources throughout the SEHB.

(http://www.sehb.ie/services/)

2.7 Traveller Community in Ireland

2.7.1 National Distribution

There are approximately 4,790 Traveller families, or an estimated 25,000 Travellers in Ireland. This constitutes approximately 0.5% of the total national population. (National Traveller Accommodation Consultative Committee Report, 1999)

2.7.1.1 Distribution in County Wexford

In 1998, 313 Traveller families were recorded as living in County Wexford. These figures, at best an estimate given the transient nature of the Traveller population, represent 1.5% of the total population. What is also significant here is that these figures rank County Wexford as having the third-highest Traveller population in Ireland, being surpassed only by County Galway and County Tipperary. (Action Plan, County Wexford Partnership, 2001).

2.7.2 Age Structure of Traveller Community

Table 2.5 National Age Structure of the Traveller Community, 1996

Age group	Travellers		Total Population	
	Number	Percentage	Number	Percentage
0-14	5,454	**50.1%**	859,424	**23.7%**
15-64	5,290	**48.6%**	2,352,781	**64.9%**
65+	147	**1.3%**	413,882	**11.4%**
Total	10,891	**100.0%**	3,626,087	**100.0%**

(1996 Census, CSO)

Probably one of the very distinctive features of the Traveller Community in Ireland is its markedly different age structure to that of the settled population. Differences in age structure are especially marked in both the 0-14 year age group and the 65+ age group. Some 23.7% of the settled population are aged 0-14 years while this rises to just over half of the total traveller population i.e. 50.1%. Only 1.3% of Travellers are over 56 years old, while 11.4% of the settled population are in this age group.

2.7.2.1 County Wexford Age Structure

The South Eastern Health Board Annual Report 1999 indicates that 370 Traveller families live within the county. This shows an increase from the 1998 figure cited above. The chart below (Figure 2.7) shows that the majority of these are children, i.e. under 18 years of age.

Figure 2.7 Breakdown of Children/Adults in Traveller Population County Wexford, 1999

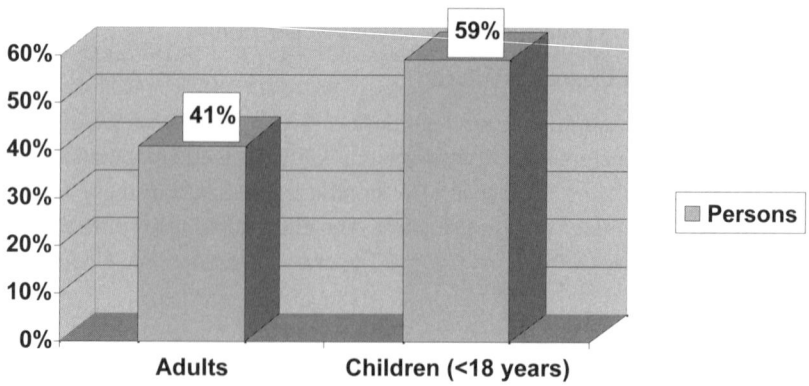

(Adapted from SEHB Annual Report, South Eastern Health Board, 1999, p19).

2.7.3 Traveller Health

The most recent national information on Traveller Health was gathered by the Task Force for the Travelling Community (1995). These data shows little differences in health statistics from the Barry et al (1991) report, despite a 4-year gap. It found the following with regard to housing and facilities available to Travellers families:

- 34% of respondents were in standard housing
- 20% had no toilet facilities
- 27% had only a shared cold water supply
- 32% had no electricity
- 40% had no bath or shower
- 18% had no refuse collection
- 47% had no access to a telephone.

Recent research by Wexford Area Council, sponsored by the Wexford Area Partnership Traveller Accommodation Programme 2000-2004, shows exceptionally low participation by Travellers in education, training and employment, and poor health and accommodation conditions. Some of the key findings of this research relevant to the Wexford area are as follows:

- Only 2.9% of Traveller children in the relevant age group were attending school in 1997.
- 41% of Traveller families had one or more members with a long-term illness or disability.
- None of the Travellers surveyed were employed at the time of the survey.
- No Traveller contacted has accessed a job as a result of a training course.
- There was a generally low uptake by Travellers of health services available, especially for antenatal/ postnatal clinics and vaccination services.

2.8 Other Cultural Minorities in County Wexford

In Wexford 459 Asylum Seekers have been given accommodation, the majority in Hillcrest (Wexford Town) and Rosbercon (New Ross). Of this total, 156 are dependent children (i.e. under 18 years). This means that among the Asylum Seeker community there is a dependency ratio of 2:1 between adults and children. (Wexford Community Development Board, 2000, p7). The Department of Justice Equality and Law Reform has recorded that 79% of the Asylum Seeker population in Ireland is under the age of 35. Consequently childbirth issues are to the fore among asylum-seeking women. Furthermore, around 20% of asylum seekers are under the age of 17. In Wexford there are 156 children seeking asylum, which is closer to 30% of the total population of this group. (Wexford Community Development Board, 2000, p8).

2.9 Parenting Alone

In order to obtain an accurate picture of parenting alone in County Wexford it is proposed here to look at the national & county figures for lone parent households, and at recent national & county figures for those in receipt of lone parent type payments in the Republic of Ireland.

2.9.1 Lone Parent Household Structure 1996

Table 2.6 Lone Parent Household Structure 1996

	WAP Area	County	National
Lone Parents (all children)	9.5%	9.7%	10.1%
Lone Parents (all children<15)	4.1%	3.5%	3.5%
Lone Parents (at least 1 child<15)	5.7%	5.0%	5.0%

(Social Inclusion Plan for Wexford Area 2000-2004, Wexford Area Partnership, 2000, p12)

Table 2.6 above shows clearly that the percentage of lone parents in County Wexford (9.7%) was lower than the national average of 10.1%. The most recent figures (end of 2001) available on lone parenting in Ireland as compiled by the Pension Services Office, Department of Social Community and Family Affairs, indicate a decrease in lone parents in County Wexford since 1996. However when one engages in a comparison by county, Wexford still ranks very high (Table 2.7).

2.9.1.1 Comparison of National and Wexford Figures for Lone Parent Households

County Wexford ranks as the 6th highest county in Ireland with regard to numbers of lone parents. Over a third of all lone parents in Ireland are based in Dublin with 3.6% of lone parents living in County Wexford. County Leitrim had the lowest number of lone parents in residence at the end of 2001.

An overwhelming majority of lone parents in County Wexford are female (i.e. 97.5%), with the remaining 2.5% being male (Table 2.7).

Table 2.7 Irish Lone Parents Statistics, Year End 2001

County	Female	Male	Total	Percent
Dublin	33,505	508	43,012	37.3%
Cork	8,774	237	9,011	9.8%
Limerick	4,066	116	4,182	4.6%
Galway	3,545	93	3,638	4.0%
Kildare	3,218	45	3,263	3.6%
Wexford	**3,187**	**79**	**3,266**	**3.6%**
Louth	3,165	57	3,222	3.5%
Donegal	3,033	86	3,119	3.4%
Wicklow	2,999	43	3,042	3.3%
Tipperary	2,791	94	2,885	3.2%
Waterford	2,706	57	2,763	3.0%
Kerry	2,267	55	2,322	2.5%
Meath	2,085	41	2,126	2.3%
Clare	1,768	65	1,833	2.0%
Mayo	1,756	69	1,825	1.9%
Westmeath	1,578	37	1,615	1.8%
Kilkenny	1,239	39	1,278	1.4%
Carlow	1,187	21	1,208	1.3%
Offaly	1,183	21	1,204	1.3%
Sligo	1,087	38	1,125	1.2%
Monaghan	926	43	969	1.0%
Laoise	938	23	961	1.0%
Cavan	794	28	822	0.9%
Longford	677	21	698	0.8%
Roscommon	602	29	631	0.7%
Leitrim	305	19	324	0.3%
Total	89,374	1,964	91,338	100%

(Department of Social, Community and Family Affairs, 2001)

(Department of Social, Community and Family Affairs, 2001)

2.9.2 One Parent Family Allowance

The number of One Parent Family Allowance payments in Wexford increased by 50% between 1995 and 1999; the national trend showed a rise of 37% for the same period.

2.9.3 Births to Teenage Parents

> "Ireland has the tenth highest teenage birth-rate in the developed world, according to a UN survey of the 28 richest countries. The study, by the United Nations Children's Fund (UNICEF), showed that 18 girls out of every 1,000 aged between 15 and 19, gave birth in 1998."
>
> (Shanahan, The Irish Examiner, 2002)

The Wexford rate of births to single mothers is slightly ahead of both the national average and the SEHB average, though it is not the highest in the South East. Approximately 97% of teen pregnancies are to unmarried mothers in the area.

A national conference on this issue in 2001 by Waterford Students Mothers Group, "In The Spotlight", was devised to act as a forum for the issues and needs surrounding teenage mothers throughout the country. It was attended by over 150 delegates from the voluntary and statutory sector, as well as by many teenage mothers, and concluded with the drawing up of recommendations towards the formulation of a state policy on teenage pregnancy.

Foremost amongst these proposals was the provision, for those young mothers who wish to continue with their education, of childcare facilities, accommodation and possible financial aid for grinds, etc. The conference was told that the absence of child care support, the time demands of combining school with motherhood, and the lack of recognition of the particular needs of the teenage mother within mainstream education were the main reasons why young teenage mothers opted out of school.

2.10 Children in Care

There are two main types of alternative care provided in the South Eastern Health Board region for children who cannot for whatever reason continue to live in their family home: residential care and foster care.

2.10.1 Residential Care

Figure 2.8 Type of Care Provided in Statutory Children's Residential Centres by Health Boards

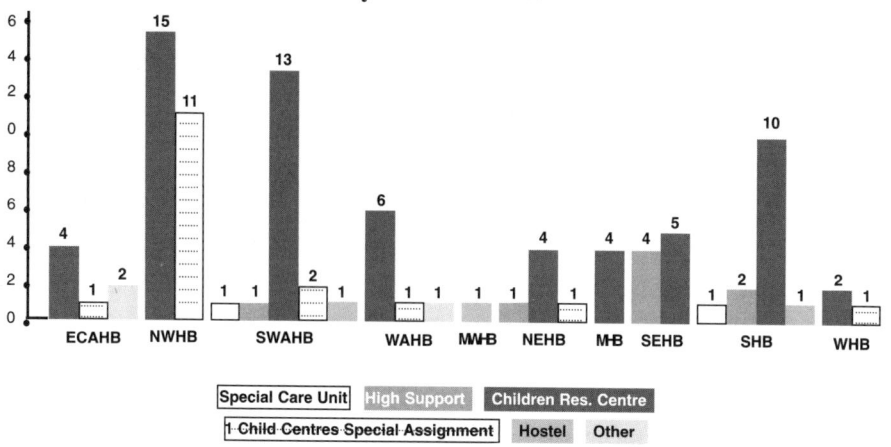

N.B. Other - After care or mother & baby home with facilities for young people in care under 18
S.H.B. includes 1 assessment centre.

(Irish Social Services Inspectorate Report, p13)

It can be seen from the above bar chart (Figure 2.8) that four high support units and five residential centres are provided by the South Eastern Health Board.

Figure 2.9 Numbers in Residential Care in S.E.H.B. Area

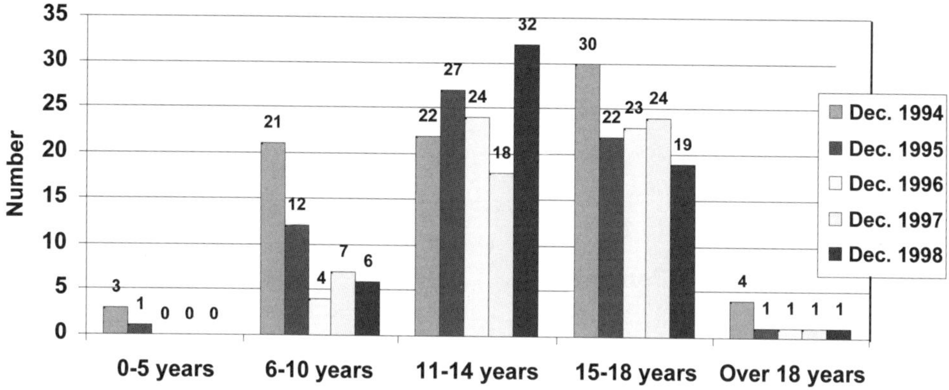

(S.E.H.B., 1999, p50)

Overall numbers in residential care have decreased between 1994 and 1998. This information reflects the regional trends in residential care in the S.E.H.B. The current figure for numbers in residential care in County Wexford is 20, the vast majority of whom are in the 12-17 year age group. (Figure supplied by S.E.H.B., July 2002).

2.10.2 Foster Care

In the Wexford administrative area the number of children in foster care has increased from 74 in 1994 to 112 in 1998 (S.E.H.B., 1999, p47). A general increase is also evident in the other administrative areas within the South Eastern Health Board, with 140 in total in foster care in County Wexford, including those being cared for by relatives (Figure supplied by S.E.H.B., July 2002).

2.11 Disabilities

An exact figure for the prevalence of disability (learning/physical/sensory) is difficult to ascertain for County Wexford. The Commission for the Status of People with Disabilities assumes that 10% of the population will have disabilities of different kinds. Thus it can be estimated that the number of people with disabilities in County Wexford is somewhere in the region of 10,400.

However, this assumes a very broad definition of disability including profound, chronic, moderate and mild disabilities. In Wexford there are 914 people with learning disabilities which are categorised on the following bar-chart. (Figure 2.10)

Figure 2.10 Categories of Learning Disability in County Wexford

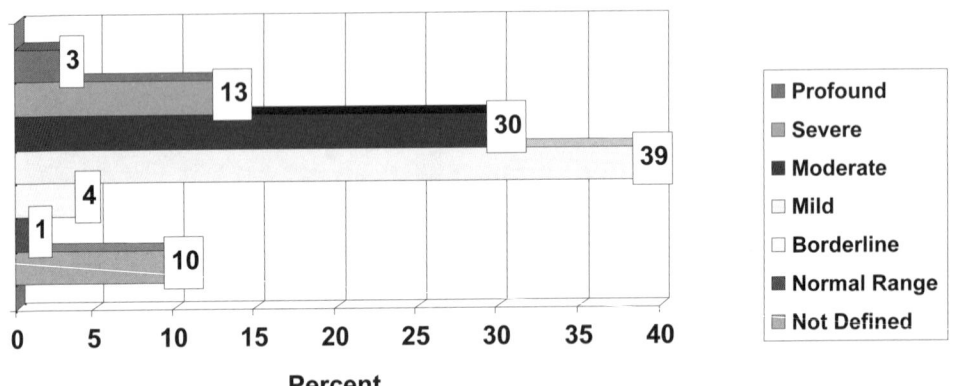

(Adapted from Commission for the Status of People with Disabilities, 1996)

The above chart (Figure2.10) shows that the most prevalent level of learning disability in County Wexford is mild, at 39% of the total. Some 13% of all learning disability is severe in nature, while 3% has been diagnosed as profound.

2.12 Substance Misuse

2.12.1 Socio-demographic Characteristics and First Treatment

According to the Health Research Board (HRB), the term drug use "...refers to any aspect of the drug taking process; however, drug misuse or problem drug use refers to drug use which causes social, psychological, physical or legal difficulties as a result of an excessive compulsion to continue taking drugs. Indirect methods encompassing the use of numbers of known drug misusers in the country, i.e. those registered for treatment, drug-related arrests and deaths etc., are currently used to approximate numbers of drug users within the general population."

(from National Drugs Strategy, Irish Government, 2001, p24)

Table 2.8 Socio-demographic Characteristics of First Treatment Contacts treated in the S.E.H.B., 1996-2000

Characteristics	1996	1997	1998	1999	2000
Male	86%	91%	85%	83%	81%
Female	14%	9%	15%	17%	19%
Under 18 years	16%	24%	14%	13%	19%
Early School Leavers	19%	19%	14%	15%	16%
Employed	26%	26%	40%	38%	33%
Average age (years)	22	23	23	24	23

(Adapted from O' Brien, Kelleher, and Cahill, 2002, p4)

The above table (Table 2.8) shows that First Treatment contacts for males has decreased in the period 1996-2000, although peaking in 1997. First Treatment contact for females has increased over the same period from 14% in 1996 to 19% in 2000. The average age of First Treatment Contacts in the period 1996-2000 peaked in 1999 at 24 years.

As can be seen from the following graph (Figure 2.11) trends in first treatment contact in the Eastern Regional Health Authority area have been decreasing since 1996 with a slight upsurge in 1999. The South-Eastern Health Board region has the same First Treatment Contact rate as the Midland Health Board, both of which are less than the Northern Eastern Health Board region.

Figure 2.11 Trends in First Treatment Contact Rates for 15 – 39 Year Olds in all Health Board Regions

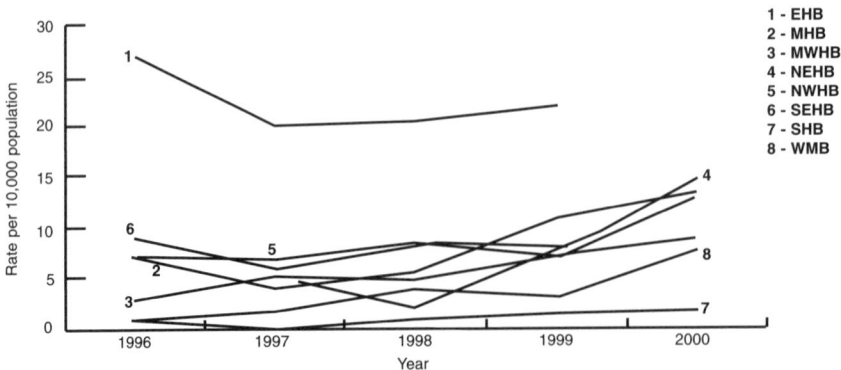

* Trends for 1996-1999 only in the EHB due to incomplete returns for 2000
** Population figures for each health board based on the Census for Population 1996, Central Statistics Office.

(O' Brien, Kelleher, and Cahill, 2002, p4)

2.12.2 Example of Service Provision

Data is available for Wexford through the SEHB's Addiction Treatment Service. Again this only reflects service attendance and not the extent of the problem socially. However, figures from such a source are '…valuable from a public health perspective to assess needs, and to plan and evaluate services' (EMCDDA, 1998 : p23).

The numbers seeking this type of service jumped considerably from 7 in 1997, to 22 in 1998. In 2000 there were 135 Wexford people attending this service. Treatment was sought primarily for misuse of 'soft' drugs like alcohol and cannabis.

Figure 2.12 Type of Drug Use in S.E.H.B. Area

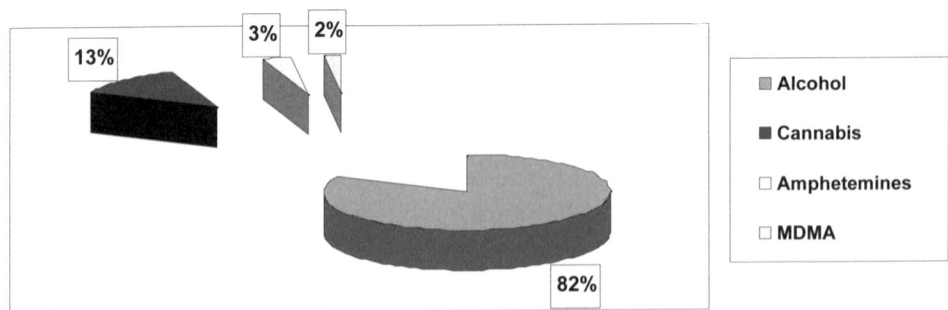

(SEHB Addiction Service 2000)

Table 2.9 Poly-Drug use in Wexford Region (Mar. 2000 – Feb. 2001)

Presenters at the Drug Counselling Service Cornmarket Project at Wexford Area Partnership

Cannabis	86%
Ecstasy	61%
Speed	45%
L.S.D.	21%
Opiates	5%
Alcohol	90%

(Figures supplied by Cornmarket Project at Wexford Area Partnership, July 2002)

The high level of alcohol use (90%) by most clients presenting for drugs counselling to the Cornmarket Project (W.A.P.) links in with trends generally in the South Eastern Health Board region. An overwhelming majority of clients used cannabis (86%) while 61% used ecstasy. These figures have remained the same since Feb. 2001 except for opiate use, which increased from 5% to 12% in the period January to June 2002.

2.12.2.1 Age Breakdown Of Service Users in County Wexford

Table 2.10 Drugs Counselling Service, Cornmarket Project at Wexford Area Partnership)

Presenters	Mar. 2000-Feb. 2001	Jan.2002-June2002
W.A.P. geographical area	61%	64%
Wexford County	39%	36%
Total	100%	100%
Age Profile of Clients using Service		
16-22 years	59%	59%
23-38 years	29%	30%
39+ years	12%	11%
Total	100%	100%
Gender		
Male	78%	68%
Female	22%	32%
Total	100%	100%

(Figures supplied by Cornmarket Project at Wexford Area Partnership, July 2002)

There has been a documented increase in the use of the Cornmarket Project by clients from the WAP geographical area, in the period Jan.2002 to June 2002 when compared to overall usage in the year Mar.2000-Feb.2001, and a concomitant decrease in usage by clients in Wexford County. The proportion of female clients has increased in the period from 22% to 32% of the total number using the service.

2.13. Education and Training

2.13.1 Early School Leavers

The most recent survey, carried out by the National Economic and Social Forum on Early School Leaving, estimates that the number of pupils leaving school early has remained unchanged since 1997; i.e. 18% of all school goers (n = 3,500) leave school annually without any qualifications (N.E.S.F., 2002).

Table 2.11 School Leaving Age (over 15) – County Wexford

	Still At School	Left Before 15	Left Aged 15-18	Left After 18	Unknown	Total
Number	8,177	18,224	40,752	9,639	1,695	78,487
%	10.4	23.2	51.9	12.3	2.2	100.0

(1996 Census, CSO)

These figures for Co. Wexford (Table 2.11) show that only 10.4% of those aged over 15 are still in education, while over 85% of the county's population aged 15 or over left school on or before the age of 18.

Wexford Area Partnership's research into this area (1998) reveals that slightly more females than males leave school early in the WAP catchment area which includes Wexford town and the surrounding area. Some 37.5% of early school leavers left between the ages of 17 and 18 years. Some left because of early pregnancy, or to take up low paid or seasonal work. Although no definite figures are provided in this research, it is interesting to note that that County Wexford has a higher rate of teenage pregnancy than the national average, although it is not the highest in the South East. (see 2.9.3 above).

2.13.2. Retention and Attainment Levels

2.13.2.1 National Overview

In 1996, exactly half of Ireland's population aged 25-64 years had left school without completing their upper secondary education. This figure compares to 62 per cent in 1989. But only one-third (34%) of those aged between 25 and 34 years in 1996 had not completed their upper secondary education. The number of young people aged 20-24 without upper secondary qualifications has declined by the equivalent of 12 percentage points (from 38% to 26%) between 1989 and 1995. Some 11% of Irish 25-64 year olds had a third level degree or equivalent in 1996, compared to 7 per cent in 1989, as against 14% of 25-34 year olds (The EFA 2000 Assessment: Country Reports).

2.13.2.2 Wexford Overview

Table 2.12 below demonstrates that while the national average for attaining a degree is 9.8%, only 5.8% of males in County Wexford and 5.9% of females have got to this level. However, completion of full second level education is higher among County Wexford females at 29.3% than among County Wexford males at 25.6%, and also than the national average of 28.8%.

Table 2.12 Educational Attainment in County Wexford

Area	Primary or less	Lower Second	Full Second	3rd level, non-degree	Degree +	Unknown	Total
Males	12210	8874	9026	2399	2029	701	35239
%	34.6	25.2	25.6	6.8	5.8	2.0	100.0
Females	10968	8187	10266	2739	2063	848	35071
%	31.3	23.3	29.3	7.8	5.9	2.4	100.0
Ireland %	28.6	20.2	28.8	9.3	9.8	3.3	100.0

(CSO Census of Population, 1996)

2.13.2.3 Third Level Participation

County Wexford ranks 16th in terms of participation at third level when compared with the other counties in Ireland, as illustrated in table 2.13:

Table 2.13 Comparison of Third Level Education Between Counties in Ireland

Counties	Population	Total no. participating	%	Rank
Galway	188,854	7,123	3.8	1
Clare	94,006	3,292	3.5	6
Leitrim	25,057	809	3.2	12
Wexford	**104,371**	**3,095**	**2.9**	**16**
Kildare	134,992	3,846	2.8	18
Donegal	129,994	3,002	2.3	26

(Dept. of Education 1998/1999)

Table 2.14 shows that Co. Wexford has a low ranking in relation to Third level participation rates, and is below the national average with regard to higher education attainment.

Table 2.14 Percentage of Population Aged 15 and over and Educational Attainment

	Wexford	National Average
In Education	10.4	12.3
Education Completed	89.6	87.7
-Primary Only	33.0	28.6
-Lower Secondary	24.3	20.2
-Upper Secondary	27.4	28.9
-Third Level (non degree)	7.3	9.3
Third Level (degree)	5.8	9.8
No information	2.2	3.3
Total	100	100

(Census of Population CSO, 1996)

2.13.3 Specific Educational Initiatives in County Wexford

2.13.3.1 County Wexford VEC Early School Leaver Provision

County Wexford V.E.C provides:

- 125 places under the Youthreach programme for early school leavers. In addition to compensatory education/training including E.C.D.L. accreditation, young people are offered progression options to Leaving Certificate Applied Programme level.
- 25 places at the Travellers Training Centre where Leaving Certificate Applied is also offered as a progression option.
- 220 places under the Vocational Training Opportunities Scheme offering Leaving Certificate, E.C.D.L. and Post Leaving Certificate courses.

On completion of the Leaving Certificate students can avail of:

- Direct Employment (in County Wexford)
- Apprenticeships (in County Wexford)
- P.L.C. Courses (in County Wexford)
- FÁS Courses (in County Wexford)
- Institutes of Technology (outside County Wexford)
- Universities (outside County Wexford)

2.13.3.2 Vocational Education Committee

The VEC provides a range of education courses at various levels. County Wexford VEC provides Post Leaving Certificate (PLC) courses, which are accredited by FETAC. There are currently twenty one different subjects offered through this programme to young people and adults. (A complete guide is available from the VEC Office, Wexford)

These services are provided in the VEC schools and, in some cases, in the Education and Training Centres. The junior and senior cycle courses provide for both compulsory and elective subjects. There is also a range of night classes available throughout the VEC schools in the county.

2.13.3.3 County Wexford Education Centre

The County Wexford Education Centre in Enniscorthy is one of 20 such centres nationally. Its principal function is to provide training, development and support for primary and secondary school teachers and for the wider school community. This service is provided to meet locally researched and identified needs of teachers, schools and communities, and the centre is also involved in providing national in-service programmes.

2.13.4 FÁS Initiatives in County Wexford

Training courses for the county are offered through FÁS, mainly from its training centres in Wexford town and Waterford city. Additional training places are provided in various locations throughout the region.

Training is made available to clients in the form of Apprenticeship Training, Specific Skills Training and Night Training. The provision of night training, allows the general public to avail of courses provided by FÁS. A range of night classes is offered in the area of computers, business and management, arts and crafts, and engineering.

The following is a sample of the main training services offered by FÁS in the county to young people:

2.13.4.1 In Centre Training

The Training Services Unit delivered courses for over 120 adults and apprentices in the year 2000 through its Training Centre in Wexford town.

2.13.4.2 Contracted Training

A number of training courses are run in the county, to facilitate people who are either unable or unwilling to travel to the training centre in Wexford town. A total of 160 people received training in this form in 2000.

2.13.4.3 Apprenticeship

Registration of new apprentices across all trades within the region reached its target of 650 minimum by the end of 2000.

2.13.5 Community Response

FÁS has a network of centres where young people aged 16 to 25 can gain valuable work experience in addition to pursuing specific certified computer training qualifications. The following Community Response programmes are currently being run in Co. Wexford:

- Windmill Therapeutic Centre, Wexford.
- Tagoat Community Council, Wexford.

2.13.5.1 Community Youth Programme

Under this programme FÁS provides training in construction skills for unemployed young people through the construction or renovation of community buildings.

- Gorey OPLA (Old People Living Alone)
- Enniscorthy OPLA
- Ramsgrange Trust
- John F. Kennedy Trust, New Ross

2.13.5.2 Community Training Workshop

This provides training and education for early school leavers aged between 17 and 25 years, to prepare them for work or further training/education. There are 24 places on the programme for this year.

2.13.6 Comment on Traveller Education Provision Nationally and in County Wexford

Lack of precise and detailed data is a complicating issue in providing services, including education, to Travellers. The National Traveller Education Officer at Pavee Point estimates that in 1999:

- 6,000 Traveller children attended Primary schools;
- 1,000 Traveller children attended mainstream Post-Primary schools;
- In the previous year (1998), 20 Traveller children had attended 6th year (Leaving Certificate Year) at Post-Primary schools.

Altogether, 600 Traveller children attended 52 pre-schools around the country in 2000, and 742 Travellers aged 15 years and upwards trained at 20 Senior Traveller Training Centres run by the Department of Education and Science. Fewer than 20 Travellers attended Third Level colleges.

According to the Action Plan, County Wexford Partnership (2001-2006), some 80% of all Traveller children aged 12-15 are not attending school. It has also been identified in this Action Plan that a majority of Travellers within County Wexford (i.e. 60%) are functionally illiterate.

2.13.6.1 National Service Provision

Table 2.15 Resource allocation for Traveller Education in Primary Schools

Resource allocation (September 2001)	Numbers
Traveller pre-schools	51
Resource teachers for Travellers	476
Special schools for Travellers	3
Junior Education Centres	6
Second-level schools in receipt of extra teaching hours	130
Senior Training Centres	28
Visiting Teacher Service	40
National Education Officer for Travellers	1

(Dept. of Education and Science 2002 Pg 17)

The above table (Table 2.15) shows that 40 visiting teachers are assigned nationally to cater to the needs of Traveller children, while provision has been made to provide 476 resource teachers for Travellers. Funding has also been allocated to provide 51 Traveller pre-schools.

2.13.6.2 Overview of Current Service Provision in County Wexford

One Visiting Teacher for Travellers is assigned to the entire county, although for reasons of population distribution, a teacher based in Carlow covers the area around and including Bunclody. The service is under-resourced at present given the numbers involved, the geographical spread of Traveller children and the many day-to-day challenges they have to face.

2.13.6.3 Pre-School Level

Fourteen years ago, two designated Traveller pre-schools were set up, in New Ross and Taghmon. These schools also cater for settled children, and the curriculum is similar to mainstream education, emphasising structured play and social skills. The school day lasts from 9.30 to 12.00 and a bus delivers the children to and from school.

2.13.6.4 Primary Level

Currently, thirty Primary schools in Wexford have enrolled Traveller children. However the number of students is in flux at any given time, since Traveller families sometimes move or children leave school.

2.13.6.5 Post Primary Level

In the last three years 13 Post Primary schools have enrolled Traveller pupils. In the school year 2001-2002, 47 Traveller pupils enrolled in these 13 schools.

2.13.6.6 Childcare and Early Learning

Family size is an indicator of high dependency. Again, Wexford has a larger average family size (3.26) than the rest of the country (3.14). This has implications for pressures on childcare in the county. In fact the National Childcare Census Report for Wexford (2001) has shown that there are imbalances in the types of childcare services provided, as well as a waiting list of 298 children for places in existing facilities. The poor provision of childcare places has a knock-on effect upon the ability of adults to access employment. (www.wexfordcdb.ie - Exclusion Report).

2.14 Youth Services

The primary aim of the 19 Local Youth Services affiliated to the National Youth Federation is to provide a co-ordinated range of services which are relevant, accessible and attractive to young people within a particular geographical area. Each Youth Service requires a core management group consisting of volunteers together with a full-time Regional Director/Manager who co-ordinates and manages the affairs of the organisation. Services are provided in a partnership with young people, volunteers, staff and other relevant local and national agencies.

2.14.1 County Wexford Youth Service Provision

As in other parts of the country, youth work is delivered by various youth and community groups. These are broadly divided into mainline youth groups, community youth projects, and community groups providing services for youth. Below are listed some of the main providers in County Wexford.

2.14.1.1 Mainline Youth Organisations

- Ferns Diocesan Youth Clubs
- Foroige
- Boys Brigade
- Girls Brigade
- Catholic Guides
- Catholic Scouts
- Scouting Association of Ireland
- Macra Na Feirme
- Girls Friendly Society

2.14.1.2 Community Youth Projects
- Enniscorthy Community Youth Project (FDYS)
- Coolcotts Community Youth Project (FDYS)
- Gorey Youth Needs
- Gorey Community Youth Projects (FDYS)
- Youth New Ross
- Traveller Youth Work (NATS)
- Young Women's Project (FDYS)
- Youth Info (FDYS)

2.14.1.3 Community Groups Providing for Youth
- Templeshannon CDP
- South West Wexford CDP
- FAB CDP

This is by no means an exhaustive listing of the groups that work with young people. Many other organisations and community groups provide either once-off events or on-going programmes. For example, among voluntary organisations the Order of Malta is not regarded as a specific youth service, but would have significant numbers of young people among its members; similarly, Youth Arts projects sponsored by community groups during local festivals often come to be regarded by the young people in the area as a central event in the year.

2.15 Juvenile Crime

In order to assess the extent of juvenile crime in County Wexford, the most recent figures from the Garda Commissioners Annual report are referred to here. In all cases it is impossible to derive figures specifically for County Wexford, as they are amalgamated with Co. Wicklow. However the figures are still very useful, as they are indicative of juvenile crime trends in the South East of Ireland as opposed to other areas of the country.

2.15.1 Types of Offences committed by Juveniles

Figure 2.13 Types of Juvenile Offences

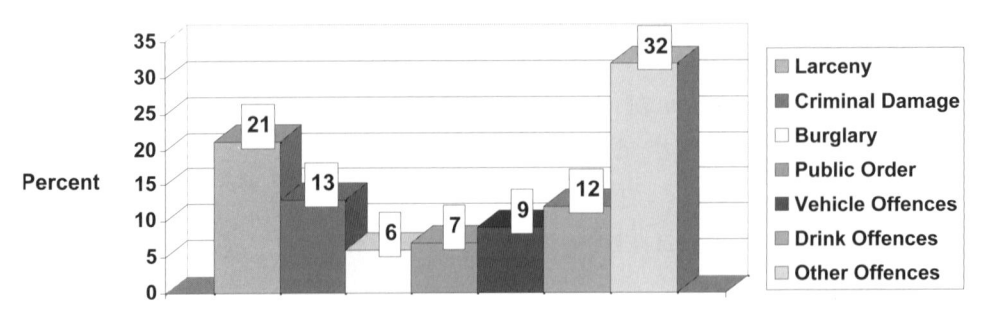

[Bar chart showing percentages: Larceny 21, Criminal Damage 13, Burglary 6, Public Order 7, Vehicle Offences 9, Drink Offences 12, Other Offences 32]

(Adapted from Garda Commissioners Report, 2000: p104)

The above chart (Figure 2.13) shows the types of offences committed by juveniles. Larceny at 32% of all crime committed is the most prevalent type of crime, with burglary being the least common of those listed here.

Larceny is the principal offence in all the regions but is particularly prevalent in the Dublin Metropolitan Region, accounting for 1,285 referrals. Vehicle and public order offences are also more prevalent in the Dublin Metropolitan Region, accounting for 757 and 501 referrals respectively. This compares to a total of 489 and 481 referrals for the other five regions.

2.15.2 Regional comparisons

Figure 2.14 Bar-Chart   Principal Offences – Comparison by Region

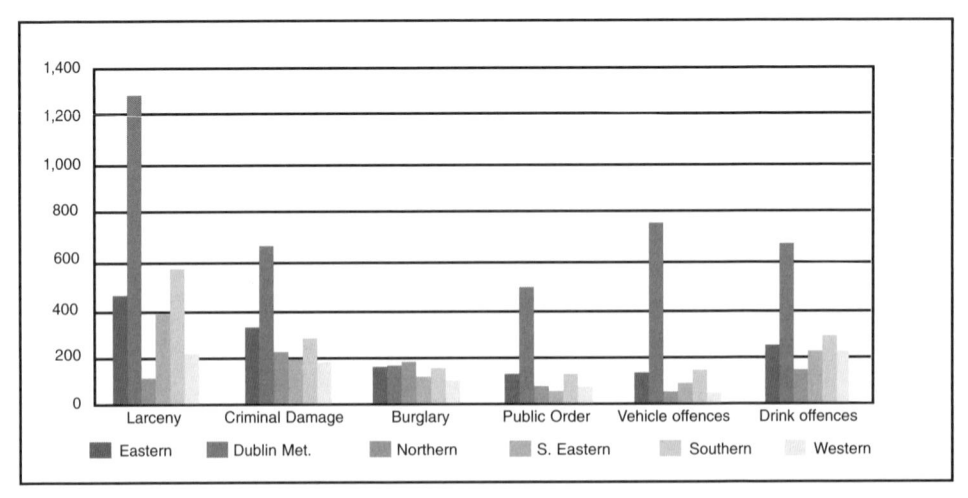

[Bar chart comparing offences across Eastern, Dublin Met., Northern, S. Eastern, Southern, and Western regions]

(Garda Commissioners Report, 2000: p107)

The above chart shows that the Dublin Metropolitan area has the highest incidence of juvenile crime. Of all types of juvenile offences committed in the South Eastern region, larceny is the most common, followed by drink offences and criminal damage. With regard to these three crime types, the South Eastern region has the third highest incidence rate in Ireland.

2.15.3 JLO Participation – Age/Sex

> *"The Garda Juvenile Diversion Programme is a national scheme operated on the basis that young offenders and society in general benefit more through having their criminal behaviour dealt with by way of caution rather than prosecution. Since the establishment of the programme in 1963, the vast majority of juveniles who benefited from a caution did not come to Garda notice again through repeat offending. The programme operates under the supervision of the Director (Superintendent) at the National Juvenile Office and is managed nationwide by specially trained Gardai who are employed as full-time Juvenile Liaison Officers (JLO's). After the juvenile has been cautioned, the JLO may maintain contact with the offender and family for a specified period of time. It may also involve referring the juvenile to other statutory agencies who are better placed to deal with the specific problems identified."*

(Garda Siochana Annual Report, 2000: p99)

Since inception, 104,170 juvenile offenders (i.e. 87.5% of the total involved), reached their 18th year of age without being prosecuted for a criminal offence.

Details of the disposal of juvenile referrals received at the National Juvenile Office during 2000 are shown by region in the following table (Table 2.16). Since some juvenile offenders were referred on more than one occasion during the year, the number of referrals is greater than the number of individual offenders. A total of 14,488 referrals were made to the Office during 2000.

Table 2.16 Disposal of 2000 Referrals

REGION		Prosecuted initially		Prosecuted on N.I.O direction		Formal caution		Informal caution		No further action	Pending	Total
		Male	Female	Male	Female	Male	Female	Male	Female			
EASTERN	Referrals	67	8	343	46	169	36	737	207	99	486	2,198
	Individual offenders	57	6	253	30	158	31	689	200	98	453	1,975
DUBLIN	Referrals	714	54	972	157	252	39	1,834	490	331	1,201	6,044
	Individual offenders	464	42	794	138	225	39	1,711	480	328	1,135	5,356
NORTHERN	Referrals	31	6	113	13	98	8	353	67	40	350	1,079
	Individual offenders	23	4	93	11	86	7	336	64	40	283	947
SOUTH EASTERN	Referrals	49	3	244	34	182	41	565	125	41	405	1,689
	Individual offenders	38	3	168	30	166	39	533	122	38	358	1,495
SOUTHERN	Referrals	78	6	458	58	145	25	605	157	119	589	2,240
	Individual offenders	68	6	334	50	134	25	582	154	118	554	2,025
WESTERN	Referrals	30	3	131	17	207	31	346	94	73	306	1,238
	Individual offenders	22	3	102	17	182	25	334	90	71	287	1,133
TOTAL for Regions	Referrals	969	80	2,261	325	1,053	180	4,440	1,440	703	3,337	14,488
	Individual offenders	672	64	1,744	276	951	166	4,185	1,110	693	3,070	12,931

(Garda Siochana Annual Report, 2000: p99)

The above table (Table 2.16) shows that there was a total of 1,689 referrals in 2000 in the South Eastern region. This is lower than for the Eastern and Southern regions, but higher than for the Western and Northern regions. Some information specific to the South Eastern region is provided below in the area comparison tables (Table 2.17 and 2.18).

Table 2.17 Details of Cautions by Region (2000 Referrals)

	Formal		Informal		Total cautions	
	Referrals	Individual offenders	Referrals	Individual offenders	Referrals	Individual offenders
SOUTH EASTERN REGION	223	205	690	655	913	860
Tipperary	70	62	66	66	136	128
Waterford/Kilkenny	99	90	464	436	563	526
Wexford/Wicklow	54	53	160	153	214	206
TOTAL	1,233	1,117	5,580	5,295	6,813	6,412

(Garda Commissioners Report, 2000: p107)

It can be seen from the above table that the total number of cautions given to individual offenders is 206 for the Wexford/Wicklow area. This comprises 24% of all cautions given in the South Eastern region. Some 526 cautions were given in the Waterford/Kilkenny area and 128 in Tipperary.

Table 2.18 Details of Prosecution by Region (2000 Referrals)

	Prosecuted initially		Prosecuted on direction		Total prosecuted	
	Referrals	Individual offenders	Referrals	Individual offenders	Referrals	Individual offenders
SOUTH EASTERN REGION	52	41	278	198	330	239
Tipperary	9	8	47	40	56	48
Waterford/Kilkenny	26	20	135	86	161	106
Wexford/Wicklow	17	13	96	72	113	85
TOTAL	1,049	736	2,585	2,020	3,634	2,756

(Garda Siochana Annual Report, 2000: p99)

The table (Table 2.18) above shows the number of prosecutions which were instituted in respect of referrals made during 2000. Prosecutions take place where juvenile offenders do not meet the requirements for inclusion in the programme. For example, offenders may be prosecuted because they have previously been before the courts, or because of the serious nature of the offence involved.

2.15.3.1 Garda Juvenile Diversion Programme in County Wexford

The following are the number of referrals dealt with under the above programme in the years 1999 and 2000.

Table 2.19 Garda Juvenile Diversion Programme in County Wexford

Area	1999	2000
Wexford District	109	108
New Ross District/ Enniscorthy District	163	128
Gorey District	35	30
Total Wexford County	**307**	**266**

The above table indicates that when one looks specifically at County Wexford with regard to number of referrals, there has been a decrease from 1999 to 2000. The decrease is most noticeable in the New Ross/Enniscorthy District, with no significant change evident in the Wexford District.

2.15.4 Probation and Welfare Statistics

> *"The number of offenders under court-ordered supervision in all categories combined decreased by 3.8%, from 5,524 in 1998 to 5,316 in 1999. The number of persons in respect of whom probation orders were made fell in 1999 by 268 (14.6%). However, the number placed on probation in 1999 was still higher than in the three years prior to 1998. The number of Community Service Orders increased by 5.8% (an increase of 73) over the 1998 figure, continuing an upward trend begun in 1998. Supervision during deferment of penalty remained virtually static (down 14, or 0.6%, over the 1998 figure). The five year trend for this type of supervision is upwards, with numbers placed on supervision during deferment up 53% in 1999 compared to the 1995 figure."*

(Probation and Welfare Service Report, 1999: p4)

With regard to probation orders made in the District Court in 1999, eight orders in the Kilkenny/Wexford area were in respect of 14 and 15 year old males, which was the highest in the Southern region outside of Cork. With regard to 16 and 17 year olds, ten probation orders were made in Kilkenny/Wexford, with twelve also being made in Cork for males in this age group.

2.15.5 Example of Specific Justice Service Provision in County Wexford

2.15.5.1 Garda Special Projects.

An Garda Síochána Special Projects is a social crime prevention initiative designed to engage with 'at risk' young people. The projects are managed by multi-agency and community based committees in each of the areas where they have been established. Projects have been set up in specific areas where the need for such intervention has been identified. The objectives of Garda Special Projects are to divert young people from becoming involved in criminal/anti-social behaviour, to provide suitable activities to facilitate personal development and encourage civic responsibility among the participants, and to work towards improving their long-term employability prospects.

In achieving the above objectives, the projects seek to support and improve relations between the local Garda and the community, and to enhance the quality of life in the area.

2.15.5.2 SAFE Project in Wexford Town

This project is running in the Coolcotts housing estate specifically for youth not otherwise engaged, and has been in operation for the last two years. There are presently 3 groups, one for boys between 12 and 14, a group for males over 18, and a group for girls between 13 and 16. It is a FAB community-based project, run in conjunction with Ferns Diocesan Youth Service and receiving funding from the Dept. of Justice. The present allocation for funding is 63,500 euro.

2.15.5.3 Cornmarket Project (Probation Service funded)

This service was formerly the Wexford Addiction Support Service prior to mainstreaming by the Probation Service. As evidenced from statistics used above, it provides a service for those engaging in substance misuse in the region. However a large component of its work also involves dealing with clients who are referred by the Gardai as presenting anti-social behaviours. Some 28% of clients who had contact with the service between March 2000 and February 2001 did so because of issues of anti-social behaviour or gambling.

2.16 Economics

There are 6,018 people on the Live Register for April 2002 in County Wexford (CSO, 2002). In urban areas of County Wexford unemployment has significantly increased. This increase in unemployment is a direct result of the high numbers of redundancies in the region. County Wexford suffered a loss of nearly 1,000 jobs in 2001, including the closure of long established industries such as Wexford Weavers in Wexford Town and the Enniscorthy plant, Wexal. The town of New Ross, once a thriving centre, has over the last number of decades become de-industrialised. Being only fifteen miles from the city of Waterford has meant that most of its labour force now seeks employment in that city, due to job losses at Stafford Shipping, Albatross, Irish Driver Harris and the closure of Hartmanns, Celtic Seafoods, Culcita and the New Ross Shipping Company (S.I.P.T.U., 2001).

2.16.1 Unemployment among Young People

It can be seen from Table 2.20 below that that the Border regions and Dublin have the highest national incidence of unemployment for both males and females under 24 years. However outside these areas, the South Eastern region including Wexford county has the highest incidence of unemployment for under 29 year olds, and the fourth highest rate of unemployment for 20-24 year age groups, surpassed only by the Border region, Dublin and the South West.

Table 2.20 Persons on the live register classified by age and sex April 2002

Sex/Age	Border	Dublin	Mid-East	Midland	Mid-West	South-East	South-West	West	Total
Males									
Under 20 years	736	950	279	240	327	570	477	377	3,956
20 - 24 years	2,278	3,867	954	795	1,190	1,746	1,965	1,298	14,093
25 - 34 years	4,079	7,819	1,789	1,352	2,167	3,057	3,825	2,497	26,585
35 - 44 years	3,351	4,895	1,433	1,197	1,627	2,564	3,136	2,281	20,484
45 - 54 years	3,310	4,254	1,184	1,151	1,504	2,564	3,008	2,231	19,206
55 - 59 years	1,088	1,732	512	397	557	763	921	743	6,713
60 - 64 years	586	1,443	319	258	371	491	614	484	4,566
Total	15,428	24,960	6,470	5,390	7,743	11,755	13,946	9,911	95,603
Females									
Under 20 years	527	772	215	232	275	448	376	264	3,109
20 - 24 years	1,591	1,978	611	597	721	1,253	1,241	916	8,908
25 - 34 years	2,893	4,278	1,376	1,154	1,486	2,349	2,644	1,652	17,832
35 - 44 years	2,614	3,312	1,255	1,099	1,428	2,195	2,143	1,777	15,823
45 - 54 years	1,706	2,377	720	703	890	1,452	1,567	1,215	10,630
55 - 59 years	545	974	261	194	282	408	496	378	3,538
60 - 64 years	283	707	132	102	177	185	245	218	2,049
Total	10,159	14,398	4,570	4,081	5,259	8,290	8,712	6,420	61,889
All Persons									
Under 20 years	1,263	1,722	494	472	602	1,018	853	641	7,065
20 - 24 years	3,869	5,845	1,565	1,392	1,911	2,999	3,206	2,214	23,001
25 - 34 years	6,972	12,097	3,165	2,506	3,653	5,406	6,469	4,149	44,417
35 - 44 years	5,965	8,207	2,688	2,296	3,055	4,759	5,279	4,058	36,307
45 - 54 years	5,016	6,631	1,904	1,854	2,394	4,016	4,575	3,446	29,836
55 - 59 years	1,633	2,706	773	591	839	1,171	1,417	1,121	10,251
60 - 64 years	869	2,150	451	360	548	676	859	702	6,615
Total	25,587	39,358	11,040	9,471	13,002	20,045	22,658	16,331	157,492

(http://www.cso.ie/publications/labour/lrabda.pdf)

In the South East region of Ireland there has been an overall increase in unemployment for males and females from June 2001 to June 2002. Of all persons unemployed in the South East region, 20% are under 25 years of age, while in Dublin and the South West some 18% of all unemployed are under 25 years of age. Specific detailed figures for the South East are provided below in Table 2.22.

Table 2.21 Changes in Numbers on Live Register June 2001-June 2002 by Region

NUTS2 and NUTS3 Regions	June 2001	May 2002	June 2002	Monthly change	Annual change	Under 25 years	25 years & over
Border, Midland & Western	49,208	51,130	54,345	+ 3,215	+ 5,137	10,827	43,518
Border	24,517	25,518	26,828	+ 1,310	+ 2,311	5,519	21,309
Midland	8,747	9,406	10,038	+ 632	+ 1,291	2,052	7,986
West	15,944	16,206	17,479	+ 1,273	+ 1,535	3,256	14,223
Eastern & Southern	91,857	103,814	109,932	+ 6,118	+ 18,275	20,582	89,350
Dublin	32,801	38,559	40,794	+ 2,235	+ 7,993	7,524	33,270
Mid-East	8,879	10,860	11,424	+ 564	+ 2,545	2,070	9,354
Mid-West	11,620	13,024	13,998	+ 974	+ 2,378	2,645	11,353
South-East	18,555	19,680	20,679	+ 999	+ 2,124	4,163	16,156
South-West	19,802	21,691	23,037	+ 1,346	+ 3,235	4,180	18,857
Total	140,865	154,944	164,277	+ 9,333	+ 23,412	31,409	132,868

(http://www.cso.ie/publications/labour/lregan.pdf)

Table 2.22 Changes in Numbers on Live Register June 2001-June 2002 – South East Region

NUTS2 and NUTS3 Regions/County/ Local Office	June 2001	May 2002	June 2002	Males			Females		
				Under 25 years	25 years & over	Total	Under 25 years	25 years & over	Total
South East	18,555	19,680	20,679	2,325	9,382	11,707	1,838	7,134	8,972
County Wexford	5,720	6,419	6,649	692	2,948	3,640	638	2,371	3,009
Enniscorthy	1,482	1,662	1,688	209	772	981	198	509	707
Gorey	841	987	1,037	100	452	552	99	386	485
New Ross	1,169	1,221	1,292	130	579	709	121	462	583
Wexford	2,228	2,549	2,632	253	1,145	1,398	220	1,014	1,234

(http://www.cso.ie/publications/labour/lregan.pdf)

Of all the areas categorised in the table above Wexford County has the highest unemployment rate at 33%. Some 21.2% of those unemployed in County Wexford are under 25 years. This compares to 19.6% in the Waterford area, 21.2% in Tipperary S.R, 20.1% in the Kilkenny area and 19.7% in the Carlow region.

2.16.2 Long-term Unemployment

Over half of those in receipt of unemployment payments are claiming Unemployment Assistance (as opposed to Benefit) in the Wexford region. This is a clear indication of the long-term nature of the unemployment in the area. Approximately 60% of unemployed men have been out of work for over two years (S.I.P.T.U., 2001). This has particular implications for life chances within a family and can leave children more 'at risk'. More than half the children 'consistently poor' in 1997 were in households seriously affected by unemployment. Almost 40% of children living in households with below half the average income were living in households headed by an unemployed person (Nolan, 2000).

2.16.2.1 Income Support

Refugees who have been granted asylum have the same rights in respect of welfare as Irish citizens, so they are entitled to payments such as Unemployment Assistance, Unemployment Benefit, etc., as appropriate. Asylum seekers (i.e. those with applications for refugee status that are under review) do not have the same welfare structure as Irish citizens, and they are paid a flat rate of payment. Asylum seekers who arrived in Ireland since April 2000 are paid under a system known as 'Direct Provision'; this amounts to approximately nineteen euros along with vouchers for food and accommodation per week.

2.16.3 GMS

While 30.9% of the national population hold medical cards, 36.5% of Wexford people fall into this category. This is again indicative of dependency in the county being higher than the national average.

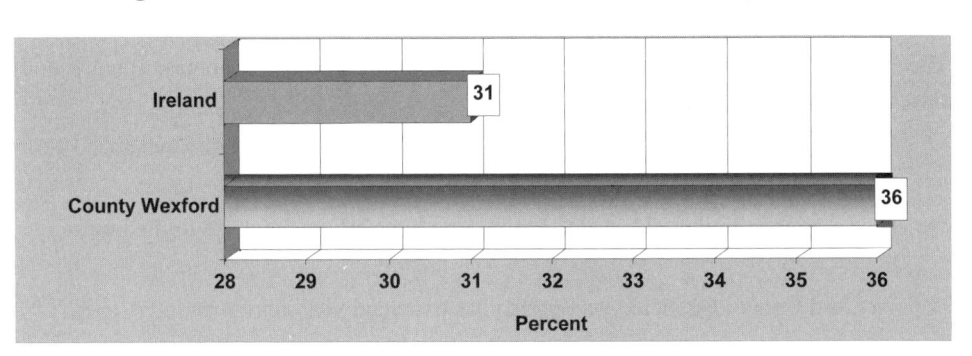

Figure 2.15 Medical Card Holders in Ireland and County Wexford

Region	Percent
Ireland	31
County Wexford	36

(DSCFA 2000)

2.16.4 Family Income Supplement

Table 2.23 Breakdown of Children in Households Below 50% Relative Income Poverty Line by Labour Force Status of Household Head, 1987, 1994 and 1997

Parental Status	1987 %	1994 %	1997 %
Employee	11.6	10.4	17.7
Self-employed	5.7	7.1	8.5
Farmer	15.5	8.3	3.9
Unemployed	52.5	47.8	39.7
Ill/Disabled	9.2	5.6	12.3
Retired	0.7	0.9	0.9
Home Duties	4.7	19.8	17.0
All	100	100	100

(Nolan, 2000)

The above table gives an indication of the employment status of parents of children in households below the 50% relative income poverty line. Unemployment is seen to be a key causal factor of childhood poverty in all three years that the Living in Ireland Survey was undertaken.

The number of families in receipt of Family Income Supplement from the DSCFA is also a good indicator of low incomes in a given area. In Wexford the DSCFA issues 750 such payments. The national trend for payments of FIS has risen by 28% since 1995; however, in Wexford the rise has been recorded at 43% for the same period. Again this would seem to imply increased financial vulnerability for families in County Wexford. (DSCFA, 2001)

2.17 Housing And Accommodation

The Bacon Report on Housing (1999) The Housing Market: An Economic Review and Assessment observed that:

- Rent inflation had increased by 17% in the twelve months prior to November 1998 in the Leinster region.
- House price inflation was in flux but in general stabilising at 4.4% in the Leinster region
- Wexford County Councils' waiting list has extended year after year.

2.17.1 Local Authority Housing

According to the Annual Housing Statistics Bulletin for the year 2001, housing output nationally, at 52,602 units, was up 5.6% on the previous year. Over 5,000 local authority houses were completed or acquired, the highest level of output for over 15 years. In addition, over 7,100 local authority houses were started. At the end of 2001, almost 7,500 local authority houses were in progress, up 47% on the numbers in progress at the end of 2000. Output under the voluntary housing programmes in 2001 was 1,253 units.

Table 2.24 Wexford Housing Statistics (Wexford Borough)

Rented	**700**	33.2%
Purchased	**1,198**	57%
In process of purchase	**195**	9.3%
Wastage (merged/knocked down/other use)	**11**	0.5%
Total	**2,104**	100%

(Supplied by Wexford Borough Council, end 2001)

With regard to Wexford Borough, some 57% of local authority housing was purchased by 2001. Just over a third was rented, and 9.3% of local authority housing was in the process of being purchased.

2.17.2 Homelessness

Table 2.25 Age of Youth Homeless in Ireland

Age	Number of Males	Number of Females	Total
Under 12 years	31	30	61
12 - 14 years	71	53	124
15 - 16 years	122	103	225
17 - 18 years	65	113	178
Total	289	299	588

(Youth Homelessness Strategy, 2001:Pg 13)

The majority of homeless male youths in Ireland are in the 15-16 year age group (i.e. 122 males), while the majority of female homeless youth are in the 17-18 year age group.

Figure 2.16 Children as a Percentage of National Total who Present as Homeless

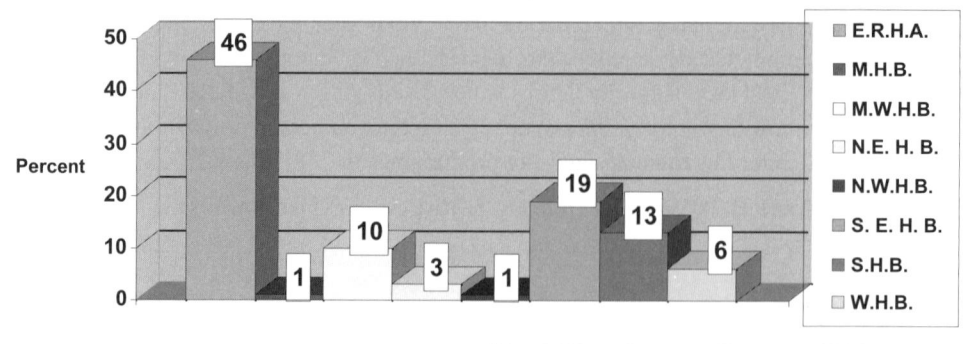

Region	Percent
E.R.H.A.	46
M.H.B.	1
M.W.H.B.	10
N.E.H.B.	3
N.W.H.B.	1
S.E.H.B.	19
S.H.B.	13
W.H.B.	6

(Youth Homelessness Strategy, 2001: Pg 13)

The greatest occurrence of homelessness for youth occurs in the Eastern Regional Health Authority Area. The next highest occurrence is in the South Eastern Health Board area at 19%, while the North Western Health Board and Midland Health Board regions have the lowest occurrence at 1%. (Figure 2.16)

2.17.3 Traveller Accommodation

Wexford County has the second highest number of Traveller families living on the roadside, i.e.110. Some 75 out of 230 families are living in standard local authority housing and 13 are living in a group housing scheme. Twenty out of 230 families are living on a halting site. This compares to 11 families living on a halting site in Waterford County, and 15 in Waterford City.

Table 2.26 County Comparison of Traveller Accommodation in Ireland

County	Standard Local Authority Housing	Group Housing	Halting Site	Roadside	Other	Total
Carlow	17	4	6	30	3	60
Cavan	26	0	18	5	0	49
Clare	32	10	18	37	10	107
Cork City	116	0	63	16	1	196
Cork County	84	16	13	45	10	168
Donegal	61	0	20	35	0	116
Dublin City	43	109	141	113	2	408
Dun Laoghaire/ Rathdown	28	24	21	23	0	96
Fingal	23	13	138	95	0	269

County	Standard Local Authority Housing	Group Housing	Halting Site	Roadside	Other	Total
Galway County	184	31	24	84	10	333
Kerry	181	2	25	16	1	22
Kildare	3	0	25	38	2	68
Kilkenny	23	3	16	12	11	65
Laois	23	1	23	15	3	65
Leitrim	2	0	21	0	1	24
Limerick City	·13	10	31	11	1	66
Co. Limerick	95	11	29	56	29	220
Longford	124	0	14	18	2	158
Louth	92	18	20	11	16	157
Mayo	90	3	8	57	2	160
Meath	54	34	16	12	4	146
Monaghan	49	0	1	1	1	57
Offaly	51	0	78	78	4	156
Roscommon	14	2	9	9	0	47
Sligo	19	1	23	23	0	59
South Dublin	77	19	160	90	18	364
Tipperary N.R.	62	0	12	36	3	113
Tipperary S.R.	36	6	18	25	4	89
Waterford City	63	0	15	14	1	93
Co. Waterford	10	4	11	12	0	37
Westmeath	47	0	30	11	0	88
Wexford	**75**	**13**	**20**	**110**	**12**	**230**
Wicklow	43	0	19	43	3	108
Total	1973	356	1100	1207	146	4790

(Report from National Traveller Accommodation Consultative Committee, 1999)
(http://www.paveepoint.ie/fs-distribution.html)

2.18 Domestic Violence

In 2000 there were 515 reported incidents of child abuse in Wexford, which included physical, sexual and emotional abuse as well as cases of neglect. This figure represents more than a doubling of the number of reports made three years before (1997), when only 239 reports were recorded. However, this dramatic rise can be explained, at least to some extent, by changes in the way child abuse is recorded and reported. Of all categories involved, it seems that reporting of emotional abuse has risen most, from 35 cases in 1997 to 108 in 2000 (SEHB Annual Report, 2000).

In order to attain local information on domestic violence, statistics from the Wexford Women's Refuge are used here as well as statistics from the Rape Crisis Centre. Wexford Women's Refuge normally works with women who have been in an adult relationship, and their usual contact with young people is not as clients, but as the children of clients. The Rape Crisis Centre does not work directly with clients under the age of eighteen without a parent being present.

Table 2.27 Wexford Women's Refuge Statistics in Year 2000

	January-June 2000	June-December 2000
Helpline Calls	260	289
New Clients	73	77
Ongoing Clients	37	44
Total	**370**	**410**

(Supplied by Wexford Women's Refuge, 2001)

Over the course of a year it can be seen that the number of calls, either by phone or directly, increased towards the end of 2000. This may be partly explained by the Christmas season, with the associated stresses and pressures on families during this time.

Table 2.28 Wexford Rape Crisis Centre Statistics

Service	2000	2001
Helpline Calls (Counselling Related)	2556	1534
New Clients	70	72
Ongoing Clients	28	23

(Supplied by Wexford Women's Refuge, July, 2002)

While the use of Wexford Rape Crisis Centre helpline has decreased between 2000 and 2001, the number of new clients has increased from 70 to 72 over the same period.

2.19 Concluding Comment

One of the most significant demographic comparisons between Wexford and the rest of Ireland is that County Wexford has relatively more old people and relatively more young people than the national average. This implies a higher dependency in these age groups in the region.

On all the key social indicators such as education, unemployment medical card status etc., Wexford fares quite poorly in comparison to national averages and other counties. One of the strongest findings from this statistical overview of County Wexford is that Wexford is significantly below the national educational attainment indicators and also below in third level participation rates. Early school leaving was strongly identified as a regional problem for Wexford youth. Lone parenting was significantly higher in the area, with County Wexford ranking 6th highest nationally for the number of lone parents in residence.

In essence all these statistical trends and others discussed within the chapter imply that youth are more likely to be 'at risk' in County Wexford than in other areas, using any of the received definitions of 'at risk' in mainstream academic/practice literature. As such, it would seem imperative to investigate these issues on a deeper level by using a qualitative methodology to engage with youth in County Wexford actually experiencing the social reality of their region. This chapter, providing a quantitative spotlight on County Wexford, highlights the fact that there are issues pertinent to youth and regional risk factors of vulnerability for youth that should be addressed. The succeeding chapters will elaborate on this by applying, in greater detail, the qualitative perspective referred to above.

References

Bacon P and Associates (1999) *County Wexford: A Strategy for Economic Development*

Barry J *Healthcare of Irish Travellers* (Irish Doctor, January, 1991)

Census Statistics Office www.cso.ie

Commission for the Status of People with Disabilities, 1996 www.wexfordcdb.ie

County Wexford Partnership (2000) *County Wexford Partnership Action Plan 2001-2006*

Dept of Education *Annual Report 1998/99* www.wexfordcdb.ie/EducationTraining.html

Dept of Education and Science (2002) *Guidelines on Traveller Education in Primary Schools*

Dept of the Environment (2001) *Annual Housing Statistics Bulletin*

Dept of Health and Children (2001) *Youth Homeless Strategy*

Dept of Social, Community and Family Affairs (2000) www.wexfordcdb.ie

Dept of Tourism, Sport and Recreation *Building on Experience National Drugs Strategy 2001-2008*

E.F.A. (2000) Assessment-Country Reports-Ireland www.unesco.org/country_reports/ireland/contents.html

EMCDDA (1998) *Annual Report on the State of the Drug Problem in the E.U.* www.emcdda.org/infopoint/publications

Garda Commissioners Report, 2000

Irish Social Services Inspectorate Report, 2001

National Childcare Census Report for Wexford, 2001

NESF (2002) Early School Leavers Forum Report No.24

National Traveller Accommodation Consultative Committee Report (1999): www.paveepoint.ie

Nolan (July, 2000) *Child Poverty in Ireland* (Combat Poverty Agency and Oak Tree Press) O'Brien Kelleher and Cahill *Trends in Treated Drug Misuse in the SEHB Area 1996-2000* Occasional Paper Drug Misuse Research Division, Health Research Board

Pensions Services Office, Dept of Social, Community and Family Affairs www.solo.ie/info/3099htm

Probation and Welfare Service Report (2001)

Report of the Task Force on the Travelling Community (Brunswick Press, 1995)

SEHB Addiction Service 2000 Statistics www.wexfordcdb.ie

SEHB Annual Report 1999

SEHB Annual Report 2000

SEHB (1998) Annual Review of Childcare and Family Support Services

Shanahan C. *'Irish Teen Births Rate Tenth Highest'* Irish Examiner, May 31st, 2002

SIPTU (2001) Submission to Southern and Eastern Regional Assembly *'Sub Regional Disparities' – the Needs and Problems of Specific Areas* (SIPTU)

Wexford Area Partnership (1998) *Responding to Early School Leaving in the Wexford Area*

Wexford Area Partnership (2000) *Social Inclusion Plan for the Wexford Area 2000-2004*

Wexford Area Partnership (2000) *Traveller Accommodation Programme 2000-2004*

Wexford Community Development Board *Quality of Life Task Group Discussion Paper (2000)* www.wexfordcdb.ie/quality_of_life_report.htm

Chapter Three
Literature Review

3 Introduction

The literature on theory and practice in the area of young people and Risk is extensive and continuously expanding. The focus in this review is on the Irish experience over recent years, viewed in the context of current approaches in the developed world to the topics of adolescence, risk taking, participation and empowerment.

The review is divided into seven sections:

3.1 Adolescence looks at the evolution of a holistic and ecological perspective on adolescence, which links the individual to the family, the community and the wider social environment.

3.2 The Risk Society summarises the key texts that define the contemporary concept of risk, focussing particularly of the ideas of Beck and Giddens.

3.3 Young People and Risk examines the situations and activities involving young people in Ireland that are generally recognised as exposing them to risk. Statistical data relating national and local experiences are summarised.

3.4 Resilience provides a brief outline of a current theory which seeks to explain the ability of individuals to overcome risk. This leads to a strategy for building resilience through those links that connect the individual to the family and the wider community.

3.5 Irish Legislation on Child Care traces the development of Ireland's statutory bodies' involvement in the lives of young people at risk through the twentieth century, and analyses the themes of inclusion and participation that underpin the National Children's Strategy and linking legislation.

3.6 Inclusion and Participation suggests an ethical framework for research with young people, and describes possible changes generated in personal identity at the individual, social and political levels through the process of empowerment.

3.7 The Conclusion to the chapter draws together the main themes that underpin the research.

Throughout the review fundamental questions of identity, personal development and behaviour are treated from an ecological perspective, based on the psycho-social theory of human development, as explained in 3.1. Adolescents' experiences are comprehended in their social linkages which centre on the individual, and extend from the immediate circle of family, peer group and confidants to the wider networks, both formal and informal, of social, community and statutory organisations.

3.1 Adolescence

Traditional societies did not generally recognise an intermediate stage between childhood and adulthood – as soon as a child became physically able to work, the hunting group, the household, the farm, the army, the factory, the mine or the ship brought childhood years to an abrupt end. In many societies, a rite of passage formally marked this transition, in a social or religious ceremony that accepted the initiate into the adult world.

'At a time when children were bought and sold for profit, subjected to extremes of corporal punishment, and generally exploited by adults as a source of wealth, the notion of a period of adolescent transition from childhood to adulthood would have been seen as self-indulgent to say the least. Adolescence simply did not exist' (Hollin, 1988: p4).

As the industrialised world became more complex, knowledge acquired a greater economic value, and formal education began to extend into the teenage years. Throughout the nineteenth century, technological advances caused a powerful middle class to emerge across Northern Europe and America, who saw further education for their children as an effective way of securing and capitalising on the wealth they were accumulating.

According to Hollin (1988), 'legal and social differences were defined in order to separate formally children and adults; a division that was complicated by the introduction of secondary schooling for 14 to 18 year olds. This newly created social group were too old to be children, but were not judged as ready to be given adult responsibilities – the adolescent had arrived' (ibid.).

So, if adolescence is to be treated as a distinctive stage in life, then it is clear that an analysis of the values and relations of the society which construct adolescence in the first place is fundamental to any useful definition. But it is also necessary to acknowledge those physical changes that occur to developing children, normally between the ages of ten and eighteen, the years we now tend to associate with the term 'adolescence':

Female

- o *Acne appears*
- o *Body hair appears*
- o *Breasts develop*
- o *Body contours become rounded*
- o *Uterus enlarges*
- o *Menstruation begins*
- o *Weight gain*
- o *Height gain*

Male

- o *Acne appears*
- o *Body hair appears*
- o *Facial hair appears*
- o *Larynx enlarges (causing deeper voice)*
- o *Genitals enlarge*
- o *Weight gain*
- o *Height gain*

(ibid.)

Every young person must also experience a series of psychological changes no less profound and radical than the more obvious physical ones. Just as a 'new' body is being formed, a whole new identity is also brought into being. The psychological changes that occur during this time contribute to the construction of a 'new' self, with its fundamentally altered beliefs, attitudes and values. Young people have to judge their own physical attractiveness, their ambitions, their ideas of what is achievable in life, their moral and ethical values; and they must also reassess their expectations of family, friends and society in general. In short, they have to reconstruct their view of themselves as men or women, and of what they expect from other men and women.

'For the adolescent these changes can be profound – although they do not have to be, as there are no rules about what can happen during adolescence – and can have marked effects, for better or worse, on the young person' (ibid, p8).

Adolescence is above all a time of transition. 'There are in fact a number of different transitions (e.g. of school, from school to work or training, to independent living, etc.) which occur during adolescence, all of which contribute to the overall process of reaching maturity ... It is important to recognise that the overall transition from child to adult is accomplished through multiple smaller transitions, all of which may be stressful or difficult in themselves' (Coleman et al in Roche and Tucker, 1997: p227).

3.1.1. Theories of Adolescence

Three mainstream approaches to the study of adolescence currently prevail:

3.1.1.1 The Biologically Determinist View

This view argues that adolescence is driven by powerful genetic and instinctive impulses. Hall's (1904) identification of puberty as the defining moment of adolescence for young people provided a firm biological foundation for the concept of adolescence that predominated over the following decades – the 'Storm and Stress' model (Roche and Tucker, 1997).

3.1.1.2 The Psycho-Analytical Approach

Sigmund Freud was largely responsible for establishing this area of study. He saw conflict, principally targeted against parents and the family, as the principal unconscious motivator of adolescent behaviour: 'Detaching himself from his family becomes a task that faces every young person' (Freud in Gay, 1995 : p745).

His influential contemporary, Alfred Adler, described the pattern of inter-generational conflict in even starker terms: 'The apparently obedient child was always in opposition to his parents; but when he has more freedom and strength, he felt able to declare his enmity' (Adler in Ansbacher, 1964 : p439).

3.1.1.3 The Social Constructionist Approach

But if, as previously suggested, we view adolescence as a social construct, rather than as an exclusively biological and/or psychological state, then the culture within which adolescence is experienced becomes a critical factor in defining the nature and characteristics of adolescence itself, '…shaped both by the legal framework and by the social and economic world in which a young person grows up' (Coles in Roche and Tucker, 1997: p99).

'Youth Culture' as we know it today has its origins in the 1950s. Teenagers in the US became an economically significant group only after the Second World War, and mass marketing (particularly of entertainment and leisure products and services) suddenly 'discovered' this burgeoning population of new consumers with time and money on their hands.

Music and film stars and style gurus acquired iconic status in this urban, hedonistic, anti-establishment cultural movement that quickly spanned the globe. Commodities, products, styles and tastes converged in affirming and endorsing the new order, and young people everywhere became avid consumers in the new mass market.

'People became nothing more than consumers…. Mass culture relied on their exploitation to exist, so a whole influx of youth-specific goods flooded the market (movies, records, magazines and TV shows)' (Garratt in Roche and Tucker, 1997 : p147).

But the 1950's was a long time ago. The nature and characteristics of adolescence have changed considerably since then, mirroring the changes brought about in the culture itself, since 'youth culture, including the idiom in which it is expressed, is not a thing but a living and changing way of life' (Rogers in Roche and Tucker, 1997: p180).

The response of the predominant (i.e. adult) culture to this emerging 'other' culture, particularly as expressed in the media, has generally been suspicious and estranging. 'Young people were blamed, and even envied, by adult society, for their loss of cultural dominance. The media has continually portrayed the young as something to be feared and envied' (ibid.).

One result of this negative portrayal of youth culture is the labelling of young people, (e.g. as delinquent, engaged in drug misuse, sexually promiscuous, etc.) in the public mind. 'The media can stir up public indignation and engineer concern about certain types of behaviour, even when there is nothing new about that behaviour or when its real threat is minimal' (Muncie and McLaughlin, 1996 : p52).

Negative stereotyping of young people has a significant impact on their social identity, on their roles, relationships and cultural activities. It also impacts profoundly on their political engagement with those very structures and systems that determine the extent and quality of young people's liberty to make decisions for themselves about their own lives.

'How we speak about young people, research into their needs, develop services for them, etc., is essentially underpinned by the views that are expressed by policy makers, those who hold sway in powerful institutions, the enforcers of legislation, professional groupings, academic writers and researchers – those able to influence and shape 'social meanings' and assist in their wider dissemination' (Tucker in Roche and Tucker, 1997 : p91).

Young people in Ireland can '…feel invisible, partly because they feel they have no voice. They resent being seen as irrelevant in the political arena, except as the receivers of protective measures to counter perceived problems. They are not viewed as contributors in any relevant way' (from the Youth Future Conference (July 2000), cited in O'Leary, 2001 : p7).

A natural response of young people to their perceived disempowerment within mainstream society is to move towards clandestine peer groups that, through an 'alternative' culture, offer them support and acknowledgement.

'As it is on the streets that most young people make themselves visible in their attempts to express their independence from adult society, it is 'the streets' that enable the creation of these cultural activities. This 'culture' interacts on the streets, and finds its expression in the style that it adopts. The high visibility of a group of young people, with shared musical preferences, fashion ideals and beliefs, leads to the creation of a 'sub-culture' (Garratt in Roche and Tucker, 1997 : p144).

But young people, if attached to a sub-culture which insists on visibility, can be stereotyped, often being portrayed as alien and threatening, particularly when the outward trappings of the subculture, (clothing, body ornamentation, social and political activity etc.), are consciously provocative.

'In the eyes of the adult world, not only are youth sub-cultures somewhat impenetrable and beyond comprehension, but they are also fundamentally corrupt (an underworld); in short they are deviant…It is adult society that creates these deviants, simply because they (i.e. young people) have broken no other rule than that which we (i.e. adults) see as the accepted dominant rules of style, behaviour and expression. Youth sub-cultures give easily identifiable teenagers a mean to rebel, but it is through style, not crime' (Garratt in Roche and Tucker, 1997 : p147).

The 'moral panic' induced in the public mind through media representation of these sub-cultures can contribute to the increased hostility and further alienation of adolescents (Muncie and McLaughlin, 1996 : p52). To take one example from an earlier time, the clashes between Mods and Rockers in seaside towns in England in the Summer of 1964, were the focus of much public outrage, initially fed by media distortion which "…resulted in an amplification of youthful deviance in both perceived and real terms. Youths began to identify with the label attached to them, and thus believed themselves to be more deviant and separate from the rest of society. They had been singled out as society's 'folk devils', and acted out that role accordingly in subsequent years" (ibid.).

The catalogue of youth sub-cultures that have come and gone since then, all inciting similar levels of moral panic in the established culture, includes hippies, skinheads, punks, ravers, new-age travellers and anti-globalisation protesters. In the same period, prominent media-driven 'issues', all focusing negatively on young people, have ranged from teenage pregnancies and sexual promiscuity, through drug misuse (including alcohol), joyriding and street crime, to hooliganism and radical political protest (ibid. p53).

But a counter-movement within the entertainment industry, of endorsing and appropriating 'youth culture', has transformed the leisure-oriented media over the same period. Stylistic innovations and social experiments among sub-cultures are ever more rapidly sanitized and absorbed by the mass culture. For today's adolescents, the more overt gestures of teenage rebellion that predominated from the 1950s through the 1980s have been largely stripped of their validity. 'By (mainstream culture's) pouncing on any sub-cultural innovation, and incorporating it into the mainstream, the movement is immediately robbed of its 'secret' appeal' (Garratt in Roche and Tucker, 1997 : p148).

So TV, radio and cinema become ever more 'youth-oriented', radical cultural innovators become corporate strategists, and today's politicians and statesmen are obliged to discuss global economic issues with rock stars. Ownership of youth culture is now more than ever in the arms of global corporations, with young people participating merely '…as passive (if enthusiastic) consumers' (ibid).

3.1.1.3.1 Sports and Culture

Due to its international promotion through the media, sport has become a global commodity which is in theory available and accessible to everyone. But as exclusive rights for brands and broadcasting rights become more monopolised and consequently more expensive, the cost for consumers also increases. The promotion of sport through the media also encourages a greater degree of passive consumption at the expense of active participation.

Sponsorship and grant aid tend to promote male sporting activities and organisations over their female equivalents, and with some notable exceptions such as tennis and gymnastics, media coverage favours male sports and personalities (Rowe, 1995). Treatment of those sports particularly associated with women often emphasise ideals of physical beauty and sexual attractiveness that mirror and reinforce the stereotypes already defined by films, TV and magazines (Haregreaves cited in Rowe, 1995).

Participation in sports offers many benefits to young people: they learn to respect their bodies, and develop fitness, dexterity, co-ordination and physical skills; they are encouraged to learn the importance of participation, loyalty, commitment and teamwork; they develop socialising skills and gain opportunities to travel outside their own area. Self esteem can be enhanced through sport; achievements can be celebrated and disappointments endured. Sports can make a major contribution to enriching and broadening the experiences of otherwise disadvantaged young people, provided they are capable of achieving a certain level of expertise.

But the promotion in certain male sports of a particular form of macho culture, with its emphasis on competition, power and success, can lead to the exclusion of those who fail to 'measure up', whether in terms of 'masculinity', commitment or physical co-ordination. Many young males choose not to participate in mainstream sports, and instead opt for alternative activities such as skateboarding, rollerblading or biking. Although these activities can be legitimately seen as equally effective in enriching the lives of their adherents, the resources and supports available in this area from statutory and commercial organisations falls pitifully short of what is currently available to more conventional sports.

Through involvement in sports dominated by a macho culture, "...boys learn early that to be gay, to be suspected of being gay, or even to be unable to prove one's heterosexual status is not acceptable" (Messner cited in Rowe, 1995 : p74). Girls and women are generally excluded from this culture except in supportive and marginal roles. Even though sport has succeeded in providing some notable gay and lesbian role models, an over emphasis on dominant male heterosexual values of competition and aggression can lead to the denigration and consequent exclusion of gay and lesbian participants.

Social class inequalities are also seen to be perpetuated by certain sports, where membership of clubs and a limited access to resources exclude those that can not afford them. While soccer, GAA and athletics are viewed by aspiring participants as offering them opportunities regardless of class background, other organised sports such as competitive swimming, tennis and golf are generally unavailable to many young people from disadvantage communities, even where facilities exist within their local area (Rowe, 1995).

3.1.1.3.2 Flexibility

There are some positive aspects however, to the establishment's appropriating and absorbing of youth culture. Increasingly, more flexible and progressive approaches are influencing mainstream thinking about adolescence (e.g. The Irish Government's National Children's Strategy (2000)), whether in analysing the 'problems' generally associated with young people, or in designing and delivering services and supports relevant and appropriate to this client group.

'Constructionists claim...that the conviction that social science can enable us to build up an objective picture of what young people are 'really' like or 'really' experience or 'really' need is misguided; there are no direct ways to know 'the truth'...What we have (and all we have) are local and contingent markers, set up in current law, guidance and practice, that simply have to be made to work until the next set of changes' (Rogers in Roche and Tucker, 1997 : p181-2).

3.1.1.4 Psycho-Social Development

One of the key figures in encouraging such an approach was John Hill, whose seminal paper *Some Perspectives on Adolescence in American Society* (1973) identified six central psycho-social themes of adolescent development (detachment-autonomy, intimacy, sexuality, achievement, identity), which he linked to bio-psychosocial factors (e.g. puberty, cognition, self-definition) and contextual influences (gender, race-ethnicity, social class) (Adams et al, 1996 : p2).

'In particular, Hill indicated that:

- issues of social class, ethnicity-race, and gender are important contextual factors in which individual development is embedded;
- biological factors of genital maturation, pubertal timing and physical growth, and changes in physical development interact with relationship roles that influence individual development;
- a comprehensive understanding of psychosocial development must include motivational, behavioural, and cognitive components' (ibid).

Because it links the life of the person to that of their environment, Hill saw his model as an ecological theory of human development. Since its first presentation to the U.S. Department of Health, Education and Welfare in 1973, Hill's paper has continued to influence contemporary research in this field. Its developmental contextual view of adolescence forms the theoretical framework of the National Children's Strategy (Government Publications, 2000).

This strategy represents the Irish Social Policy planning guide on services and supports to Irish children for the next decade. Its 'whole child perspective' involves the 'dynamic interaction of three aspects' of the child's life: 'the child's own capacities; the multiple interlinked dimensions of children's development; and the complex mix of formal and informal supports that children rely on' (ibid., p25).

These aspects are further developed in identifying nine dimensions of childhood development:

- Physical and mental well being;
- Emotional and behavioural wellbeing;
- Intellectual capacity;
- Spiritual and moral wellbeing;
- Identity
- Self-care
- Family Relationships;
- Social and Peer Relationships;
- Social Presentation.

(ibid., p27).

The Vision of the Strategy, in emphasising themes of inclusion and participation, reflects a positive, progressive understanding of childhood and adolescence '...where children are respected as young citizens with a valued contribution to make, and a voice of their own; where all children are cherished and supported by family and the wider society; where they enjoy a fulfilling childhood and realise their potential' (ibid., p4).

This research project – on young people's perceptions of their own needs and of the responses by service providers that they consider appropriate to meeting those needs – is in part motivated by the request in the strategy for 'better research and information on children (which) is urgently required to improve the quality and effectiveness of the services and supports being provided to them and their families' (ibid., p38).

The 'urgency' of this requirement expresses a prevailing anxiety among agencies and social commentators that many children and young people today are vulnerable, exposed to unacceptable levels of risk, and lacking sufficient support and protection. But how vulnerable in fact are young people in to-day's world? Is their exposure to risk greater than that of previous generations of young people? And are young people necessarily more 'at risk' in the modern world than their adult counterparts?

Before we can properly examine the relationship between youth and risk, we must first examine how vulnerability and exposure to risk has become ingrained in everyone's day-to-day reality; how, by merely participating in modern society, each of us, whether adult or young person, inevitably comes to accept risk as an unavoidable and ever-present aspect of our lives.

3.2 The Risk Society

We live in age of constant anxiety and insecurity. We learn to accept that political and economic forces, over which we have little if any control, can nevertheless impact in powerful and unpredictable ways on our daily lives. International commentators (particularly Beck and Giddens) have argued that our psychological acceptance of risk is different in quality from that of previous generations, because, through enjoying our modern economic circumstances and lifestyle, we have in some sense colluded in promoting our own vulnerability.

In a more innocent time, when the concept of risk was not interiorised to such a degree, when the general concept of risk could still retain a certain heroic glamour, Sigmund Freud wrote in Thoughts for the Times of War and Death: 'Life is impoverished, it loses interest, when the highest stake in the game of living – life itself – may not be risked' (1915, ibid.).

The necessity to take risks would seem to be an essential aspect of our very existence. Erich Fromm in The Fear of Freedom (1942) speaks of the two forms of freedom necessary for growth and autonomy – as the child becomes more free to develop and express its individuality, it is simultaneously freeing itself from a world which offers it security and reassurance. Breaking free from the control and protection of others is fraught with risk, and every step is perilous; but it is nonetheless necessary if the child is to become the adult. Indeed, for Fromm, 'the very helplessness of Man is the basis from which human development springs; man's biological weakness is the condition of all human culture' (ibid., p26).

Ulrich Beck defines risk as '…a systematic way of dealing with hazards and insecurities' (Beck, 1992 : p21), and argues that the acceptance of risk and the practice of 'risk management' are essential if one is to actively participate in modern society.

Beck argues that in the developed world, our relationship to risk has fundamentally changed. Throughout human history, both naturally occurring and socially determined hazards (such as disease, flood, famine, war, oppressive political or economic systems, etc.) had traditionally moulded the fates of individuals and groups. But in today's post-industrial age, our technological mastery over nature obliges us, both as individuals and as members of post-modern society, to manage an acceptable level of risk in our day-to-day lives.

Thus, in our changing employment patterns, in our exploitation of the environment, in our use of pesticides, medicines and drugs, in the preparation of our food, in all those areas of life touched by modern technology, we constantly and consciously expose ourselves to a certain level of risk, and make decisions based on our evaluation of that risk. 'In contrast to all earlier epochs (including industrial society), the risk society is characterised essentially by a lack: the impossibility of an external attribute of hazards. In other words, risks depend on decisions; they are industrially produced and in this sense politically reflexive' (ibid., p183). So there is no longer an 'other' which we can criticize or blame as being the author of our fate; we carry within us not only the sense of risk, but also the responsibility for creating that risk.

The sociologist Anthony Giddens regards risk as global and ongoing: 'To recognise the existence of risk or set of risks is to accept not just the possibility that things might go wrong, but that this possibility cannot be eliminated' (Giddens, 1990 : p111). He speaks of 'the runaway, juggernaut character of modernity' which, although driven by human beings, always threatens 'to rush out of control and rend itself asunder' (ibid., p139).

Caught in this predicament, Giddens argues that our attitude to abstract systems (i.e. systems which rely on expert knowledge), based as it must be on partial knowledge only, is inevitably ambivalent, as it combines both a respect for the sophistication of such systems together with a scepticism regarding their supposed omnipotent power. Ironically, this ambivalent acceptance of modernity is seen by Giddens to reawaken in us the ancient sense of dread, of Fortuna or Fate; '…a feeling that things will take their own course anyway, thus reappears at the core of a world which is supposedly taking rational control of its own affairs' (ibid., p153).

Giddens sees trust as our way of coping with such ambivalence in our everyday lives. For him, trust is a form of 'faith' linked to '…confidence in the reliability of a person or system, regarding a given set of outcomes or events' (ibid., p34). Because we lack full information, we must trust 'abstract systems' (e.g. money, science, medicine, banking, travel, power-supply, etc.), which utilise expert knowledge we do not possess, and over which we have little or no personal control. 'In conditions of modernity, attitudes of trust towards abstract systems are usually routinely incorporated into the continuity of day-to-day activities, and are to a large extent enforced by the intrinsic circumstances of daily life' (ibid., p90).

Risk and trust intertwine. Patterns of risk are regularly presented to us within a surrounding framework of trust, from investing in the stock market to playing dangerous sports, and '…in all trust settings, there is always a balance between trust and the calculation of risk' (ibid., p34).

Given that risk is a product of our everyday activities and the management of risk an ongoing imperative of modern life, we should therefore view risk as a continuum, a spectrum of hazard, and the limits of acceptable risk as socially constructed, contextual and necessarily relative. As one investigation into adult risk-taking within a specific cultural framework concludes: 'Risk boundaries delimiting 'perceivably normal' courses of action remain highly flexible and dynamic…Adherence to particular rules of conduct is therefore not…clear-cut' (Monaghan, Bloor, Dobash and Dobash, 2000 : Conclusion 6.3).

Consequently, we need to regard terms such as 'taking risks' and 'risky behaviour' as laden with culture-specific judgements, individual interpretations, and subjective meanings.

3.3 Young People and Risk

For young people, the limits of acceptable risk are regarded as different from those that adults can competently manage. Parents, and those in loco parentis, naturally tend to see their charges as more vulnerable than themselves, and adopt 'protective' strategies to defend them against the risks inherent in the 'adult' world. But is the parent or guardian always best equipped to decide which approach is most appropriate, or even effective? And if adult intervention is 'badly' managed, is the young person always obliged to respond with obedience and deference? And what of those adults who attempt to exert unreasonable levels of power and control? Or of those who exploit children through economic or physical abuse? In short, are adults invariably in the best position to measure 'acceptable' levels of risk that young people in their 'care' are likely to encounter?

Most western states refrain from awarding full rights of autonomy to adolescents until they reach eighteen years, on the basis that anyone under that age is not yet sufficiently competent in making 'mature' choices or decisions, and therefore requires protection. The Irish State, for example, reserves the right to intervene when it judges that insufficient protection is offered to the child by its immediate family, under the Child Care Act, 1991.

However, many studies have challenged this assumption of young people's lack of competence, and demonstrate that 'once most teens reach middle adolescence (age 16) they seem to apply similar decision-making processes as do adults...' (Melton cited in Adams et al, 1996 : p45).

But there is also a wealth of evidence to indicate that 'prior to age 16, most teens display a good number of deficiencies in their decision making skills, although this may vary with topic or situation; for example, early adolescents are less likely to consider future consequences or to recommend consultation with specialists, when arriving at major decisions' (ibid, p50).

Bell & Bell (1995) argue that taking risks is a necessary aspect of adolescent behaviour, as one aspect of the process of exploring one's own self, of shaping one's own identity, through making decisions and taking initiatives. They identify three types of risk-taking:

- Developmentally enhancing (e.g. rock climbing, canoeing);
- Dangerous (e.g. joy riding, unprotected sex);
- Life-threatening (e.g. fighting with knives or guns)

(ibid., p167).

There is also an important distinction to be made between active and reactive risk-taking: 'Active risk taking might be associated with positive adaptations, successes and resourcefulness, rather than simply being a reaction to stressful circumstances, even though it may put the individual at substantial personal risk to health and safety' (Anderson et al in Bell & Bell, 1995 : p169). These authors suggest that distinguishing between the two '...will require a consideration not only of the context, but also of the individual's perception of, and reaction to that context.' (ibid.)

So our perceptions of levels of risk appear to be subjective and situational. In consequence, the adolescent judges the risk margins in any activity in relation to predicable gains and losses for him or herself. Nevertheless, certain factors do prevail in society, and within families, that are seen to increase levels of risk taking among adolescents. Bell & Bell (1995) categorise the negative factors involved as follows:

Individual Factors:

- Low academic performance
- Poor self esteem/ self image
- Underestimating one's own vulnerability
- Lack of skills to resist peer pressure
- False perceptions of actual risk
- Ignoring factual information
- Seeking immediate rather than deferred rewards

- Risk of imprisonment
- Regular pattern of re-offending

Family Factors:
- Poverty, social exclusion
- Low socio-economic status
- Low level of parental support and control
- Parental involvement in risk behaviours
- Parenting Styles
- Maladaptive family situation
- Parental denial
- Lack of parental knowledge of consequences of specific behaviours
- Family isolation
- Pattern of problems with law enforcement agents

Environmental factors:
- Relative poverty
- Lack of resources
- School structures
- Transition between schools
- Prevalence of substance abuse
- Absence of positive role models
- Patterns of peer initiation
- Ageing population
- Relationship with law enforcement agents
- High level of social welfare dependence

(ibid).

Bell & Bell (1995) argue that these factors are cumulative in effect; that any single factor is relatively insignificant in assessing risk, but risk increases exponentially with every extra factor that applies. So, for example, a child who experiences four of these factors has sixteen times (i.e 2x2x2x2) the exposure to risk as the child for whom only one factor applies.

Many of the **Individual** factors cited above will be dealt with in the next section on **Resilience**. Before moving to this topic, we first examine the influence on adolescent development of **Family** and **Environmental** factors, under three separate headings: Social Influences, Health Issues, and Active Risk Taking.

3.3.1 Social Influences

Poverty is a major negative risk factor in both social and domestic terms, and levels of poverty among young people in Ireland are relatively high. The 1996 census recorded 1,071,972 people living within the state under the age of 18, which, at 29% of the total, represents the highest proportion of children in any EU population (CSO Census, 1996). Ireland also has the highest percentage of households with children within the EU, at 43% (National Children's Strategy, 2000 : p16).

One in four of these children live in poverty (NAPS, 1997 : p43). Ireland has the second highest level of child poverty in the EU, and the highest concentration of child poverty outside the United States (Eurostat, 1997). In the South-East, 'nearly one fifth (19%) of children aged less than 15 years…live in the most deprived District Electoral Divisions' (SEHB, 1998 : p31).

Although the nature and causes of poverty may be complex, its effects on children's lives are all too clear. 'The multi-dimensional nature of child poverty means that it impacts on all aspects of children's lives' (National Children's Strategy, 2000 : p63). Children's health suffers: 'virtually all aspects of health are worse among children living in poverty than among children from affluent classes' (SEHB, 1998 : p31). But children are placed at risk in other ways too. 'Poor children have been shown to do less well educationally…, are vulnerable to homelessness and delinquent behaviour and have fewer opportunities in life' (NAPS, 1997 : p47).

Clearly, reducing levels of poverty would have a profound impact on removing unacceptable risk from children's lives. 'Child poverty is a denial of the basic right of a child to an adequate standard of living…It is not an individual problem, but a structural one, arising from inadequate income' (Combat Poverty Agency, 1999 : p7).

Promoting **employment** opportunities is one effective way of tackling poverty. 'Employment is recognised as the best way out of poverty for families' (National Children's Strategy, 2000 : p63). Lack of job opportunities has long term consequences for society, and particularly for young people. 'It is generally recognised that most young people who are unemployed, or in low paid jobs, will be at risk of poverty, and may live in persistent poverty' (NYCI, 2001 : p5).

While the Irish economy has made impressive gains in the past decade, not least in the area of job creation, politicians and economists alike acknowledge that County Wexford has not benefited from the Celtic Tiger to the same extent as its more successful neighbours (Wexford People, 15/05/02). This assessment is confirmed by unemployment rates in Co. Wexford, which are higher than the national average: (Table 3.1)

Table 3.1 : Unemployment Rates in Wexford vs. National Average

Unemployment Rate	Co. Wexford	National
Male	18.4%	16.4%
Female	13.6%	12.0%
Total	16.8%	14.8%

(Dept. of Social, Community and Family Affairs, 2001)

The Bacon (1999) Report on Co. Wexford points to present weaknesses in this county's employment structures, associated with:

- a high dependence on agriculture,
- a concentration on traditional industries,
- relatively little foreign investment and
- an underdeveloped tourism industry.

(Bacon, 1999).

Unemployment in Co. Wexford is not evenly distributed but localised, and can be deeply rooted in particular areas (McMahon et al, 1998).

An established link exists between **unemployment** and **educational attainment**, where again, Wexford is seen to be relatively disadvantaged, with lower attainment rates at both second and third level than the national average (See Chapter Two, 2.13)

The Bacon Report states that 'higher levels of education and training enhance both earning and employment prospects' (Bacon, 1999 : p55), and that in the future, education is likely to become even more important in securing employment. Current trends suggest that 'knowledge workers' will become the dominant group in the workforce within the next twenty years.

'Knowledge workers' will have specialist skills and will be highly mobile. Flexibility, frequent changes of job and continuous re-education through e-learning and seminars will become the norm; competitiveness within professions and job insecurity will be much more pronounced (Drucker, 2001). In such conditions, a high level of formal education will be essential in order to secure well paid employment. A reserve workforce, comprising early school leavers and those who lack the ability to 'sell' their skills, will face a lifetime of sporadic and poorly paid employment (Galbraith, 1992).

Current educational provision at second level in Ireland is not meeting this challenge, and significant gaps are evident, particularly in the area of **early school leaving**. Of the 70,000 school leavers in Ireland in 1996-97, almost one in five left without a Leaving Cert, and 3.5%, or 2,500, left with no qualification whatsoever. An additional 800 failed to transfer from primary to second level (Dept. of Education & Science Statistical Report, 1998/99).

Although half of all students nationally are from a working class background or with unemployed parents, 88% of early school leavers come from this sector (NESC Report no.11, 1997). When asked for their views, early school leavers in Wexford 'thought school was irrelevant, they didn't get on with teachers, felt themselves to be 'behind' others, and felt that they were not succeeding and didn't belong there' (McMahon et al, 1998).

In addition, national access to third level education is unequal, 'with school leavers in some middle class areas ten times more likely to go to college than those from poorer areas' (HEA Report by Prof. Patrick Clancy cited in The Irish Times, 26/03/02). In Wexford, 'costs may well be a limiting factor on demand, as there are no third level facilities in the county' (Bacon, 2001 : p41), and while Co. Wexford's income levels 'are among the lowest in the country...educational attainment is similarly low' (ibid.). In fact, only three counties (Donegal, Louth and Monaghan) have a higher proportion of early school leavers than Wexford (ibid., p40).

Risk factors associated with poverty, poor educational attainment and limited employment prospects can impact significantly on young people's health: 'A considerable amount of young people experience poverty, lack of social support networks, family breakdown, educational/professional challenges, (and) low standards of nutrition; all of these affect healthy growth and development' (NCCHC, 2000 : p23).

3.3.2 Health Issues

Perhaps the most prevalent (and certainly the most publicised) of adolescent behaviours that challenge propriety is their use and misuse of drugs. Although 90% of young Irish people agree with the statement that '**smoking** is bad for your health' (Dept of Health, 1996), one child in five between 9 and 17 is a 'regular' smoker (HBSC, 1999). Ireland still comes out 'top or close to it, in most of the smoking categories' in a European school survey (ESPAD, 1995).

Figures in the South-East are, if anything, higher. A SEHB 1998 study of school pupils aged 9-17 indicates that 'nearly one in four (23%) are current smokers', with higher ratios in the older (15-17) age group where 31% of boys as against 32% of girls are current smokers (SEHB, 1998 : p17). More boys in lower social class groups smoked, but there was no similar trend for girls (ibid.).

Anecdotal evidence suggests that adolescents start drinking **alcohol** at an earlier age, and drink more often and in greater quantities than in previous decades (Sheridan, 2002). A recent study showed a 41% increase in the amount of alcohol consumed in Ireland in the decade between 1989 and 1999. This compares with a fall in consumption in ten EC countries during the same period, and an increase of less than 5% in the remaining four (Interim Report of the Strategic Task Force on Alcohol, cited in the Irish Times 29/05/02).

Seven out of eight 16 year old Irish students surveyed by ESPAD had drunk alcohol in the previous twelve months, with two-thirds admitting to having been drunk at least once

(ESPAD, 1995). Apart from the health implications of alcohol abuse, the association of drunkenness with violence and anti-social behaviour add further risk factors (Sheridan, 2002). In 1999, the Gardai made over 1,400 charges against juveniles on drink-related offences, and a further 1,300 charges on public order and assault offences, and the pattern is increasing (Garda Siochana Annual Report, Dept of Justice, 1999 : p93).

These figures place Irish teenagers' alcohol consumption second highest in Europe (ESPAD, 1995), and yet appear to underestimate young people's levels of drinking 'when compared to the results of regional studies' (Youth as a Resource, Dept of Health and Children, 1999 : p12). In the South-East Region, one in three school pupils reported that they had been drunk at least once, with the proportion higher in boys, and in the older age groups. Over a ten year period (1987-1998) in this region, 'alcohol consumption has risen dramatically, especially in the older age groups' (SEHB, 1998 : p19).

Three out of five seventeen year olds who have left school are 'regular drinkers', with slightly lower levels for their counterparts still in school (Dept. of Health and Children, 1999 : p12). One study found that 'early school leavers were at high risk of increased drinking levels, and possibly problem drinking' (ibid.).

Illicit drug use is also common in Ireland, with 37% of 16 year olds having used **cannabis/ marijuana**, 16% having used another illicit drug, and 7% having used tranquillisers or sedatives (ESPAD, 1995). Treatment statistics indicate a marked difference in drug choice between clients under 15 and older users; those under 15 who were referred for treatment chiefly use cannabis (58%), volatile inhalants (20%) and opiates (17%), whereas for older clients, opiates predominate (Youth as a Resource, Dept. of Health and Children, 1999 : p12). The use of opiates is more prevalent among inner city unemployed youths, but these drugs are readily obtainable everywhere (SEHB Survey, 1998). In a study of a drug treatment programme in the Dublin area, 58% of respondents were early school leavers and 83% were unemployed (Dept. of Health and Children, 1999 : p12).

In the South-East, 23% of 15-17 year old male students had admitted using drugs in the previous month, as opposed to 15% of 15-17 year old females (SEHB Survey, 1998). The most frequently used drugs were solvents (227 users), cannabis (108) and magic mushrooms (98). It is important to remember that 'substance abuse is normally experimental in nature, and only a small percentage will develop an addiction. However substance abuse and dependence in the 15-24 age group is frequently associated with mental health disorders such as depression' (NCCHC, 2000 : p27). A further risk factor is the link that young people may establish with criminal elements to secure their supply.

Of the 135 clients who attended the *Community Counselling Service* in Co. Wexford, only 7% were under twenty years old, but 33% were between 20 and 30. The majority of older clients had begun misusing drugs and alcohol in their teens (Co. Wexford CBDI, 2002 : p6). A significant proportion of those receiving counselling (38%) are either unemployed or on a training course (ibid.). The age profile of clients of the *Wexford Addiction Support*

Service was similar. In its first year of operation, this service based in Wexford Town saw 69 new clients, who generally abused cannabis, ecstasy or alcohol, with a gender breakdown of 78% male and 22% female (The Cornmarket Project, WAP, 2002).

However gender-specific issues have been identified that inhibit women drug misusers from seeking assistance and support. These issues are embedded in social contexts. Particularly in areas where there is a traditionally low level of education, inadequate housing and poverty, and where the roles of carer and home-maker are culturally assigned to females, women often put the needs of partners, husbands and children before their own '…to the detriment of their own health and well being' (Butler and Woods cited in Maycock, 2000). The fear of being labelled "unfit" mothers if identified as drugs users often leads women to greater secretiveness in their drug misuse, and Mayock (2000) reports several cases of drug misuse among female-only groups.

If the stigma attached to addiction is a greater issue for women than for men, then statistics indicating a predominance of younger males seeking help from agencies may mask the reality on the ground. Consequently, assumptions based on these figures may lead to an underestimating of the prevalence of drug misuse among younger females.

Adolescents are perhaps more responsible and more restrained in regard to **sexual activity** than is popularly acknowledged. In a Galway study of school-going teenagers, 29% of the males and 15% of the females admitted to having had sexual intercourse (McHale, 1994, cited in Youth as a Resource, Dept of Health and Children, 1999). A later Cork study (Alliance, 1998) suggested higher figures (32% of males and 22% of females having had sex by the age of 16), but also noted that 55% of males and 70% of females aged 15-17 said they were still virgins (cited in Youth as a Resource, Dept of Health and Children, 1999). Condoms were used by 59% of the sexually active males, and by 70% of the sexually active females (ibid., p16); nevertheless 'in Ireland, rates of STIs in general have been increasing' (NCCHC, p26).

The SAVI Report (2002) indicates the prevalence of **sexual abuse** in Ireland. From interviews with over 3000 adults, its findings indicate that close to a quarter of all males and almost one in three females have experienced sexual abuse as children. (see Table 3.2)

Table 3.2 : Types of Unwanted Sexual Experiences by Age at Abuse (child<17 years), categorised by Most Serious Level of Abuse Experienced.

Most Serious Levels of Sexual Abuse/Assault Experienced	Male	Female
Child Pornography	2.7%	0.8%
Indecent Exposure	4.7%	9.2%
Contact Abuse (no penetration)	12.0%	12.8%
Attempted Penetration	1.5%	2.0%
Penetration/ Oral sex	2.7%	5.6%
% of Total	23.6%	30.4%

(McGee et al, 2002 : p68)

Although the number of **teenage pregnancies** has not increased greatly since 1970, only 5% of new mothers under twenty were married in 1997, compared to 50% in 1970. This has consequences for the household's income levels, as '…children of adults parenting alone face a higher risk of poverty' (National Children's Strategy, 2000 : p18.) In 1996, the SEHB 'had a higher rate of teenage pregnancies than the national average, with 338 births to teenage mothers, 98% of whom were single' (SEHB, 1999 : p10). **Abortion** rates for teenagers 'have changed little since the mid 1980s' (NCCHC, 2000 : p27). The majority of patients attending the STI clinic in Waterford in 1998 were over 20 years old, but the number of those under 20 have increased each year since 1996 (SEHB, 1998 : p77). There is no published evidence available of organised teenage **prostitution** in Co. Wexford.

Diet regimes figure more in the lives of young females (12%) than young males (4%), and 28% of females admitted a wish to lose weight, as against 18% of young males (Youth as a Resource, Dept of Health and Children, 1999). Disorders such as **anorexia** and **bulimia** are to some extent culturally driven, but their prevalence is hard to quantify because of their secretive nature. Overall quality of diet, which can have a major influence on physical and intellectual development, is clearly related to socio-economic background: the Murphy-Lawless (1992) study found that average-income families 'had better quality food, larger portions and greater variety' than families depending on welfare, who 'relied heavily on cheap filler foods like potatoes and white bread' (cited in NAPS, 1996 : p55.)

Although most Travellers claim to have regular contact with the settled community, Travellers are still marginalised and 'very high proportions of Travellers claim to have direct experience of **discrimination**' (Citizen Traveller Survey, 2000).

'In terms of mental health, nearly 10% of 15-24 year-olds appear to suffer from signs of **depression** that are clinically recognised' (NCCHC, 2000 : p25). 'Mental Health disorders are much more common amongst disadvantaged groups in society' (ibid.). National admissions to psychiatric hospitals for those aged 19 and under totalled 859 in 1996, '…with considerably more coming from the unskilled manual group than any other background' (Youth as a Resource, Dept of Health and Children, 1999 : p15.) Other factors that can contribute to a sense of **isolation** include sexual orientation, ethnic background, physical or intellectual disability, family lifestyle, and living in a remote or poorly serviced area.

'Between 1980 and 1995, the **suicide** rate for males doubled…Suicide is now the most common cause of death among 15-24 year-old males in Ireland…and is particularly a rural phenomenon' (P.MacGiolla Bhain, *Magill Magazine*, 2001 : p15). Para-suicide (i.e. severe self-harm or attempted suicide) is more common in urban areas, is as frequent among females as males, and is more associated with high density rented housing, limited education and unemployment (Youth as a Resource, Dept of Health and Children, 1999 : p15.)

3.3.3 Active Risk Taking

There is a strong association between social class and risk of **injury** and death from injury, with those from lower socio-economic backgrounds being far more vulnerable to a wide range of injuries and accidents (Youth as a Resource, Dept of Health and Children, 1999 : p16.) In 1993, 40% of all childhood deaths nationally (aged 1-14) were from injuries. Of these, 48.6% were from **traffic accidents**. Drivers aged 24 or under were involved in a quarter of all fatal and injury accidents in the state in 2000, but were held responsible for 60% of accidents where contributory factors were reported (NRA, 2001). The number of 18-24 year olds killed in road traffic accidents was much higher than for any other age group. Weekend nights are the most common times for young driver accidents to occur, and the most frequently cited contributory factor in fatal two car accidents is speed. (ibid.)

Young people are not generally sufficiently **safety-conscious**. The SEHB report on *Our Children's Health* (1998) concludes that the '…usage rates of proven safety aids' (e.g. safety belts (40%) and cycling helmets (under 10%) '…are disappointing and warrant efforts by all agencies to educate and promote their use' (SEHB, 1998 : p24).

The national figures on **juvenile offenders** for the year 2000 indicate that larceny (21%), criminal damage (13%), alcohol-related offences (12%) and motoring offences are the most common causes of court appearances by juveniles (see Chapter 2, 2.15). One fifth of all referrals which led to a prosecution or caution involved female offenders (ibid.)

Figures relating to the previous year (1999) indicate that 85% of all juveniles given court orders (for more serious or persistent offending) were male, and that the rate of offending tends to peak between the ages of 15 and 16:

Table 3.3 : Age of Juvenile Offender 1999

Age	17	16	15	14	13	12	Under 12
%of Total	18%	23%	22%	15%	9%	5%	8%

(Garda Siochana Annual Report, 1999, p89-90).

Evenings are the most frequent time for offences to occur: 'The majority of the activity (69%) occurred fairly evenly across the hours from 2pm to midnight, with activity at its highest between 8pm and 10pm' (ibid : p90).

Of all offenders given a court order (as opposed to a custodial sentence) in the District Courts in 1999, one male offender in every six, and one female offender in every eight was under 18 years old (Probation and Welfare Service Report, 1999 : p29).

Being **homeless**, whether by choice or circumstance, leaves young people vulnerable. 'Homelessness is more than lacking material items, it is also a cause of mental distress, characterised by insecurity and low self-esteem' (Dept of Health & Children, 2001 : p11.)

Between 1998 and 2000, the number of homeless young people in the South-East Region increased from 65 to 110 (ibid. : p13), with 'family problems' or 'emotional/ behavioural problems' identified as the primary causes as to why 'they believed that their home was not a place they could reasonably occupy' (SEHB, 1998 : p52). In County Wexford, 19 young people were designated as homeless in 1998; 11 were given hostel accommodation and 7 assisted independent accommodation (ibid.)

Young people who arrange to stay with friends or relatives ('sofa surfing') can have the same sense of homelessness, but may not come to the attention of support services, and their numbers are far harder to quantify. Also, older adolescents may choose rented accommodation or a squat, in preference to staying in the family home, but again can avoid contact with services.

However being exposed to factors of vulnerability in adolescence does not inevitably lead to long-term difficulties in adult life. It is important to remember that 'only a minority of at-risk children ... experience serious difficulties in their personality development' (Hauser et al, cited in Rak & Patterson, 1996). More focused investigation of those factors that assist young people to overcome negative life circumstances has given rise to a theory of **Resilience** that offers insights into the ways and means by which young people can and do triumph over adversity to achieve full autonomy. 'Resilience provides most vulnerable children with their key to building positive integrated adult lives' (ibid.).

3.4 Resilience

Resilience can be defined as 'the healing potential that may lie naturally within children, in their normal daily experience or their social networks' (Gilligan, 2001). Resilient children display a capacity to rise above adversity, to recover from negative experiences and to overcome often formidable obstacles to healthy growth and development. Inherent and acquired personal qualities, family factors, and supports in their social world can all contribute to nourishing 'the wellsprings of individual strengths' in these children (Yawney, 1999).

From the 1970's, Garmezy, Anthony, Werner and Smith, Rutter and others studied populations of children and adolescents at risk, focusing not on the casualties of negative life-experiences, but on those who managed to survive and overcome challenging or threatening circumstances. The purpose of such studies was to identify the qualities that enable resilient children to overcome those obstacles that hinder others from realising their potential.

The literature points to the existence of a variety of protective and compensatory factors common to the lives and experiences of resilient children. These factors contribute to the process of building resilience at one of three levels: the individual, the family and the wider community, or in the Yawney model, *'interpersonal, intrapersonal and environmental'* (Yawney, 1999).

3.4.1 The Individual

Rak & Patterson identify 'seven characteristic personal qualities common to resilient children:

- An active evocative approach to problem solving;
- An ability from infancy to gain others' positive attention;
- An optimistic view of their experiences;
- An ability to maintain a positive view of life;
- An ability to be alert and autonomous;
- A tendency to seek novel experiences;
- A proactive perspective.'

(Rak & Patterson, 1996)

Wolin and Wolin (1993) also identify a variety of aspects: 'insight, creativity, humour, relationships, morality and initiative'; and Wahlsten (1994) offers the following profile: 'Resilient children have been shown to be more intelligent, more easy-going, more independent and easier to handle' (both cited in Yawney, 1999).

Whether it is the child's 'instinctive' behaviour that creates the desired adult response, or the positive adult influence that reinforces these 'attractive' qualities in the child, is a moot point; but the unsettling conclusion must be that charm, beauty and a pleasing disposition, even at this age, carry distinct advantages for the 'fortunate' child. Happily, life experiences can also provide other opportunities to build resilience.

3.4.2 The Family

Rak & Patterson in looking at family conditions, record the most significant aspects for building resilience as:

- The age of the opposite-sex parent (for a girl, an older father; for a boy, a younger mother);
- Four or fewer children, spaced more than 2 years apart;
- Focused nurturing and little separation from the primary caretaker during the first year of life;
- An array of alternative caretakers when required;
- A multi-age network of kin available to the adolescent at risk, for counselling and support;
- Sibling caretakers or a same-age confidante in childhood;
- Structure and rules in household during adolescence.

(Rak & Patterson, 1996).

Gilligan (2001) sees the family as an extremely powerful agent for promoting self-esteem and self-efficacy. 'Acceptance by people whose relationship the child values, and the accomplishment of tasks the child values, contribute towards their positive self-esteem, their sense of self-worth'. He identifies sources of resilience within the family as:

- social support,
- positive parental childhood,
- good parental health,
- good relationship with sibling,
- education,
- workrole

(Gilligan, 2001).

Howard and Johnson (1998) identify 'the consistency and quality of care and support experienced by the child within the family' as providing protective factors. Families also help to develop coping skills. 'Family context was of crucial importance to the child's development of coping strategy, as lack of support from the parents reduced the child's possibility to revise and develop his or her coping ability' (Montgomery et al cited in Yawney, 1999).

3.4.3 The Wider Community

Environmental supports can produce potential role models and mentors to the child beyond their own family – in schools, clubs, community centres, health and social services, churches and the local neighbourhood (McElwee, 1996). 'Resilient children…often had the possibility of attaching to people outside the family and seem to be able to nourish even from limited contacts with positive people' (Sundelin, Wahlsten, cited in Yawney, 1999).

Furthermore, the wider community offers opportunities for 'nurturing children's sense of belonging and accomplishments, and in preserving positive threads in their lives' (Gilligan, 2001).

Schools play a significant role in most children's lives, providing a rich social and cultural environment, with many possibilities for building self-esteem and affirming positive behaviour. 'Schools that have good academic records and attentive caring teachers can contribute to developing qualities of resilience' (Howard and Johnson, 1998).

But 'good academic records' should not be the only criterion. 'Education must encompass all aspects of the 'whole child' perspective. While it is important that all children leave school with a suitable qualification, the wider focus of education on social, emotional and behavioural wellbeing and physical and mental health is also recognised' (National Children's Strategy, 2000 : p53).

Gilligan also points to the importance of spare time activities in building competence and a sense of achievement in children at risk. 'Such spare-time activities may embrace sport, cultural pursuits, the care of animals, environmental protection and part-time work' (Gilligan, 2001). Work experience programmes and part-time work can also play a part here, provided the job is productive and the worker's contribution acknowledged (Murphy, 2000).

Protective factors operate cumulatively. 'The more protective factors that are present in children's lives, the more likely they are to display resilience…Cumulative protective factors work in the opposite direction (to adverse experiences)…and may have disproportionately positive effects' (Gilligan, 2001).

Intervention need not be carefully planned or structured. 'Neither major special efforts nor special skills are required to demonstrate care and attentiveness – simple acts will do' (Howard and Johnson, 1998). Gilligan refers to the 'turning point', a critical time in a young person's life, when one perhaps spontaneous positive experience may prove to have far-reaching consequences. At a turning point, 'the ripple effect of one strength being unearthed or harnessed may ultimately set off a positive spiral of change in the whole system that is a child's life'(Gilligan, 2001).

There is no single method or approach available to building resilience. 'It is hard to generalise about the most effective ways to mobilise and implement protective factors; they will be individual and particular to the circumstances in which the children find themselves' (Howard and Johnson ,1998).

Resilience fosters in the young person a capacity to engage successfully with the wider society, and trust in abstract or expert systems, as we have seen, is fundamental to that engagement. Organisations dealing with young people, being in themselves expert systems, are in a powerful position to influence their clients' ability to trust abstract systems generally.

According to Giddens, the nature of the engagement at an access point, where the lay person meets the representative of the system, is of fundamental importance, as '…attitudes of trust, or lack of trust, towards specific abstract systems are liable to be strongly influenced by experiences at access points' (Giddens, 2000: p90). Because vulnerability is inherent in any contact at such access points – lay scepticism on the one hand against professional expertise on the other – trust is critical to promoting a successful outcome. Otherwise, for the lay person, '…bad experiences at access points may lead either to a resigned cynicism or, where this is possible, to a disengagement from the system altogether' (ibid., p91). Consequently Giddens views access points as being both 'places of vulnerability' and also 'junctions at which trust can be maintained or built up' (ibid., p88).

Giddens argues that trust in any relationship is dynamic and ongoing; it is '…a project to be worked at by the parties involved, and demands an opening out of the individual to the other. Where it cannot be controlled by fixed normative codes, trust has to be won, and the means of doing this is demonstrable warmth and openness' (ibid., p121).

According to this analysis, effective contact between service providers and young people at access points needs to be based on two guiding principles: a mutual *'opening out of the individual to the other'*, and *'demonstrable warmth and openness'*. Such a formulation has clear implications for the strategies of engagement that service providers ought to adopt in working with young people.

It is clear that at each level (individual, family and community), practical and effective intervention can offer opportunities to build resilience and reduce risk for the vulnerable child. Voluntary and statutory services already provide a variety of programmes that can help to build resilience among young people in Co. Wexford as elsewhere:

- Programmes that build initiative, self-esteem and social integration, activities that offer positive and affirming experiences, and the committed involvement of supportive adults in the community can all assist in empowering the individual child.

- Supports to parents, education and training in parenting skills, improved financial and housing conditions, and increasing employment opportunities can all reinforce positive family influence.

- Encouraging community solidarity, improving neighbourhood facilities and infra structure, developing stronger links within the community and between the community and the schools, social and health services, the police and local and national agencies can help provide positive environments for children, lessen their level of exclusion and reduce their exposure to risk.

The *Family Commission Report* (1998) suggests that 'an approach which is empowering of individuals, builds on family strengths, enhances self-esteem and engenders a sense of being able to influence events in one's life, has significant potential as a primary preventative strategy for all families facing the ordinary challenges of day to day living, and has a particular relevance in communities that are coping in a stressful environment' (Dept. of Social, Community and Family Affairs, 1998, p16).

Issues of access to services remain, and real problems around empowering the most disadvantaged both within and outside established communities must be faced. The aspirations expressed here can be realised only through planned and consistent investment of resources, and any measure of success cannot be assessed in twelve months.

The legislation which enables and funds such a progressive approach has had a long evolution. We have travelled far from the repressive approach traditionally associated with childcare institutions and structures. To understand where we are, we must look back to where we have come from, if only to get a sense of how new and therefore how fragile is the prevailing perspective on the nation's responsibilities towards its young people.

3.5 Irish Legislation on Child Care

The Children Act, 1908 consolidated all 19th century legislation on child care in Ireland and provided the legal basis for the array of childcare services and institutions provided throughout the 20th century by religious orders, local authorities and referral agencies such as the ISPCC (Buckley, Skehill and O'Sullivan, 1997).

3.5.1 The Voluntary Sector

The "moral panics" associated with youth culture (see 3.1.1.3) can be traced back at least to the Industrial Revolution when, through rapidly developing towns and cities, the presence of large groups of adolescents, particularly working class males, was viewed by the middle classes as a threat to public order, morals and values.

In response, youth organisations were established in England as elsewhere to work with young people. Their initial purpose was to improve moral behaviour, encouraging young people to undertake responsible roles in society and become good citizens. The majority had a religious aspect to their work, and their leaders were considered to be role models for the young people in their charge. Examples of such organisation include the Young Men's Christian Association (YMCA), established in 1844, the Young Women's Christian Association (YWCA), established in 1877, and the Boys Brigade, established in 1883.

The early twentieth Century saw the founding of the Boy Scouts (1907) and shortly afterwards, the Girl Guides. Gender roles that applied in the wider society were reinforced by these organisations, as evidenced in the view of the founder of Scouting, Robert Baden Powell:

"The girls' branch is more important, since it affects those who will be the mothers of future generations of boys" (cited in Jenkinson, 1996).

All such organisations are run on a voluntary basis. Their approach can be seen as a conservative one, operating more as mechanism for socially controlling young people than for promoting social justice or equality (Hurley and Treacy, 1993).

In the Irish context, youth work has continued through the past century to be based upon volunteerism. The debate regarding the purpose of youth work has been ongoing however, and significant movement has occurred within organisations, particularly in recent years, towards structures that are more inclusive and participatory.

The Bruton Report (1977) and the O'Sullivan Report (1980) emphasised the need to focus on the personal development of young people, albeit within the prevailing structures. Both reports identified young people as being capable of personal change, but failed to identify a role for them in promoting societal change. Bruton (1977) was first to officially acknowledge the need for full-time workers to support and collaborate with volunteers. However, due to changes in government during this time, these reports' proposals were never fully implemented.

The Costello Report (1984) offered a more critical perspective on the purpose of Youth Work, regarding it primarily as promoting the empowerment of young people. The report acknowledges prevailing social inequalities, and encourages young people both to critically examine their own position in society, and through engagement and participation, to challenge these inequalities. Again this report's recommendations were never implemented, but its recognition of the need for active participation by young people themselves in Youth Work structures and practices has permeated many policy documents produced since then, up to and including The National Children's Strategy (Irish Government, 2000).

The Irish Youth Work sector has traditionally been seen as fragmented and lacking a unifying identity. Organisational structures and models of practice vary (Hurley and Treacy, 1993 and Staunton, 1996); affiliation of organisations to different national bodies (Jenkinson, 2000) and competition for funding have also contributed to its disunity. This lack of cohesion has been cited by a succession of governments as negatively influencing the provision of funding for the sector (Jenkinson, 2000).

The Youth Work sector gained a statutory footing for first time through the Youth Work Act (2001), and now comes under the remit of the Department of Education and Science. In the act, Youth Work is defined as:

"A planned programme of education designed for the purpose of aiding and enhancing the personal and social development of young persons through their voluntary participation, and which is –

(a) complementary to their formal, academic or vocational education and training; and

(b) provided primarily by voluntary youth work organisations.

(ibid.)

While voluntary participation is viewed in the act as a vital principle of youth work, other sectors that have adapted Youth Work methods to their practice may nevertheless retain a compulsory element to participation. So although many government departments do play a significant role in youth provision (such as Enterprise & Employment, Health & Children and Justice, for example), their position vis-à-vis the voluntary nature of their clients' participation differs substantially from that of most Youth Work organisations (Jenkinson, 2000).

As we have seen, the emphasis in Youth Work policy has shifted away from models that promote social control and towards the enabling and empowerment of young people to seek greater social justice for themselves and their peers. However changes in policy within organisations do not necessarily transfer smoothly to practice on the ground (Jeffs and Smith, 1987). Consequently, the vibrancy and dynamism inherent in youth culture may not necessarily be mirrored in Youth Work practice, where emphasis on process for its own sake can often be subordinated to projected goals and outcomes.

3.5.2 The Statutory Sector

Until the 1950s, the numbers of children in institutional care in industrial schools, reformatories, orphanages and foster homes averaged between 7,000 and 8,000 at any given time, and declined gradually thereafter. The *Task Force on Child Care Services*, 1980 commented that '...the most striking feature of the child care scene in Ireland was the alarming complacency and indifference of both the general public and various government departments and statutory bodies responsible for the welfare of children. This state of affairs illustrated clearly the use by a society of residential establishments to divest itself of responsibility for deprived children and delinquent children' (cited in Buckley, Skehill and O'Sullivan, 1997).

But attitudes and terminology were gradually changing. Through the seventies and eighties, the concept of the 'depraved child' was steadily being replaced by that of the 'deprived child', as more enlightened theories of child development gained ground. 'Rather than focusing almost exclusively on the *physical* needs of the child, the need to incorporate *emotional and psychological* dimensions in promoting the welfare of children, gained acceptance' (Buckley, Skehill and O'Sullivan, 1997 : p8).

In the nineteen nineties, the national response to child abuse scandals made the need for reforming legislation and improved services to children even more urgent. 'The decade of the 1990s was one where our society recognised its failure to protect our children from abuse both in the community and in the institutions maintained by the state' (National Children's Strategy, Irish Government, 2000 : p61)

And so the role of the state in child care, which had for two centuries been marginal, (Buckley, Skehill and O'Sullivan, 1997 : p10), underwent dramatic changes after 1970. *The Health Act (1970)* established eight Regional Health Boards, each incorporating a number of Community Care Areas. Responsibility for industrial schools and approved voluntary homes had devolved from local authorities and religious institutions to the Departments of Health and Education by 1984. Over two decades the number of social workers employed by the Health Boards, by local authorities and by voluntary agencies increased substantially, from 235 in 1974 to 726 in 1993 (Buckley, Skehill and O'Sullivan, 1997 : p11). The Department of Health, in its *Child Abuse Guidelines* (1987), promoted transparency in its procedures and co-ordination of resources and expertise in its decision making, and advocated inter-agency and inter-professional co-operation and case conferencing in resolving cases of children at risk.

The *Child Care Act*, 1991 finally replaced the 1908 Act, and was fully implemented by 1997. The Act imposes on each Health Board a statutory duty of care to promote the welfare of children up to the age of 18 in its area. 'There has been a significant increase in social work personnel ...and a number of services have been developed for assessment, treatment and family support work, in order to both respond to the needs of victims of child abuse, and to address primary and secondary intervention' (Buckley, Skehill and O'Sullivan, 1997).

In the last decade, an array of interventions and programmes has been introduced by other government departments to complement the developments brought about in the Child Care Act. The *National Children's Strategy* (Irish Government, 2000) attempts to provide a framework for future legislation and for the development of supports and services to children.

The *National Children's Strategy* involves eight government departments in all, and particularly those with responsibility for children: Education & Science, Health & Children, Social, Community & Family Affairs, and Justice, Equality & Law Reform. So it carries significant legislative weight. The participation of expert Advisory Panels and extensive consultation with service providers and other stakeholders (including children themselves) was intended to ensure that the Strategy would identify and respond to many of the issues affecting young people at risk in Ireland today.

Its main virtue is that it provides a serviceable framework for planning and delivering services and legislation in the area of childcare for the coming decade. The *Three National Goals* identify what needs to be done; *operational principles* are defined, which direct and guide the actions to be taken; and finally, the *mechanisms* for realising the goals, requiring partnerships at national and local level, are spelt out in some detail.

The Three National Goals are:

- **Children will have a voice in matters which affect them and their views will be given weight in accordance with their age and maturity.**
- **Children's lives will be better understood; their lives will benefit from evaluation, research and information on their needs, rights and the effectiveness of services.**
- **Children will receive quality supports and services to promote all aspects of their development.**

(National Children's Strategy, 2000 : p30)

Within the framework provided in the Strategy, a range of legislative and service provision for children's welfare has been implemented in recent years, with an emphasis on consultation, inter-agency co-operation, and participation of young people themselves in decision making. Among the most significant developments have been:

The Task Force Report on the Traveller Community (1995). This report makes recommendations to promote inclusion of the Traveller community in the wider society without compromising their unique culture.

The National Anti-Poverty Strategy (1997). This strategy promotes the involvement of the voluntary and community sector in tackling social exclusion, early school leaving, unemployment and family income support.

The Education (Welfare) Bill (1999) sets up a system where educational welfare officers monitor and advise boards of management on school attendance issues. Schools themselves must draw up and implement programmes and strategies to tackle non-attendance and early school leaving among students. The importance of inter-agency consultation and involvement of parents at all levels is emphasised.

The Youth Homelessness Strategy (2000) provides a framework for interventions with young people who are either homeless, semi-homeless or in inappropriate accommodation.

The National Health Strategy (2001) gives young people a voice on issues that have a bearing on their health.

The Youth Work Act (2001) obliges local Vocational Education Committees to co-ordinate and manage youth work programmes which will be contracted out to voluntary agencies and which will complement the formal education services. A Voluntary Youth Council acting as a forum for all voluntary youth work groups will advise the VEC, and one fifth of its members must be under 20, ensuring a voice for young people.

The Children Act (2002) raises the age of criminal responsibility from 7 to 12 years, and provides a framework for the development of welfare provision for children involved in criminal activity, involving the Probation Services, the Gardai and the Health Boards. The concept of restorative justice and the use of family welfare conferences in drawing up action plans for young offenders are new initiatives in this area.

3.6. Inclusion and Participation

The UN Convention on the Rights of the Child (United Nations, 1990) affirms the child's right to hold and express opinions. *Article 12* confirms on the child '…who is capable of forming his or her own views, the right to express those views freely in all matters affecting the child, the views of the child being given due weight in accordance with the age and maturity of the child.' *Article 13* declares: 'The child shall have the right to freedom of expression; this right shall include freedom to seek, receive and impart information and ideas of all kinds…'

The National Children's Strategy (2000) has as its third goal: 'Children will have a voice in matters which affect them and their views will be given due weight in accordance with their aims and maturity'.

In order to provide meaningful research on what happens in young people's lives, it is clearly necessary to talk to young people themselves, and to listen to their opinions, experiences and feelings. 'In respecting children's competencies, the implication is that ethically sound techniques can add to the value of research' (Thomas and O'Kane, 1998 : p336).

But the power relationship between adults and young people has implications for how issues such as confidentiality, consent and potential exploitation ought to be handled.

'Research with children has largely resulted in objectification, and the denigration of the value of children's own potential contribution to research and to a body of knowledge about how they develop and experience the world' (Hogan and Gilligan, 1997 : p5).

Four key ethical principles that apply in research involving young people are suggested:

Table 3.4 :   Ethical Principles of Research with Children

Types of Right	*Research Ethic Principles*
1. **To satisfactory development and well being**	The purpose of the research should contribute to children's well being, either directly, or indirectly through increased understanding of children which can help adults who are responsible for children.
2. **To protection from harm**	Methods should be designed to avoid stress and distress; contingency arrangements should be available in case children become upset or situations of risk or harm are revealed.
3. **To appropriate services**	Children should whenever possible feel good about having contributed to research as a service which can inform society, individuals, policy and practice.
4. **To express opinions which are taken account of**	Children should make informed choices about: – agreement or refusal to take part – opting out (at any stage) – contributing ideas to research agendas and processes, both for individual research projects and to the research enterprise as a whole.

(ibid. p20)

There is an increasing international trend for programmes directed at young people to involve the young people themselves at all levels – in their design, content and delivery mechanisms, and in their management and monitoring (Senderowitz, 1998 : p1). However, there can be different forms of participation, '…from full participation in decision making to forms of "pseudo-participation" where there is a pretext of participation but really no decision making power is shared' (CWC, 2001).

In a major study of decision making by young people in care in England and Wales, the researchers developed 'a range of participatory techniques designed specifically to allow children to participate on their own terms and to discuss decision-making matters that were relevant to their own lives as they saw them' (Thomas and O'Kane, 1998 : p338).

Potential interviewees had full information on the research, were encouraged to discuss it with their caretakers, could choose if and for how long they would participate, and had as much choice as possible over the research instruments and direction of their interviews (ibid, p339).

Any model for anti-oppressive practice must serve to *empower* the participants. 'If empowerment practice is to be effective it is essential to understand the process which leads from feeling powerless to powerful' (Dalrymple and Burke, 1995 : p52). The core of this process is at the level of *feelings*, focussing on personal biography and analysis of life experiences, and promoting a sense of ownership of one's life and the confidence that comes from being taken seriously. The second level, the level of *ideas*, is where a change in consciousness emerges as initiative develops, increasing the participant's sense of personal power and strength. The third level is that of social and political *action*, which '…may be about changing legislation or policies, but can equally be about the small changes that may effect the life of one individual…making a difference in the world around us' (ibid., p53)

These levels are not segregated but interdependent. Empowerment is an ongoing process, and changes can often occur at the same time at various levels and so enhance one another. Risks and setbacks are inevitable, and supports are required to avoid a return to the former state of powerlessness (ibid.). But empowerment is a key component of resilience, both at individual and community level, and critical to the process of tackling discrimination and exclusion.

3.7 Conclusion

In extending the psycho-social model of personal development into the areas of resilience and empowerment, we have attempted to connect the need that all young people have to be acknowledged, consulted and involved in decision making, with the themes underpinning much of the progressive thinking influencing current and prospective legislation and service provision.

Any attempt to overcome risk factors in communities must recognise that poverty, social exclusion and their impact on educational attainment and employment prospects have a critical influence on young people's futures. Remedial programmes and activities must acknowledge and challenge these forces if they are to be really effective.

The process of empowerment involves changing awareness and questioning accepted values and systems. The empowering of young people, through their taking on real authority and autonomy in decisions concerning their own lives, may in the short term increase the risk of mistakes being made. But mistakes are not exclusive to the young. And the wish for power and autonomy is the essence of adolescent yearning. It is through developing their own resilience and self-esteem, through experiencing personal responsibility, through actively participating in social and political reform within and beyond their community, that young people can *themselves* reduce the levels of risk to which their environment and culture exposes them on a daily basis.

Chapter Four
Research Design and Methodology

4. Introduction

This chapter outlines the decisions taken and implemented to progress the research from its initial proposal stage to its realisation as a complete project. The information is presented in ten sections:

4.1 Research Families looks at research epistemologies and identifies the approaches agreed for this project.

4.2 The Ethical Framework was ratified by the Steering Group prior to conducting the study. It was essential that the ethics were based upon good practice guidelines (See Literature Review 4.6) that promote positive experiences for all involved.

4.3 Boundaries of the Study were established by the Steering Group to provide definition and maintain the focus of the project.

4.4 Sampling describes different sampling methods and identifies the reasons for selecting the methods used in this project.

4.5 Data Collection and Design provides details regarding the pre-planning of engagement strategies and details the data collections tools used to gather information from participants.

4.6 Data Management outlines the thematic framework employed to collate raw data in order to extract meaning from the information supplied by participants.

4.7 Bias Proofing Day describes the consultative process employed to seek to ensure that the recorded perceptions and opinions of participants were not lost or distorted by the researchers' analysis.

4.8 Delimitations looks critically at various aspects of the project, including the pilot project, questionnaires, focus groups and time constraints.

4.9 Study Trips is a brief outline of existing projects in Ireland working with similar target groups which the researchers visited as an information gathering exercise.

4.10 Conclusion summarises the main elements of the methodology, emphasising the principles of equality and participation which underpinned the process of recording the perceptions of young people regarding supports available to them in their own environment.

4.1 Research Families

The epistemologies of Positivism and Human Interpretativism underpin different research families. Positivism, a functionalist perspective, studies causal relationships by using systematic gathering of precisely measurable data to test pre-determined hypotheses, and is generally referred to as quantitative research (Bilton, 1997).

Advocates of Human Interpretativism argue that rich sources of data and knowledge are excluded form research investigations by using quantitative methods. Qualitative research methods utilise collection tools that enable participants to provide data around their experiences, attitudes, feelings and perceptions. Such details are seen to be obtained by the researchers becoming immersed in the social situation of the people being studied.

Throughout a qualitative research process, researchers observe and interact with the research participants and detailed notes are kept of these interactions. It is from these recordings that researchers are able to identify emerging themes and concepts. However, as additional information is gathered, these themes and concepts may change, develop and expand. Therefore, qualitative research involves a back and forth process, which leads to a theory only when adequate data has been collected. Theories resulting from this process are seen to be less generalisable than quantitative equivalents, but they are intended to supply a richer and deeper understanding of the reality of the people being studied.

Considering that the aims of this research project included the need to gather information directly from and with young people, a qualitative research approach was selected as the more suitable.

4.1.1 Organic Growth of the Project

The original proposal to conduct a 'Collaborative Action Research' was debated at various Steering Group meetings. It was decided that it would not be a feasible methodology for the following reasons:

- The researchers felt that the genuine "action" of facilitating young people to design, implement and evaluate possible solutions for the statutory and voluntary organisations would be impossible, due to the time-scale and the number of agencies involved in the initiative.

- If agencies did agree to operate pilot programmes, would resources, premises, staffing and existing decision-making structures facilitate the authentic participation of young people? If not, such a form of research would be open to legitimate criticism, and undermine the validity of the project.

Nevertheless, the research question provided by the Steering Group required the project to obtain the perceptions of young people on current services, and to assist young people to identify their own needs and ways of meeting those needs. However, the project did not require the implementation and evaluation of proposed new services during the research, so the Collaborative Action Research method was not seen as prescribed.

This led to the decision by the Steering Committee to utilise 'Participatory Narrative Inquiry' in place of Collaborative Action Research.

Although a different methodology, Participatory Narrative Inquiry is an approach that also belongs to the qualitative research family, and is underpinned by the principles of participation and equality. As such, this research approach facilitates both researchers and participants to bring their own views to the research process.

As Miles and Huberman (1994) state, "researchers are no more 'detached' from their objects of study than their informants." At the outset, this recognition that the researchers' own biases can influence outcomes and interpretations of interactions caused measures to be designed to safeguard against the loss of the young people's point of view and meanings. (See 4.7 Bias Proofing Day)

4.2 Ethical Framework

Following discussion, the Steering Group ratified and agreed an Ethical Framework for this study (16th July, 2001) which is based on the current guidelines of the Sociological Association of Ireland and the Psychological Association of Ireland. The ethical considerations are presented under the following headings:

- Consent
- Confidentiality
- Storage of information
- Respect
- Working with young people under influence (alcohol, drugs or substance usage)
- Prevention of harm
- Equality proofing.

4.2.1 Consent

Young people with whom the researchers come into contact will be informed of the nature and purposes of the work at the earliest possible opportunity. In the case of detached work (see 4.3.2 below) this will be at the stage where the researchers attempt to engage with or are first approached by young people. In the case of the thematic entry points (see 4.3.2 below) this will be outlined during the initial outreach/contact phase or by gatekeepers if they are being used.

Written informed consent is to be sought from all young people at or above the age of 15.

Written consent is to be sought from young people and parents/guardians of young people under the age of 15.

Consent is to be sought at the data collection stage (focus groups) rather than at the initial data collection stage.

The research will obtain written consent from young people and/or their parents/guardians before the stage of formal data collection begins. No data received before this stage will be recorded or used in the research process without the researchers obtaining full retrospective consent.

The principle of informed consent will necessitate the young people being informed of details of the following prior to being asked to give written consent:

- The rationale behind the research.
- The methodology being used.
- The level of ownership and participation to be afforded young people in the research process.
- The level of ownership and participation of young people in the analysis and findings from the research.
- Policies to be observed during the research in relation to confidentiality.

This will be provided in both written and verbal forms in order that literacy barriers can be overcome and all communication, written or verbal, will be appropriate to the age and developmental level of the young people concerned.

4.2.2 Confidentiality.

All participants in the research will be guaranteed confidentiality during and following the research. Names of participants will be concealed and coded referencing will be used.

On all issues of confidentiality, the research will apply the *Children First* guidelines (Dept. of Health and Children, 1999) as adopted by the Board of Wexford Area Partnership. This includes the reporting of information disclosed by young people of abuse they have suffered, and any genuine suspicions of abuse that the researchers develop during the research. Young people will be informed of this condition at the stage of initial contact.

4.2.3 Illegality

Crimes of a certain degree of seriousness, whether ongoing or likely in the future, would be reported. These would include crimes against other people or crimes meriting a custodial sentence on conviction. All crimes observed by the researchers would have to be reported, but admission of past crimes need not be reported.

4.2.4 Storage of Information.

All data and associated documents, tapes etc., will be stored securely in the premises of the Wexford Area Partnership for a period of five years. Wexford Area Partnership and the SEHB will control access to the data, which cannot be accessed without the consent of both parties.

No access will be allowed to raw data. Data will be used for the purpose for which it was collected, and in the development of any projects that arise out of the research. Once the five years storage period has elapsed the data will be destroyed.

4.2.5 Respect

In the collection of data the researchers will at all times have regard for the rights and dignity of all participants. The researchers will report the data in a professional manner.

4.2.6 Working with young people under the influence of alcohol, drugs or other substances

The researchers will at all times have regard to issues of safety in relation to working with those under the influence of any drugs or stimulants. The researchers will judge each situation on its own merits and reserve the right not to work in any situation where they feel it is unsafe to proceed.

Any data received from young people who are deemed to be under the influence of drugs or stimulants may nevertheless be used, but this context will be noted in the reporting of such data.

4.2.7 Prevention of Harm.

The research shall not intentionally use methods which place the participants in physical, emotional or psychological danger.

4.2.8 Equality Proofing

The Equality Status Act 2000 prohibits discrimination on grounds of gender, marital status, family status, sexual orientation, religious belief, age, disability, race and membership of the Traveller Community. Informed by the legislation, the research will not discriminate against any young person for any reason. The research will not reinforce existing inequalities in its methods.

The research recognises urban and rural differences, and will ensure that social exclusion is not reinforced by methods used during the study.

4.3 Boundaries of the Study

It was agreed by Steering Group that young people between nine and eighteen years of age should be included in the study. The range of factors that the agencies required to be investigated during the study meant that additional criteria needed to be applied to the target age group, in order to establish study boundaries that would be realistic, reliable and valid within the set parameters of time-scale and budget.

To assist the Steering Group to establish such study boundaries, the researchers were requested to provide details of a representative sample of both urban and rural areas of County Wexford. A profile of each area was submitted to the Steering Group, including population figures, the number of statutory and voluntary services available for youth within the area, and access criteria of the services on offer.

This information enabled the Steering Group to then establish study boundaries, by applying markers that resulted in the final selection of the areas and approaches to be used by the researchers. This process is detailed in the following section.

4.3.1 Application of Markers

Markers are a set of criteria that can be applied to an overall research question to define study boundaries, and to progress the project from a conceptual stage to actual operation. For the purpose of this study four markers were utilised:

- Marker One – Urban and Rural
- Marker Two – Population and geographical spread
- Marker Three – Type and availability of current services for young people
- Marker Four – Methods of engagement a) Thematic b) Detached

These markers were utilised and resulted in the selection of particular geographical areas that are detailed in the following sections:

Marker One

It was agreed at Steering Group to include both rural and urban youth in the study, and two urban areas and two rural areas in the county were selected. In addition, a further urban and a rural area were identified as alternative sites that could be used if the research process was blocked or deterred in any of the selected areas.

Marker Two

Population distribution and a geographical spread of the four regions within the County were used to refine the selection of rural and urban areas. This marker resulted in the decision to work within one larger and one smaller urban area, and one larger and one smaller rural area.

Marker Three

The type, number and access criteria of current services available to young people in each area were used as the third marker. It was decided to target one urban and one rural area that evidenced services for young people, and one urban and rural area that did not.

Marker Four

The participation of young people was recognised early in the process as a crucial element of the research. To gain access to the target group two engagement methods were agreed, Thematic Entry Points and Detached Street Work.

4.3.2 Engagement Methods

Detached work

The definition of detached work for the purpose of this study has been adapted from work published by the Welsh Youth Agency, and is as follows:

> *"Detached work" is a broad term used to describe an approach to engage with young people, who may be or may not be accessing existing youth provisions. The researchers will initially engage with young people on the streets, those who use public spaces, such as parks or other public facilities, etc. These young people may have become "detached" from conventional youth provision either because they reject these services, are excluded from them or are unaware of them"*
>
> (Wales Youth Agency, 2001 : p4).

Thematic Entry Points

Thematic Entry Points were to be used to contact young clients of existing services. Steering Group representatives submitted potential thematic entry points for debate. These included Juvenile Justice, Teen Parenting, Mental Health Issues, Illegal Drug Use, Alcohol and Substance Misuse, Suicide, Out of Home (defined as young people homeless for short or long periods of time), and Semi-Homeless (e.g. those living in Bed and Breakfast accommodation).

While Potential and Early School Leavers was not originally proposed, it was subsequently offered as a further thematic entry points that did not potentially exclude any specific group of young people or reinforce existing inequalities, thereby accommodating the requirements of the study.

Subsequently, the Steering Group ratified the following thematic entry points:

1) Young People Involved in the Juvenile Justice System, and

2) Potential and Early School Leavers.

It was acknowledged that both these target groups usually exhibited multi-traits of being "at risk". These thematic entry points also ensured that a sufficiently large target population would exist within each geographical area to enable the researchers to recruit an adequate respondent sample within the time scale, and also that no specific group would be constructively excluded.

Juvenile Liaison Officers Scheme (JLOS)

The Juvenile Liaison Officers Scheme is a service working with young people in the Juvenile Justice System. A member of the Garda Siochana known as the Juvenile Liaison Officer (JLO) works with young people and their families for an agreed period of time. The emphasis for the JLO is to delay or divert a young person from entry into the criminal justice system. The scheme deals with crimes or offences involving juveniles in one of two ways, Prosecution and Diversion.

1) Prosecution

Prosecution following a conviction is usually avoided unless:

- The juvenile in question has been previously convicted;
- The person's conditions do not meet the requirements of the diversion programme;
- The crime is of a serious nature, which results in the DPP deciding to prosecute;
- The juvenile's name and address cannot be confirmed, in which case a prosecution may be initiated and an adjournment sought to allow for the preparation of a file.

2) Diversion

The convicted young person avoids prosecution by being included in the Garda Juvenile Liaison Scheme. The offender receives an official caution and is then placed under JLO supervision. To avail of the diversion programme the young person must:

- Be under 18 and over 12
- Admit to the offence
- Have no previous cautions
- Have the agreement of parents or guardians that they will accept the help and advice of the Gardai.

Early School Leavers and Potential Early School Leavers

The Wexford Area Partnership has previously conducted research into early school leavers (McMahon et al, 1998). Their definition of an early school leaver as *"a young person who leaves school without completing the senior cycle"* (ibid., p8) will be adapted for this study to also include potential early school leavers in the respondent sample. In many schools, programmes specifically designed to meet the needs of potential early school leavers are in operation, and participants are usually identified as an 'at risk' group (ibid.)

The application of the marker resulted in the following selection of areas and specific engagement method to be used:

South Region (See Appendix 3)

In the southern region of the county, Wexford Urban was selected. The population of Wexford Urban area in 1996 was 9,533 including 1,768 young people between the ages of 0 – 14 years and 1,655 young people between the ages of 15 – 24 (Census, 1996). It is a large urban area with existing statutory and voluntary services for mainline youth and specifically targeted youth. A thematic entry point of Juvenile Liaison Officers Scheme was used to access the young people.

North Region (See Appendix 3)

In the northern region of the county the Gorey Urban area was selected. This area has a population of 1,039 which included 225 young people between the ages of 0 –14 years and 155 young people between the ages of 15 – 24 (Census 1996).

The initial research into areas within the county compiled for the Steering Group revealed that the number of both statutory and voluntary services available to young people in this area was seen to be limited. The Steering Group selected the detached method for the researchers to engage with young people in this area.

North-West Region (See Appendix 3)

In the north-west region of the county, Bunclody (also known as Newtownbarry) was selected. This is a larger rural population of 923 people, which includes 244 young people between the ages of 0 –14 years and 151 young people between the ages of 15- 24 years (Census 1996), and provides services to the surrounding rural area.

The thematic entry point of potential and early school leavers was allocated to working with young people in this geographical area.

South-West Region (See Appendix 3)

In the south-west region of the county, Campile (also known as Kilmokea) was selected, with a small rural population of 373, which includes 101 young people between the ages of 0 –14 years and 75 young people between the ages of 15 –24 years.

The cross section of areas within the County compiled for the Steering Group revealed that the number of both statutory and voluntary services available to young people in this area was seen to be limited. To balance the study the detached method of engaging with young people was selected for this area.

4.4 Sampling of Respondents

The definition used for this study of young people 'at risk', and the methods of contacting the target group through thematic entry points and detached work, meant that for the purposes of the study, any young person who the researchers came into contact with was a potential respondent.

Sampling is a method of selecting potential respondents for the research. There are two main approaches to sampling – Probability and Non-Probability (Blaxter, 1996). Probability sampling is used when a whole population can be identified (e.g. a national population) and any member has an equal chance of being selected. Participants may be selected randomly or by systematic methods and this approach is usually associated with quantitative research. (Further reading Blaxter, 1996)

Non-Probability sampling is used where the research population is difficult to identify, or knowing the exact population is not considered necessary. The sampling methods used in this approach facilitate the researcher to select typical or interesting cases, and enable potential sample respondents to volunteer to be involved in the process.

The combination of both detached work and thematic entry point enabled the research to use a range of sampling methods, as outlined in the following sections.

4.4.1 Number of Respondents by Detached Work and Area

The sampling methods varied slightly between the two geographical areas where detached research work was deployed. Due to the time-scale, "gatekeepers" were used to assist with the mapping of both areas, through locating known "hang outs" of young people. No engagement with young people was attempted at this stage.

Once the detached work commenced and initial engagement was made, it was then possible to use snowball sampling which enabled the researchers to gain access to a wider target group. Subsequently, purposive and voluntary sampling was used to recruit respondents for the focus groups.

4.4.2. Number of Respondents by Thematic Entry Points and Area

Convenience sampling (Blaxter, 1997) is an approach that selects potential participants from a particular group. This method enabled the researchers to maintain a gender balance, and to snowball into other contacts from the initial sample recommended by the gatekeeper.

A total of 125 young people were enrolled for the current year with the JLOS in the south region of Wexford Town and its hinterland at the time of the study.

In the North-West region of Bunclody, potential and early school leavers were used as a thematic entry point. The second level schools had identified 85 young people that had either recently left school or were at risk of not completing the senior cycle. Access to a sample of those identified by the gatekeeper enabled the researchers to snowball from these initial contacts into a wider population of young people in the area.

4.5 Data Collection and Design

In general it is recognised that qualitative research methods reduce data subsequent to its collection. Therefore it was essential to establish an effective method of data management from the outset which would also facilitate later analysis (Padget, 1998).

Data required by the research project included information on engagement strategies, on young people's perceptions of current supports available to them within their environments, and on facilitating young people to explore their own needs,.

Prior to commencing any collection of data, the Steering Group and WAP ratified a Code of Practice and arranged an insurance policy both for the researchers and for potential respondents.

4.5.1 Engagement Strategies

The definition of engagement as used in this research is the voluntary interaction of a young person with the researchers.

4.5.1.1 Detached Methods – Engagement Strategies

The detached method involved three stages of working with young people. These were familiarisation, engagement and conducting the focus groups.

Planning in Detached Areas

Familiarisation involved going out to the different areas to review existing facilities and amenities such as local shops, cafes, schools, clinics, sports clubs, parks, etc. The researchers made themselves known to service providers in the area by personal introduction, networking through the Steering Group and Collaborative Group, and issuing information to the local press.

Following this familiarisation process it was then possible to establish a work pattern for engaging with young people. This included identifying areas where young people appeared to congregate and the times that young people frequented these areas. The work pattern had to be flexible to facilitate the inclusion of a wide cross section of young people within the area, but for the researchers, commitments and arranged appointments they made had to be rigorously adhered to in order to build up trust among those contacted.

Recording of Data in Detached Areas

Field notes on engagements in detached areas included details about dates, times, weather, use of venues if applicable, methods of work, and approaches taken in engaging with young people.

Analysis of Data

The researchers constantly discussed and critically reviewed experiences from the fieldwork to refine their methods of approach, identify strengths and weaknesses of their work and plan follow-up sessions. These views are presented in the Findings chapter.

4.5.1.2 Thematic Entry Points – Engagement Strategies

The target groups of JLOS participants and Potential and Early School Leavers had previously been identified as 'at risk' by service providers, and as probably already experiencing varying degrees of exclusion from their communities and from existing systems.

Background reading provided the researchers with information regarding the possible needs of these young people. The principles of participation and equality that underpin the overall approach demanded that the young people would be involved in decision-making regarding how they were to be included in the research process. However the researchers were also aware that these target groups might find such involvement in decision-making a new and difficult concept.

Potential participants who may already experience social exclusion often require supports to participate in such work (Croft & Beresford, 1996). Therefore methods were devised that could allow for investigation of the two engagement strategies while also providing the participants with positive experiences and opportunities for personal empowerment.

Planning –Thematic Entry Points

Planning involved a number of stages prior to engagement with the young people.

Gatekeepers were initially contacted to assist with the identification of the target groups. The gatekeepers then informed potential participants that the researchers would be making contact with them.

Subsequently the researchers made both written (See: Appendix Four) and personal contact with each of the potential participants and their parents/guardians. This provided an opportunity for the researchers to outline the purpose and ethics of the research to the potential participants and to invite them to become involved in the research process. A date for the first session was agreed with the participants and a follow-up letter circulated.

The sessions were designed as an informal way of conducting interviews which could generate youth led themes. The young people were facilitated to agree amongst themselves on arrangements around the types of activity they might opt for, within set budget and time-scale constraints.

Activities were used as a means to an end, where the researchers were able to gain information regarding issues that were important to the young people, and the young people gained new experiences through activities and from their involvement in the decision-making process.

The researchers' interaction with the young people also provided information and insights into how they spend their leisure time and with whom. It was from this interaction that linking or 'snowballing' into a wider research population not directly involved in these services was made possible.

Recording Details of Engagement Methods

Again, field notes were recorded to supply information on effective engagement methods, dates, times, weather, and use of venues where applicable.

Analysis of Data

Constant analysis was conducted by the researcher in a continuous reflective process to identify the effectiveness of different approaches and to suggest modifications of practice.

4.5.2 Youth Perceptions and Needs

The youth-led focus of the study meant that the researchers had to speak and interact directly with young people. The data collection tools utilised were selected to facilitate direct participation of each target group. A number of collection methods were implemented, as described in more detail in the following section. These were used with the intention of providing a holistic picture of the social reality of these young people, so that recommendations arising from the later analysis of the data could reflect a "whole child perspective" (National Children's Strategy, 2000).

> *"Interviews/questionnaire and observational methodologies and the application of multi-trait, multi-method strategies...are fundamental to a developmental contextualist perspective"*
>
> (Adams et al., 1996 : p7).

Combining these collection methods maintained a consistency between the four geographical areas of the study and between the two engagement strategies.

4.5.3 Data Collection Tools

Each of the data collection tools is discussed in detail in the following sections, and their relative advantages and disadvantages considered. The range of tools used included:

- Participant Observation
- Activity Based Interview
- Questionnaires
- Individual Sessions
- Focus groups
- Retrospective Consent

4.5.3.1 Participant Observation

Advantages of Participant Observation

To ascertain young people's perception of their own needs and to provide information on their lifestyles, it was essential to meet young people "on their own turf". The social reality for young people is their everyday lives, and social facts are embedded in social interaction (Miles and Huberman, 1994). These meanings are most often discovered "…by hanging around and watching people carefully and asking them why they do what they do" (Erickson, cited in Miles and Huberman, 1994 : p4).

Disadvantages of Participant Observation

The exclusive use of participant observation would require long-term observation that the time scale of the study could not facilitate.

The researcher's own background, experience and bias may result in the interpretation of data becoming skewed, unless methods of triangulation are included in the research design to prevent the young people's perceptions being misrepresented (See:4.7 Bias Proofing Day).

The Use of Participant Observation

Participant Observation was used during the initial stages of mapping the research areas, and to gather data in subsequent engagements.

Participant Observation in the Detached Areas

Participant observation was used in the initial stages of the engagement process :

1) to establish membership of peer groups;
2) to establish links between different peer groups;
3) to prevent premature selection of individuals for focus groups;

4) to provide background information on the lifestyles of young people;

5) to establish youth generated themes and issues (Friere cited in Hope and Timmel, 1984) which would be incorporated with those identified by the statutory and voluntary sectors in the formulation of the Topic Guide for the final phase of data collection.

Participant Observation in the Thematic Entry Points

In the areas of thematic entry points (i.e. JLOS and potential and early school leavers), participant observation was conducted during both the initial introductory phase and the subsequent activity-based interview sessions.

The data gathered through participant observation served a number of purposes:

1) to identify norms and values as they developed within the group;

2) to provide background information into the lifestyles of young people;

3) to establish youth generated themes and issues (Friere cited in Hope and Timmel, 1984) which would be incorporated with those identified by the statutory and voluntary sectors in the formulation of the Topic Guide for the final phase of data collection.

4.5.3.2 Activity Based Interview

Interviews usually fall into three categories: structured, associated with quantitative research, semi-structured, normally used in qualitative research and unstructured, involving an open and free dialogue (Blaxter, 1996).

Unstructured interviewing took place around an activity which provided an informal setting for interaction between participants and researchers. It was seen as a method that could attract and involve participants who might be reluctant to participate in more structured settings.

Advantages of Activity Based Interview

The participants were invited to discuss and decide on what activities they would like to do, which involved them in decision-making and promoted co-operation. This procedure openly valued the participants' opinions and provided a potentially empowering experience for them. The activity also provided a forum for interaction among participants who might not otherwise socialise or interact outside their own peer group. The activities themselves offered opportunities to the young people to broaden their experiences.

Disadvantages of Activity Based Interview

The usefulness of the method very much depends on the researcher's skills in recognising and extracting meaning from the dialogue.

A programme combining activity-based sessions with more structured interviews could result in inconsistent attendance among the group's members, as they would select the more attractive activities.

Activity-Based Interview with Thematic Entry Points

Activity-based interviewing was used as a method of work only within the Thematic Entry Point of the JLO system. The convenience sample of clients of the JLO may or may not have known each other prior to the research. Thus, it was important to provide a forum to build trust within the group as well as between participants and researchers (Benson., 1997 & Prendiville, 1995).

The information gathered in the first stages of group development was intended:

1) to provide an insight into the everyday language, attitudes and behaviours of the young people;
2) to encourage dialogue to elicit the feelings of the participants on issues and experiences that emerged in the dialogue (Friere cited in Hope and Timmel, 1984);
3) to establish youth-generated themes that could be included with those identified by the statutory and voluntary sectors in the Topic Guideline for the final phase of data collection.

4.5.5.3 Questionnaires

Questionnaires are associated with both quantitative and qualitative research. In quantitative research, a questionnaire with closed-end questions normally requires the respondent to select an answer from a predetermined list, and does not provide any opportunity for adding further information. The National Census is a familiar example.

In qualitative research, questionnaires can include open-ended questions around core issues. The phrasing of questions can also provide opportunities for the respondents to supply additional information, if they wish. Such questionnaires are more suited to eliciting 'rich' data (Blaxter, 1996).

Use of Questionnaires during the Research

The questionnaire was intended as an introductory exercise for the focus groups. It asked questions around themes of age, gender, social class, ethnicity and race. Further questions on leisure and social activities provided a method of cross referencing basic knowledge about behaviours that had been identified at the initial stages of data collection.

However the questionnaires were only used in two focus groups and were then eliminated from the process, as problems arose due to the literacy levels of some participants. The likelihood of creating negative experiences for them was contrary to the principles of the project. The implications of this decision by the researchers are discussed under the Limitations section. (See:4.8).

4.5.5.4 Focus Groups

Focus groups were used by sociologists during the Second World War to investigate the effects of military propaganda films on viewers. The focus group model made it possible for the facilitator to identify the feelings engendered in the participants by selected phrases or scenes. Therefore focus groups were used to gain an understanding of attitudes rather than trying to measure them (Luntz F., 1994).

The subsequent post-war consumer culture adapted the use of focus groups, using academically trained market researchers, to gain an insight into consumers' perceptions and attitudes regarding products and services. Politicians have also recognised the usefulness of focus groups which are increasingly used to review the public's likely reaction to different methods of presenting information prior to campaigns (ibid.)

A Focus Group for the purpose of this study is defined as:

> *A group of young people purposefully bought together to discuss a combination of a priori material and generative themes of the research.*

Advantages of Focus Groups

The interaction within the group has the potential to reveal group beliefs, attitudes, feelings and experiences about various issues. Compared to observation only, these interactions provide the opportunity to gather larger amounts of information over a short period of time (Gibbs A., 2001).

The focus group is a method that involves the direct participation of the young people themselves (Croft & Beresford, 1992). It is underpinned by the principle of equality and it values the young people as 'experts' in identifying their own needs and issues. Thus, it has the potential to encourage young people to look at their own lives, and at ways of improving things for themselves.

Disadvantages of Focus Groups

Gibbs (2001) states that the homogeneity of the group is important for the development of trust, and in enriching subsequent interactions of the group members. Although considerable time had previously been spent in identifying peer groups for purposeful and voluntary sampling, the very open ended nature of the method meant that 'successful' outcomes (i.e. meeting the researchers' goals) could not be guaranteed.

The forum of open group discussion may be found intimidating by some people, especially around sensitive issues. Therefore the option to avail of an individual session was offered to all participants at the end of the each focus group session.

Although the participants were encouraged to respect confidentiality, information offered in this apparently secure setting might be later divulged outside the group.

Use of Focus Groups in the Different Areas

The researchers recorded the participants' interactions and responses to issues, using the pre-formulated Topic Guide based on the issues identified by young people and agencies.

Conducting two focus groups, one female and one male, in each of the geographical areas provided an opportunity for collecting data from a representative population balanced on both gender and geographical lines.

4.5.5.5 Individual Sessions

Any young person could request an informal individual session, in line with good practice guidelines. Two researchers would attend any such session. The data collected by this method would be mainly individual views.

Advantages of Individual Sessions

Individual sessions provided the opportunity for young people who found group situations intimidating to voice their opinions. These individual sessions also provided a mechanism for equality proofing, by providing a forum for any young person who might have specific needs or issues of a private nature.

The inclusion of individual sessions was also designed to be empowering for young people, as their individual opinions could be seen to be valued as complementing the group opinions.

Disadvantages of Individual Sessions

The researchers needed to be very clear about boundaries in this context, being careful not to take on the role of counsellors.

The potential for interaction is limited compared to the focus group.

Individuals may bring up issues other than the previously youth-driven generative themes. It was decided that it would be at the discretion of the researcher either to follow-up such issues or to recommend further research.

Individual sessions were used in one geographical location only (see Limitations section. 4.8).

4.5.5.6 Retrospective Consent To Use Information from Initial Stages of Data Collection

The provision of retrospective consent in the ethics of the research was designed to facilitate the use in the final analysis of data relating to a specific issue or topic which might be presented during the initial stage of data collection.

Although the interaction in focus groups can reveal 'rich' data around a number of issues, there would always be the possibility that a particular issue previously identified as significant might not be raised or responded to at the focus group. Retrospective consent provided safeguards against the loss of such potentially valuable information.

Summary

The combination of data collection tools and engagement process is intended to provide opportunities for young people both to lead and participate in the research project. The complexity of young people's lives requires that a variety of methods be employed to gain insights into their issues, and to provide flexibility in the researchers' interactions with them. Figure 4.1 identifies the stages of the research process, from the first engagement to the final stages of data collection in focus groups.

Figure 15. Research Process from Engagement to Data Collection by Focus Group

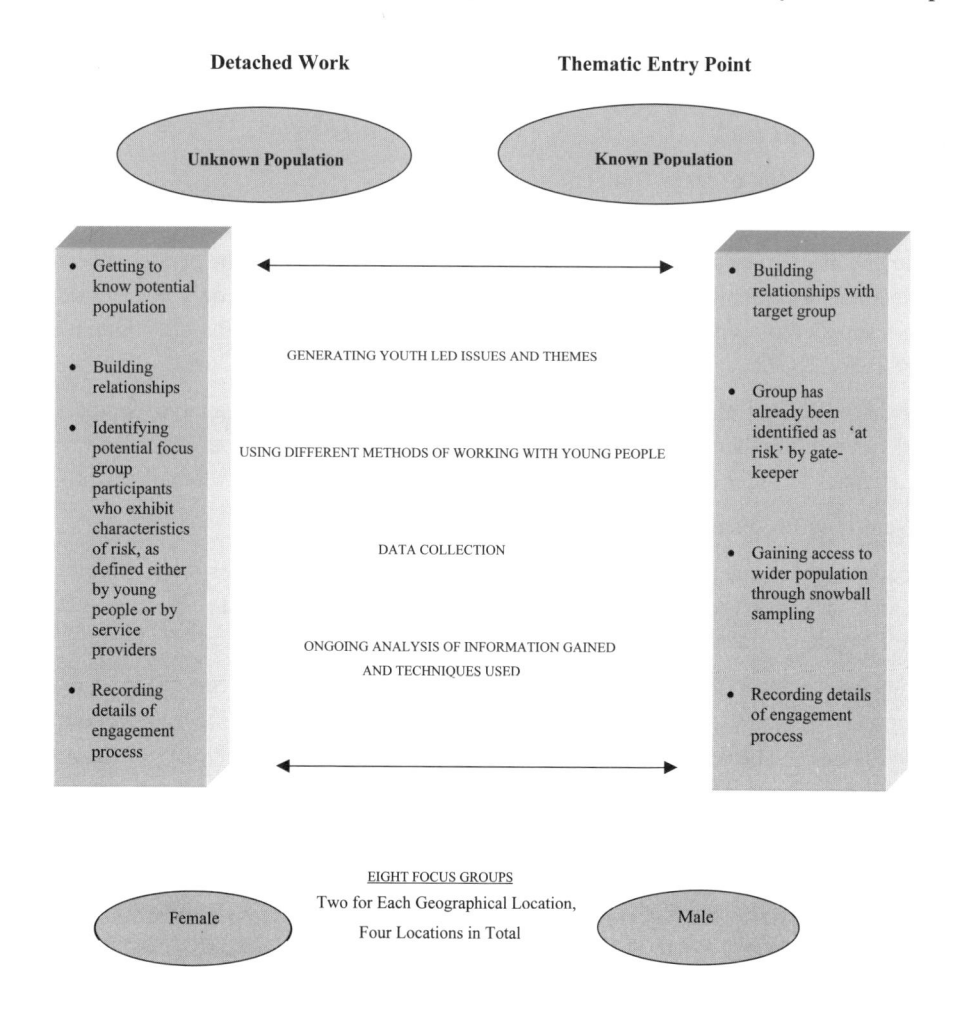

Detached Work — Unknown Population

- Getting to know potential population
- Building relationships
- Identifying potential focus group participants who exhibit characteristics of risk, as defined either by young people or by service providers
- Recording details of engagement process

Thematic Entry Point — Known Population

- Building relationships with target group
- Group has already been identified as 'at risk' by gate-keeper
- Gaining access to wider population through snowball sampling
- Recording details of engagement process

Central process (between both columns):
- GENERATING YOUTH LED ISSUES AND THEMES
- USING DIFFERENT METHODS OF WORKING WITH YOUNG PEOPLE
- DATA COLLECTION
- ONGOING ANALYSIS OF INFORMATION GAINED AND TECHNIQUES USED

EIGHT FOCUS GROUPS
Two for Each Geographical Location,
Four Locations in Total

Female / Male

4.6 Data Management

The use of both detached and thematic entry points resulted in significant amounts of raw data. Field notes averaged sixteen pages of type per session. To ensure that the information was preserved accurately, it was important that the data management process was both efficient and capable of preserving the confidentiality of participants.

The *Thematic Framework Analysis* used for the study is a method of analysing qualitative data by content, through a process of summarising and categorising. This method enables the researchers to identify similarities and connections between the data and to ascertain meaning, without the original data being corrupted. The researchers' ability to effectively interact with and to interpret the data is informed by their involvement in the initial participatory narrative inquiry.

The data collection tools were used in two separate stages – identifying youth-led issues, and recording of focus groups. The data management process of each stage is detailed in the following sections.

4.6.1 Initial Stage of Data Collection

The initial stage of data collection was intended to identify issues that were important to young people. To ensure that the research process was youth-led, young people needed to be facilitated to identify issues they considered important, as using only pre-determined issues supplied by service providers would negate their direct participation. (Green cited in O'Leary, 2001).

The data collected at this stage was managed on three levels: pre-analysis preparatory work, identifying themes, and combining of these themes with those already identified by the agencies in order to create a Topic Guide for subsequent use with focus groups.

Pre-analysis Preparatory Work

In both thematic entry points and detached work, detailed field notes were made by the researchers. These notes were then transcribed, with each area and respondent given a specific code to maintain confidentiality.

A summary contact sheet (Appendix 5) was attached to each transcript. This facilitated the researchers to record salient points and whether these were youth-raised or researcher-raised issues. The term 'youth-raised issue' is defined for this study as: *"an issue that was spoken about by the young person, prior to any suggestion by the researcher."* A 'researcher-raised issue' is defined as: *"an issue that was raised or led by the researcher."*

Identifying Themes

The identification of themes was a lengthy process that involved familiarisation with the material and its subsequent gathering and organising into distinct thematic units.

Familiarisation

The transcripts were read thoroughly three times to ensure that the researcher had become immersed in the data. On the third reading, notes were inserted in the margins and recurring issues and particular topics of interest were highlighted by theme in the text.

Arrangement of Themes

As recurring issues and topics were identified, they were included in the contact summary sheets, to provide a visual method of tracking data back to the original source. As this process made it possible to quickly identify youth-raised issues, the researchers were able to recognise recurring themes emerging that could then be incorporated into the Topic Guide for later data collection through focus groups.

Table 4.1 Numbers of Young People who Participated in the Development of Youth Led Themes (by area)

Area	Females	Males	Total
One – Urban	32	39	71
Two – Urban	24	36	60
Three – Rural	22	35	57
Four – Rural*	41	61	102
Total	119	171	290

* Thematic Entry Point into large youth population

4.6.2 Focus Groups

The focus groups were used as the final data collection method, and it was from the records of these engagements that the main findings and analysis of the report are taken. As well as providing an effective way of ascertaining young people's perceptions, the structure of the focus groups also confirmed to the participants that their opinions were valued, and maintained the 'youth-led focus' of the research process.

The focus groups produced significant amounts of data, which was managed in four phases:

1) Pre-analysis Preparatory Work;
2) Constructing a Thematic Framework;
3) The Application of the Framework to the Data;
4) Mapping and Interpreting the data.

Pre-analysis Preparatory Work

Respondent Identification, Transcription and Tracking

To ensure the anonymity of the participants, while also enabling the researchers to track the order of the contributions to the discussion, each focus group and each of its members was given a respondent code. The discussions in the focus groups were recorded on audio-tape, given an identification code and transcribed verbatim. On average the transcribing took 14 hours of typing per 1 hour of taped interview.

Data Analysis

From the transcripts it was possible to proceed to an analysis of the data. The identification of themes was a lengthy process involving a number of stages: familiarisation, analysis and arrangement of themes.

Familiarisation

The transcripts were read through three times to ensure that the researcher had become immersed in the data. On the third reading, notes were inserted in the margins and recurring themes and particular topics of interest highlighted, using the same procedures as adopted during the initial stages of data collection (4.6 above).

Constructing a Thematic Framework

When the familiarisation process was completed and the notes of each transcript reviewed, key issues and concepts were identified that could be examined and referenced. A thematic framework was constructed which sought to incorporate the research aims, the themes identified by the service providers, and the emergent issues of the young people themselves, both in the preliminary work and during the focus groups themselves. Appropriate quotes were then extracted from the transcripts and arranged in data matrices under the established thematic framework headings. (Appendices Six to Thirteen).

Thematic Framework

Risk and Resilience (Appendix 6)	Risk Youth Perception of Risk	Resilience Resilience Factors	
Health (Appendix 7)	Associated Behaviours Different behaviours affecting short and long term health	Development of Health Services for Young People Perceptions, Awareness and Access	Services Suggested by Young People
Education (Appendix 8)	Attitudes Positive and Negative Aspects, Future Plans	Perceptions of extra-curricular activities	Alternative Education Development of Educational Services
Youth Services (Appendix 9)N	Private Sector	Voluntary and Community Sector Awareness, Appropriateness and Development of Services	Self-organised Activities
Justice (Appendix 10)	Illegal Activities Identified Illegal Activities Perceptions of Illegal Activities	Knowledge of the Justice System Garda, Custody, Court Sentences and Identified Services	
Independence (Appendix 11)	Family Monetary Supports, Practical Supports And Behavioural Boundaries	Peer Groups Relationships One to One Community	Employment
Culture (Appendix 12)	Use of ICT's and Media	Different Backgrounds and Changes Community	Activities / Arts Spiritual Beliefs
Political Involvement (Appendix 13)	Perception of involvement in decision making	Development of participation strategies to involve young people	Engagement Approaches
Engagement Strategies	Detached Methods	Thematic Entry Point	Findings for Practice

111

4.7 Bias Proofing

Measures to prevent the distortion of the participants' perceptions through the processes of recording and researchers' analysis were effected through a Bias Proofing exercise involving both professionals nominated by the steering group and young people.

Participants in Bias Proofing Exercise

Seven adults, five males and two females, had been proposed for the exercise by the Steering Group for their experience in working with and on behalf of young people in services associated with the group's member organisations.

The young people were recruited by the researchers from the four geographical locations involved in the study. There were seven participants, four males and three females. Two of the participants (one male and one female) were new to the process; three (one male and two females) had been involved at the initial data collection stage; and two (both males) had participated in one of the focus groups.

This selection procedure was seen as fulfilling the researchers' commitment to check back with young people regarding the contents of the final report. It also maintained the principles of participation and equality that applied throughout the research (see 4.2.8 above).

Bias Proofing Process

A plenary session provided a summary of the project and set goals for the day. Two workshops, one comprised of adults and one of young people, reviewed the findings and analysis of key topics selected by them for discussion. These workshops were facilitated by the researchers. At the closing session the groups rejoined to provide feedback on their deliberations and to outline possible recommendations of the research.

The exercise also offered young people the opportunity to ask direct questions of adults who represented services that had often been characterised by their peers during the research as faceless and anonymous (See:Health Services Findings 5.2).

The research consultant acted as rapporteur for the Bias Proof day.

4.8 Delimitations

This section outlines the limitations of the study, considered under the following headings:

- Pilot Project
- Pilot Taped Interview
- Questionnaires
- Focus Group
- Time constraints
- Scale constraints

4.8.1 Pilot Project

A pilot project was conducted using a thematic entry point, which focused on a small number of young people involved in an Arts Project. The main purpose of the pilot was to ascertain whether the proposed open-ended question approach for the research would elicit sufficient information relevant to the research aims and provide adequate opportunities for young people to raise their own issues.

The pilot would also examine the engagement approaches to be used by the researchers, and to test their effectiveness as a team.

The researchers individually compiled field notes and transcripts of the session. Subsequently, the salient themes identified by each were critically discussed, to establishing the reliability of their interpretation of data.

4.8.2. Pilot Taped Interview

At the initial stages of data collection within a detached area, a gatekeeper approached the researchers with information about the perceived behaviours of a group of young people. This provided the researchers with an opportunity to conduct a pilot taped interview.

The respondents, three young males between the ages of thirteen and fifteen, together with their parents, gave their consent to participate in a taped recording of a focus group meeting. It was agreed that the tape could be used at the discretion of the researchers in the final data analysis. Ultimately, the data was not included in the final analysis.

Conducting a pilot taped interview fulfilled a number of purposes. It enabled the researchers to test the recording equipment and procedures. It provided a test of how topics might be introduced into the session, including both 'youth led' and 'service provider' issues. It helped ascertain whether young people would actually reveal authentic details of their activities and attitudes to services in similar research environments.

4.8.3. Questionnaires

Questionnaires completed by focus group participants were intended to measure the validity of the researchers' observations of behaviours and contextual situations made at the initial data collection stage. However it became evident early on in the research process that some young people had low literacy levels, and that the completion of a questionnaire would be difficult for some, giving them a negative experience of the process. Therefore the researchers decided after the first focus group not to use the questionnaires again.

4.8.4 Focus Groups

The process of building trust with respondents and recruiting to the focus groups proved successful in all but one area. Here young male participants withdrew from the focus group despite having given prior assurances that they would co-operate. Full details of the session are given in the Findings section (5.10). Individual interviews were afterwards used to supplement the data collected up to the point of withdrawal. The data collected for this area should be regarded as arising from individual views rather than as gathered via group interaction.

4.8.5 Time Constraints

The time scale of the study was a relatively short period of twelve months. In view of this, an initial proposal to employ collaborative action research was reviewed, and the Steering group agreed instead to employing an alternative approach, that of qualitative participatory narrative inquiry.

This shift in methodology was principally due to limitations previously outlined (See: 4.1 Organic Growth of Project). However the focus on young people had to remain a vital element of the research. The need to engage meaningfully and build relationships with young people in the four regions might have benefited from having more time available.

4.8.6 Scale Constraints

The small scale of the study, involving 290 participants at the initial stages and 43 in the focus groups, although providing rich data, may limit the generalisability of the findings to the whole population of Wexford youth.

However the information yielded on effective engagement strategies for use by agencies and services can be adapted and used across the different sectors.

4.9 Study Trips

A number of study trips were conducted to gain knowledge that would complement, inform and assist the research process. These included visits by the researchers to Focus Ireland servicing homeless people and to The Gaff, Galway a youth café, and by a member of the Steering Group on behalf of the Collaborative Group to an E.U. study visit on youth work practices in European cities.

Focus Ireland operates a Street Outreach Service that comprises three elements:

- The Streetwork Service
- Follow-up Contact Service
- Advocacy Work

It also provides supports for out-of-home young people under the age of eighteen through The Loft and for over eighteens with the Nightlight project.

The purpose of the study trip was to meet members of a street team to gain an insight into the preparation, equipment and insurance requirements for street work prior to commencing the fieldwork in Wexford.

The Gaff, Galway

This Health Board funded youth initiative in Galway City provides a high quality venue offering a café, a chill out area and other spaces to work with young people. A young people's committee involved in managing the project were not available to meet the researcher on the day of the visit, but the project co-ordinator was interviewed.

The opinion of the researchers is that this is an innovative response to a large urban youth population, but its adaptability to a smaller youth population may be inappropriate, considering this project's findings in relation to stereotyping and ownership of services by particular groups. (See:Youth Services Conclusions, 5.10.4)

E.U. – Youth Work in Cities: Possibilities, Challenges and Obstacles

Literature and examples of models of practice were obtained by the SEHB representative at this conference. The researchers reviewed the contents of the information pack for possible use in the development of models of engagement and practice.

4.10 Conclusion

The research methodology was designed with the purpose of maintaining a 'youth-led' focus throughout the research process, underpinned by the principles of participation and equality. The methods and approaches used were intended to provide opportunities for young people to become involved in the process, and offer their opinions on their own terms. To ensure that the information, perceptions and feelings of young people were not lost or distorted by the researchers in the writing up of the report, a review mechanism was included in the design from the outset of the research.

Chapter Five
Research Findings

5. Introduction

In this chapter the findings of the research are identified by topic. The sequence of topics presented follows the Thematic Framework (see Table 4.2) compiled from the issues identified by the different agencies and by young people themselves during the preparatory stages of the research. A profile of each focus group precedes each set of findings, detailing the age, gender and location of participants.

As outlined in the Introduction and Methodology section, focus group discussions were extensive, and yielded significant amounts of information. In compiling data matrices using direct quotes from the transcripts of the taped interviews, it was possible to arrange the data in a thematic framework consisting of nine subsections (See: Data management of Focus Groups, 4.6.2).

It is important to highlight at this point that if any section is viewed as an isolated topic, rather than as inter-connected within the overall thematic framework, the complex interplay of ideas and behaviours that more fully reveal the reality of young people's lives will be missed.

The research findings identify the eight focus groups as F1, F2, F3 and F4 for those with female participants and M1, M2, M3 and M4 for male groups. The findings are presented under nine topic headings in the order shown below:

5.1 Risk and Resilience Findings are presented regarding the types of risk identified and young people's perception of risk. This section then presents findings regarding resilient qualities of some of those contacted during the research.

5.2 Health is an extensive section that provides an insight into associated behaviours (e.g. alcohol and drug use, sexual relations, etc.), before presenting the young people's perceptions of the Health Services currently available to them, their own needs, and their suggestion of strategies to meet those needs.

5.3 Education explores the experiences of participants in primary and secondary schools and in training facilities, their attitudes to school and their future plans.

5.4 Youth Services findings are presented under the three main headings of Awareness, Appropriateness of Service and Development of Services.

5.5 Justice findings are comparatively brief, and focus largely on the relationship between young people and the Gardai.

5.6 Independence findings present young people's perceptions of gaining their independence, and their views on the Family, on peer groups, relationships and employment.

5.7 Culture The development of adolescents is seen to be embedded in cultural contexts. The meaning and perceptions that these young people have of their own culture provides one essential facet of a holistic perspective on their lives.

5.8 Political Involvement relates the participants' views and experiences of current decision-making mechanisms in society, and possible ways of promoting participation by young people.

5.9 Engagement Strategies relates the experiences and observations of the researchers during the research process, and offers an analysis of the effectiveness of detached and thematic entry points in practice.

5.10 Conclusion offers a summary of the main findings.

Focus Group Profiles

The focus group participants were recruited through the contacts made during the initial data collection stage. Prior to commencing each focus group, individual and parental consent had been obtained, and the procedures and ethics of participation explained and agreed on. The participants' understanding of these was then verbally confirmed at the beginning of each recording.

A total of 43 young people from the four areas participated in the focus groups. A breakdown of their gender, age and location is presented in the following tables.

Table 5.1 Focus Group Participants by Gender, n = 43

Area	Females	Males
One	6	8
Two	5	6
Three	3	3
Four	5	7
Total	19	24

Table 5.2 Age Range and Mean Average Age of Focus Group Respondents

Area	Females	Average Age (F)	Males	Average Age (M)
One	13 – 17 years of age	14.5	14 – 17 years	**14.75**
Two	15	15	13 – 16	**15**
Three	12 – 13	12.5	10- 13	**12**
Four	16 –17	16.5	16-17	**16.5**

Table 5.3 Number of Respondents in Urban & Rural Location by Area

	Urban	Rural
One	14	
Two	11	
Three		6
Four		12
Total	**25**	**18**

5.1 Risk and Resilience

5.1.1 Introduction

This section looks at two aspects of youth behaviours, Risk and Resilience. The first section presents the female and male respondents' perceptions of Risk. The second section considers Resilience factors exhibited by female and male participants during the research process.

5.1.2 Risk Findings

Female Findings

F3 (average age 12.5, rural)

These young girls did not see themselves as involved in anything risky, or as being 'at risk'. They associated risk with activities of older teenagers such as smoking, drinking alcohol and taking drugs. They did not believe they would get involved in these activities when they got older.

F1 (average age 14.5, urban), F2 (average age 15, urban) and F4 (average age 16.5, rural)

The respondents from these focus group were able to list off both immediate and long-term risks associated with particular behaviours such as alcohol consumption, drug misuse etc. However they supplied this information in a detached and indifferent manner, and stated that young people, even when aware of the risks, *"do these things anyway"* (F1 Respondent).

Physical risks identified included physical harm and even death through alcohol-related asphyxiation and the use of certain drugs (such as Ecstasy). However the participants did not generally associate these 'risks' with their own behaviour.

The young people did view being caught by their parents (while drunk or shoplifting, for example) as a real risk. This concept of risk chiefly centred on the imagined response of their parents.

Male Findings

M1 (average age 14.75, rural), M2 (average age 15, urban), M3 (average age 12, rural) and M4 (average 16.5, rural)

All males identified situations and factors that placed them in physical risk. The younger respondents identified two main risks for themselves - being bullied by older males in the locality, and being unable to resist peer pressure from older males. For example, in climbing high buildings under the 'encouragement' of older youths, one respondent stated: *"You'd be shittin' bricks"* (M3 Respondent).

Other activities that they were involved in were not identified as risky at all, but were seen as just *"messin'"*. These included driving cars, using peg guns (*"It's a peg of steel with an elastic band"* (M3 Respondent), falling off bikes, and breaking limbs. Many of these activities proved a source of amusement to the respondents during the discussions.

Older respondents (M1, M2 and M4) also identified immediate physical risks associated with being drunk or *"high"*, and these included climbing high buildings and lying on railway tracks, or being in cars with drunk drivers.

Emotional risks identified by the groups involved their relationships with people who were "sly" (M1 Respondents). They readily linked trust and risk; *"But still, the whole thing is if you trusted them or not."* (M1 Respondent)

5.1.3 Resilience Findings

Female Findings

F1 (average age 14.5, rural), F2 (average age 15, urban), F3 (average age, 12.5 rural) and F4 (average age 16.5, rural)

In general, the female respondents had positive relationships in the different contexts of family, community and school, and particular examples of resilient behaviours were clearly identifiable during the discussions.

The respondents' overall experiences of the Education System caused them to view it as unfair, but they could still state: *"But we manage all right though, I think"* (F1 Respondent), supported within the group with *"We do manage."* (F1 Respondent)

Within their peer groups, these respondents were able to maintain and promote individual opinions, suggesting their ability to resist peer pressure at least to some degree.

From an agency perspective the young women in F1 would exhibit an accumulation of risk factors. As a group they were attached to only one service, Compulsory Education, which they attended irregularly and would often avoid by *"mitching"*. Only one of the group's members accessed sports.

Being conscious of parental disapproval and likely sanctions could also be viewed as a resilience factor for these participants, as considering consequences is a key element in decision-making around risk taking.

Members of another focus group demonstrated coping skills where family separation has occurred, by drawing on both parents to obtain support. For example: *"Yeah when you have fights with your ma, you can go live with you're da, and when you have fights with your da you can do the opposite."* (F2 Respondent)

Resilience

Male Findings

M1 (average age 15, urban), M2 (average age 15, urban), M3 (average age 12, rural) and M4 (average age 16.5, rural)

Although males acknowledged their positive relationships with family members and in other contexts, some groups and individuals openly offered negative views about themselves, and identified difficulties in coping with these negative perceptions. For example, one respondent who had achieved significant sporting success spoke about this only in relation to his perceived failings in other areas *"...as I'm not good at anything else."* (M2 Respondent)

The majority of the respondents in one focus group (M1) related experiences of negative relationships within the family context, although individuals were still able to identify positive feelings towards family members; *" You still love them."* (M1 Respondent). Their negative attitudes permeated other contexts such as education and employment. However these young people still attended school, if irregularly, and sought and obtained employment when they needed to.

A respondent who had experienced a number of negative situations in his own life was able to identify an individual within a service who, from his point of view, had once made a crucial intervention: *"Well what she did for me, she saved me."* (See 5.2.3.1). This young man was able to identify a positive experience within a very negative context.

5.2 Health Findings

5.2.1 Introduction

The Health section is quite extensive and is presented under the following sub-sections

- Associated Behaviours
- Other Medical Issues
- Identification of Health Services
- Perception of Current Health Services
- Development of Services.

5.2.2 Associated Behaviours

Associated behaviours include alcohol, drugs and substance misuse, and practices relating to sexual health. Female focus groups are presented first (indicated by the letter F), followed by male groups (indicated by the letter M).

5.2.2.1 Alcohol

Female Findings

F3 (average age 12.5, rural)

This group did not use alcohol, cigarettes or other drugs, but stated that a pupil had once brought beer on their school bus, indicating that primary school students can have ready access to alcohol.

The participants agreed that teenagers in their area probably were involved in drinking, drugs misuse and smoking. The perception of this group was that older adolescents did these things because they were *"upset or bored."*

There were a number of public houses in the area that the young people would frequent only to use the toilet, or with older family members to have soft drinks, *"not a proper drink"* (F3 Respondent).

F1 (average age 14.5, urban), F2 (average age 15, urban) and F4 (average age 16.5, rural)

These female respondents all viewed alcohol consumption as a regular social group activity that usually occurred at the week-ends. Some referred nostalgically to their cider drinking sessions *"...when we were younger..."* (F1 respondent)

Similarities that featured across the locations included the consumption of alcohol *"for a bit of excitement"*, (F1 respondent). The manner and types of alcohol consumed was governed by the amount of money available; *" ... Well I go out once during the weekend so that would be, well if I was goin' out for a good night out, I'd bring sixty or seventy (Euro) just to make sure I have enough to go out."* (F4 Respondent)

None of the participants had problems in obtaining alcohol. Some frequented pubs with their parents (F4 Respondents); others got friends over eighteen to buy their alcohol, which they drank in public places such as parks, school grounds, street corners, river banks or laneways (F1 and F2 Respondents). The type of alcohol drunk ranged from spirits (particularly vodka) and alco-pops (Barcardi Breezers, Smirnoff Ice) to inexpensive beers such as Dutch Gold. On occasion, a friend's house would become 'free' for a house party, and this was considered *"lucky"* (F1 Respondent).

Alcohol

Male Findings

M3 (average age 12, rural)

The participants stated that they did not consume alcohol themselves, but were aware of the places where older teenagers congregated, such as tennis courts, playing fields, the train station and laneways. The respondents knew that drinking and smoking occurred at these venues because of the evidence of empty cans, broken beer bottles and cigarette ends.

M1 (average age 14.75, urban), M2 (average age 15, urban) and M4 (average age 16.5, rural)

The male respondents in each of these focus groups agreed that the consumption of alcohol was a normal social activity that occurred at the week-ends. The M4 respondents preferred pubs to public spaces, stating: *"it's just a bit of crack, bit of a laugh, somewhere to go to"*. Members of this group also attended nightclubs.

The preferred venue for consumption of alcohol varied in the younger M1 group, with the majority stating that they enjoyed *"sculling cans in a field"*, and some behaviours induced by intoxication were considered *"fun"*, such as *"running around a field with your trousers around your ankles"* (M1 Respondent).

Their choice of drink varied from spirits to inexpensive beers. An approximation of the amount of money required by those who frequented pubs and nightclubs was put at between 40 and 50 Euros for normal weekend activities (M4 Respondent). None of the male focus groups reported difficulties in obtaining alcohol.

5.2.2.1.1 Consequences of Alcohol Consumption

Female Findings

F1 (average age 14.5, urban), F2 (average age 15, urban) and F4 (average 16.5, rural)

The groups separated the consequences of consuming of alcohol into two broad categories: Health Risks and Social Behaviours.

Health Risks identified as associated with alcohol consumption were possible unconsciousness, sickness and death through asphyxiation, *"kidney failure, brain damage and that it could kill you"* (F2 Respondent). These were listed off spontaneously, with little discussion arising on the topic.

Social Behaviours were often associated with boundaries set by the family. As one F4 respondent stated, *"I wouldn't be a real alcoholic. If I was out, my mam says to me "Two at the limit", and Daddy is the same, he'd go mental if he knew. 'Cos you are not able to mind yourself if you are falling around the place and you make a holy show of yourself."* And *"If I was going out, I'd have to go with someone else; my mother wouldn't let me go on my own like – I'd have to go with my brother or something."*

Close shaves of almost being caught drinking were recalled with amusement in another focus group: *"I was up in the park one day (drinking), and my mother walked through; we had to hide in the bush."* (F1 Respondent)

Other social behaviours identified included *"...when you're drunk you just act stupid"*, (F2 Respondent) and *"...you always get jeered the next day if you do something, like."* (F2 Respondent) But it was agreed that it was usually *"a laugh"* (F2 Respondent), even though the amounts consumed would often result in some participants *"...fall*(ing) *over ourselves"* (F1 Respondent).

Monitoring of amounts consumed was evidenced in one location, when friends would intervene to prevent someone from becoming too drunk. *"We take the drink off them and we'd say stop, like."* (F1 Respondent). This type of action was confirmed by one of the respondents who had been drinking in the school grounds: *"They wouldn't let me finish my drink."* (F1 Respondent)

Another concern was that the Gardai occasionally became stricter about under-age drinking. A number of young people in one location had been fined, and their parents obliged to go to the barracks. In another area a related observation was made: *"I don't go evenings very often, but into X (a nightclub), you don't get in every time. It depends whether the guards are around"* (F4 Respondent).

Consequences of Alcohol Consumption

Male Findings

M1 (average age 14.75, urban), M2 (average age 15, urban) and M4 (average age 16.5, rural)

The males' perception of the consequences of alcohol consumption varied slightly from that of females in that they identified primarily physical risks.

One group (M4) related situations that occurred in their night club, when violence was a risk *"...just, like drunken rows and stuff like that. People, not just teenagers like, people cause trouble, and then they* (i.e. nightclub staff) *say 'You're barred'."* Violence also occurred after the club closed. These encounters were often viewed with amusement by the group, with one M4 respondent stating *"I'd run away very fast!"* These young males emphasised that it is not only young people who cause rows when under the influence of alcohol.

Another physical risk identified by M4 respondents was drunk driving. Different strategies here caused a difference of opinion, with some limiting the risk *("That's if they weren't too bad like"*), but one suggested : *"If you were in a circle of good friends, you wouldn't be really paying attention, like. Like you'd have a few pints yourself and you'd say "Ah sure, we're going there anyway like. Save a couple of quid on the taxi, get in the car where they're goin'."* This was supported by others: *"We often got into a car with a lad and he'd be paralytic."*

M1 Respondents highlighted the issue of contraception, where the need to use a condom would often be ignored when young people were intoxicated.

5.2.2.2 Substance and Drug Misuse

The findings regarding substance and drug misuse is presented by individual focus group, as differences in the values and norms of participating peer groups were pronounced.

Female Findings

F3 (average age 12.5, rural) did not offer any specific information on this topic, other than that they knew that older adolescents were involved in drinking, drug misuse and smoking.

F1 (average age 14.5, urban)

All these participants shared a strongly negative view of drugs and substance misuse, stating *"It's stupid"* and *"Never do it"*, and regarded it as unacceptable behaviour within their all-female peer group.

They went further, applying the negative label *"druggies"* to a male peer group that they knew used drugs on a regular basis, and stated that for this reason, they chose not to associate with them. The *"druggie"* group were accredited with *"ownership"* of a particular youth service in the area, which meant that these respondents would not access this same service under any circumstances.

However they acknowledged that a male peer group that they did associate with *"smoked a bit of hash a few times"*. But these young males were considered acceptable (*"they're not druggies"*), because their drug use was occasional only; they were *"not popping pills or not E's or all that"*.

Access to drugs was clearly easy for these respondents, if ever they did decide to use them. One respondent within the focus group witnessed a drugs search by the Gardai, which had resulted in two arrests. However the respondent declined to provide details of the incident, urging the group to move on to the next topic.

F2 (average age 15, urban)

Initial comments on this topic were muted and reserved. But in this tentative opening stage the young people were able to list the health risks associated with drug and substances misuse, which they had not done in the discussion about alcohol.

However one respondent then said *"Come on, woman!"* which broke the ice, and the discussion became more open and revealing. In general the young women agreed that most young people were *"using"*, some of them "just sitting there laughing, and they think they're deadly like, going around telling people *'Oh I does this'*, and *'I does that'*, like". This suggests that the use of drugs is associated by some young people with acquiring street credibility.

The group stated that most young people would know where to obtain drugs if they wanted them, but thought that the main substances used were *"hash and speed"*.

F4 (average age 16.5, rural)

This group did not offer any contribution regarding substance or drug misuse, but focused on the belief that young people, particularly young women, smoked cigarettes to look *"cool"*. One young woman spoke about how she had her first cigarette in fifth class in primary school and developed a regular habit after that. As a seventeen year old she now smokes an average of twenty a day.

(Although the F1 and F2 groups did not identify cigarettes as health risk, a number of respondents in each of the focus groups smoked during the interview.)

Substance and Drug Misuse

Male Findings

M3 (average age 12, rural) offered no knowledge of substance and drug misuse other than that older adolescents used them.

M1 (average age 14.75, urban) and M2 (average age 15, urban)

The discussion regarding their knowledge of drugs produced different reactions. Some were noticeably guarded about the topic, while others were more open and stated that drugs shouldn't be illegal. A younger respondent (who attended primary school) had witnessed older males ordering their *"smoke"* (M2 Respondent) by mobile telephone. He believed that the older males thought he did not understand what they were doing.

The M1 group offered the following analysis: *"No, but like, thing is like, in today's young society is ...who does drugs and doesn't do drugs, like."* On further exploration, the group saw it as possible to identify and label groups by their relatively 'open' use of drugs, but the participants were sure that those who were stereotyped as 'non-users' in their locality often did in fact 'use'.

5.2.2.2.1 Consequences of Substance and Drug Misuse

All Groups combined

Generally females did not consider the consequences of substance and drug misuse in the discussions, and as many did not "use", they therefore did not consider themselves at risk. Some identified drug misuse with a street credibility.

In contrast some young males identified **mental health** risks such schizophrenia, paranoia and **physical risks** including lying on train tracks or climbing high buildings when "high". However this knowledge did not prevent them from "using." The risk of being searched by the Gardai was also cited by respondents (See: Justice Findings 5.5)

5.2.2.3 Sexual Activity

Core questions regarding sexual health were removed from the question formula for focus group F3 and M3 due to the low average age of the respondents. F3 (average age 12.5, rural) offered no information and M3 (average age 12, rural) made only one comment.

Female Findings

F1 (average age 14.5, urban), F2 (average age 15, urban) and F4 (average age 16.5, rural)

All the respondents of these focus groups acknowledge that sexual activity was common among their school populations and within their locality. All sixteen female respondents of these three focus groups personally knew at least one female under the age of fifteen who had become a mother, identifying seven young mothers in total.

Across all the locations the perception of these young women was that early motherhood would not be a desired personal choice. They felt that the responsibilities of motherhood would be more appropriate when they were older and they wished to experience life fully prior to having children.

Sexual Activity

Male Findings

M3 (average age 12, rural)

At the time of the focus group none of the young males had entered a one-to-one relationship, although one stated he *"nearly had a girlfriend."* In fact the group tended to have a negative view of females generally, and especially of adult females on the basis that they were *"big nosy neighbour(s)"*, who were there to interfere with and spoil their fun.

M1 (average age 14.75, urban), M2 (average age 15, urban) and M4 (average age 16.5, rural)

Sexual references were constantly used to describe situations, topics and people, either positively or negatively. Respondents in these groups said that they were sexually active, but most did not disclose whether they participated in full sexual intercourse. None were fathers at the time of the study. One seventeen year-old stated that he had been with a prostitute in a neighbouring town area on several occasions.

5.2.2.4 Safe Sexual Practices

Contraception

Female Findings

F1 (average age 14.5, urban), F2 (average age 15, urban) and F4 (average 16.5, rural)

A common view across the locations was that contraception should be the responsibility of both females and males. However it was also acknowledged that this was often not the case. If a pregnancy resulted *"fellas wouldn't be bothered sticking by you like.....they think they can do whatever they want and get away with it"* (F2 Respondent). Another focus group thought that both females and males were unsure of safe sexual practices: *"Like, the lads are saying, 'Oh, you'll be all right with me'...and yet they don't know what they're doing themselves."* (F1 Respondent) A consistent view across the locations was that their parents would be disappointed if they became pregnant.

Contraception

Male Findings

M1 (average age 14.75, urban), M2 (average age 15, urban) and M4 (average age 16.5, rural)

Some of the respondents viewed the threat of parents as sufficient reason to practice safe sex if they made a girl pregnant: *"they'd kill me"* (M1 Respondent). Pregnancy prevention, rather than risk of exposure to a sexually transmitted infection, was seen as the priority for taking precautions such as using a condom.

Prevention of Sexually Transmitted Infections

Female Findings

F1 (average age 14.5, urban), F2 (average age 15, urban) and F4 (average 16.5, rural)

One group (F1) listed Sexually Transmitted Infections, but did not offer insights into how they would obtain treatment. In another Focus Group participants would seek assistance from the local hospital, suggesting *"when you go up there like, you probably would be embarrassed, but when you start talking to them you wouldn't"* (F2 Respondent).

Male Findings

M1 (average age 14.75, urban)

Although it was stated that it was possible to become infected, *"There's some you couldn't clean up like, but sure, if you got AIDS or something..."* (M1 Respondent), a number of respondents stated that when intoxicated, they would often ignore the need to use a condom.

5.2.2 5 Sex Education

Female Findings

F1 (average age 14.5, urban), F2 (average age 15, urban), F4 (average 16.5, rural)

The participants' levels of sexual awareness varied considerably, with some focus groups stating that young people gained most of their knowledge regarding sexual activity from *"...the street, no matter what age you are."* (F1 Respondent). Yet they agreed that information gained from peers might prove inaccurate.

They also thought that the content of programmes that teachers delivered in Personal Development classes in school was inconsistent. Some teachers did provide detailed information on relationships and contraception and were open to questions put to them by the students, but others discussed friendships only, or focused on topics the participants considered irrelevant.

In contrast another focus group were knowledgeable about sexual health, which they learned about mainly through a programme in their school: *"Like there is people that are going around to the schools and talkin' and talkin' about safe sex, which is good, 'cos you kinda get to know more information about what to do"* (F4 Respondent).

However the group also acknowledged that *"there is still people getting pregnant you know. You don't really know what can stop it. Mainly it's yourself, for thinkin' what to do and you should know what to do, you know"* (F4 Respondent). This view was echoed in another location when a respondent stated about young women who didn't take precautions, *"But sure, they're stupid; they know what they're doing. If they don't want it, they know to use protection."* (F2 Respondent)

In one group the option of abortion was discussed by the young women's who offered the following scenario: *"I think the worst thing is if your friend did tell you and she didn't want anybody else to know and she wanted to have an abortion. Where would you be then?"* (F4 Respondent) This would represent a real conflict of values for these young women, but the course of action they would take was not decided.

N.B. Male groups did not offer any suggestions regarding sex education.

5.2.2.6 Sexual Health

F1 (average age 14.5, urban)

These young women spoke about their own experiences during puberty, and the fact that they all found it *"embarrassing"* to attend a male doctor. One respondent recalled a visit to a male doctor, and identified the practise of having a female nurse attending as offering a protection both to her as a patient and to the male doctor. The group stated that they felt they had little choice in the matter, as only male doctors operated in their area. One respondent stated that if unwell, *"I won't go to the doctor, just wait for the problem to pass"*.

N.B. Male groups did not offer any suggestions regarding sexual health.

5.2.3 Other Health Issues

Discussions in this area focussed on the issues of Mental Health and Eating Disorders.

5.2.3.1 Mental Health

Female Findings

F1 (average age 14.5, urban), F2 (average age 15, urban), F3 (average age 12.5 rural) and F4 (average 16.5, rural)

The respondents' awareness of mental health issues appeared limited. For some, mental health meant to be *"happy"* (F1 Respondent), and spending time with their friends and enjoying themselves achieved happiness and well-being. In contrast other young women were aware of depression and acknowledge that they would sometimes feel *"down"*, (F2 Respondent) but would usually speak to their friends about anything that was troubling them. They were aware of counsellors being available through the Health Board, *"but sure they won't do nothing for you really."* (F2 Respondent)

The school counsellor was identified as a person who offered advice and assistance for those who found themselves in difficulty or crisis: *"Yeah, you could ask for a list of names without giving any information. I'm sure she would ask, but if you don't want to talk to her, you don't have to, like"* (F4 Respondent)

Mental Health

Male Findings

M1 (average age 14.75, urban) and M4 (average age 16.5, rural)

In the focus groups M1 and M4 the issue of para-suicide and suicide were discussed in some depth. One participant stated that he had previously attempted suicide by taking an overdose. During his stay in hospital doctors had considered admitting him to a mental institution. The young man related how his admission was prevented only by the intervention of a doctor who *"...went up and goes: 'That young lad's not going into that fucking place – two days in it and he'll be fucked up in the head!'"*. According to him the doctor's intervention was crucial: *"Well, what she did for me, she saved me"*.(M1 Respondent)

The group's empathy towards this person was evident during this part of the discussion, the prevailing mood of humour and sarcasm became quieter and gentler, and other members agreed that often they too did not know what to do, and could sometimes feel depressed.

They could relate to the predicament of young men who attempt suicide: *"Most people don't want to, most people just do it to get attention"* (M1 respondent) and *"Most think they're not getting enough attention"* (M4 respondent). It was seen as important for friends and services to offer support *"...just to let them know that they're wanted or something"* (M4 Respondent).

School Counsellors were discussed in relation to education services available (See: Education Section). However, the group believed that the school Counselling Service was *"stupid"* (M1Respondent) and ineffective.

5.2.3.2 Eating Disorders

Female Findings

F1 (average age 14.5, urban) F2 (average age 15, urban) and F4 (average age 16.5, rural)

In general young women were aware of eating disorders, and believed that a desire to look thin is driven by the media and by peer pressure. One respondent explained: *"'Cos you see other girls thin, and you just envy them. You'd say "Oh, look at the figure on her and look what she can wear when you're that thin", and like "I wish I was like that", you know what I mean?"* (F4 Respondent). In one group, respondents showed concern for one of their peers who they believed did not eat adequately; the young women's response was *"It's not true lads, I'll eat when I want to eat, not when you want me to eat."* (F2 Respondent)

Conflicting opinions were expressed by individuals in different focus groups regarding the disclosure of suspected cases of anorexia and bulimia to parents or a trusted adult. Some viewed informing the parents/adult as a betrayal of the friend's trust, while for others the health of the friend was the priority, even if it meant the cost of the friendship.

However all three focus groups knew where to access information leaflets regarding eating disorders, which *" give you a number an' all on the leaflet to ring."* (F1 Respondent)

A closing comment in one focus group was that they were aware of healthy eating habits that they had learned about during *"Home Economics"* classes, but felt *"girls will always have an obsession with their figures"* and that healthy eating was *"...more so not about how healthy they are going to be,* (but) *how thin they can get."* (F4 Respondent)

Eating Disorders

Male Findings

M4 (average age 16.5, rural)

Only one of the young males focus groups offered any explanation of eating disorders, and they identified a clear gender difference, as illustrated in the following interaction :

Respondent D: *Girls are very conscious of their weight, that's why most of them smoke as well.*

Researcher: *And what does that come from, the fact that girls are more conscious of their weight?*

Respondent E: *Because of all the supermodels.*

Respondent D: *Girls would be more remarking about each other.*

One of the respondents went on to recount the case of a young female he knew who developed an eating disorder, and who now at the age of nineteen, was seriously ill: *"They said her stomach was after closing completely this time"* (M4 Respondent).

Attitudes expressed towards this young female varied from understanding to total lack of sympathy, and some felt it would be none of their business if they became aware of someone suffering from an eating disorder.

5. 2. 4 Current Health Services Identified

Throughout the focus group discussions a number of services were identified by females and males, and these are presented in table 5.4 It is important to note that females identified more services than males, and that younger participants (F3 and M3) identified more services than their older counterparts. Also rural focus groups identified a number of community based health initiatives that were not identified by those in urban areas.

5.2.5 Perceptions of Identified Health Services

Table 5.4 below lists all the health services identified by participants as being currently available within the county.

Table 5.4 Identified Health Service by Focus Groups

Type of Services Identified			
Female	**Focus Group**	**Males**	**Focus Group**
• Doctors	• All	• Chemists	• M3
• Hospitals	• All	• Doctors	• All
• Addiction Supports Services	• F3	• Hospitals	• All
• Childline	• F3	• Counsellors	• M1/M3
• Information via the Internet	• F3	• Health Centre	• M3
• CURA	• F4	• Day Care for Elderly	• M3
• SMART	• F4	• Hospice Care	• M3
• Dentist	• All	• Foster Care	• M3
• Clinic	• All	• Respite Care	• M1
• Sexual Health Programme in Schools	• F4	• Crumlin Children's Hospital	• M4
• Speech Therapists	• F2		
• Baby Clinic	• F1/F2		
• Social care	• F1		
• Family Welfare Supports	• F1		
• Counsellors	• F2		
• Chemists	• F2/F4		

Female Findings

F1 (average age 14.5, urban), F2 (average age 15, urban), F3 (average age 12.5, rural) and F4 (average age 16.5, rural)

In general the identification of services by respondents was either through personal experience or through contact with others who had used the service. The opinions regarding health services were very limited with mixed reactions ranging from *"okay"* (F1 Respondent) to *"stupid"* (F2 Respondent).

Male Findings

M1 (average age 14.75, urban), M2 (average age 15, urban), M3 (average age 12, rural) and M4 (average age 16.5 rural)

Again identification of services appeared to be linked to personal experience or through contact with someone who had used the service. However their perceptions of current identified health services, both positive and negative, were more comprehensive than those offered by female respondents.

Positive comments included praise for a local doctor who was considered excellent, as he had responded immediately to a late night call from the home of one participant. Foster Care and Respite Care availed of by respondents from different areas were appreciated, as they provided breaks from home and access other amenities (e.g. swimming pools, cinema, etc). However the respondents who used these services stated that they always liked to return to their family home.

Some negative attitudes were expressed towards school counsellors from male respondents in both rural and urban areas, identifying the services as "stupid" and one counsellor as "ignorant". Female respondents were less negative, acknowledging the opportunities the service offered for those who might need information or support.

Hospital services came in for criticism which focused on long waiting time in Casualty Departments and for X-rays, and that services needed extra staff, more resources, and should be offered locally in rural areas. The cost of visiting the doctor was also cited as a negative: *"They charge too much though, don't they?"* (M4 Respondent)

5.2.5.1 Accessing Current Identified Health Services

Female Findings

F1 (average age 14.5, urban), F2 (average age 15, urban), F3 (average age 12.5, rural) and F4 (average age 16.5, rural)

A view expressed in all focus groups was that it was the role of their parents to access services for young people if they were in need of health care. The respondents viewed the family as a support, to *"look after them"* (F1 Respondent). This caring role was particularly identified with mothers. However, younger female participants (F3) also saw Childline and information via the Internet as services that young people could access themselves.

The young people didn't identify any specific statutory or voluntary health provision as being responsible for their health. However once the young women had accessed a service, they illustrated awareness of ethical considerations in doctors' appointments, where a female member of staff needed to be present during examinations by a male doctor. They thought more female doctors were needed.

The identification of Social Care arose through a discussion regarding Justice, when a participant spoke of having personal contact with an individual who had accessed social care services. This service was described as a home where the young person lived, as a result of being in trouble.

The F1 participants regarded Personal Development classes in school as mainly concerned with exploring friendships, relationships and sex education, but that saw them as confined to the school context, and not as a component of a more "holistic" approach to health care. The young people's expectations of these classes were often left unmet, as they stated that the delivery of these sessions was inconsistent and very much depended upon the input and attitude of the teacher.

N.B Male participants made only one contribution in regard to the accessing of services, where parents accessed health services on their behalf.

5.2.6 Development of Health Services

Four suggestions were promoted by young people, three by females and one by males. These are outlined in the following section.

Female Findings

F1 (average age 14.5, urban)

It was generally felt that a specific service for young women should be established, giving teenagers information on biological changes, sex education and other general medical needs, to be staffed by female personnel.

The respondents suggested that a more structured and comprehensive sex education programme would be advantageous for young people. However, there was a disparity among the respondents regarding the ideal age of any target groups for such programmes, preferred options ranging from 5th & 6th Class in primary school to 16 and 17 year olds.

F4 (average age 16.5, rural)

The favoured proposal in this group was *"a phone line or something, just for young people with problems who feel that they can't go to friends. Some people might feel that they haven't got friends, but if there was a phone service or something that they could chat to about the littlest problems or the biggest problems..."* This was confirmed by another in the group :*"Yeah, someone to go to."*

Male Findings

M1 (average age 14.75, urban)

The main proposal for new health services in this group concentrated on a crisis service for young people that would be available as a walk-in facility. The respondents varied in their ideas of who should operate such a service; some thought that young people were best suited, reasoning that those of a similar age would be *"doing the same shit"*; therefore a peer-education approach would be most acceptable. Others expressed no preference as regards age of staff, but generally urged a service that could be trusted by young people.

5.3 Education

5.3.1 Introduction

The Education section details findings from each of the focus groups under the sub-sections list below:

- Attitudes to School
- Social Interaction
- Examination and Non-Examination Years,
- Transition and Leaving Certificate Applied Programmes,
- School Size and Identity
- Extra-Curricular Activities and Service within School
- Future Plans
- Alternative Education

5.3.2 Attitudes to School

Female and Male Findings

All Groups

A common feature of the focus group discussions was an initial reaction that school was *"boring"* (F3 Respondent), but as the conversation and discussion developed, a general consensus emerged that school was also enjoyable and, given the choice, all respondents would attend.

However some respondents were aware of young people who felt negative about school, and one group recalled a case of arson that occurred in their local primary school (M3). They believed the action of the young males involved was motivated by their poor relationship with teachers in the school.

5.3.3 Social Interaction

Female Findings

F3 (average age 12.5, rural)

These young people enjoyed the social interaction within school, and the way that school offered routes into other activities, such as swimming and drama productions. Some did not participate in the swimming classes due to the cost.

As a group they appeared quite sociable, and liked most people in their classes. But they were also aware that not all students enjoyed school in the same way, with some being bullied and occasionally hit by others.

F1 (average age 14.5, urban), F2 (average age 15, urban) and F4 (average age 16.5, rural)

The majority felt that the non-examination years were enjoyable, and that it was possible to *"have a bit of a laugh"* (F2 Respondent), indicating that they liked the social element within the education system. An in-depth analysis of the social system operating within school was offered by one focus group (F1), who clearly identified a framework of peer groups loosely based upon social class.

Three main types of groups seem to be identified by this focus group: *"Druggies", "Posh Ones"* and their own friends and associates. The Druggies according to these participants were a group that used drugs openly and were usually too *"high"* (F1 Respondent) to communicate with; some of these had been suspended from school for *"dealing"* drugs (F1 Respondent). (See: Justice Section)

They associated the 'Posh Ones' with extra curricular activities such as the Student Council and the debating team: *"They don't talk to you, associate with you like..."* as *"...they kind of think they're too good for us like."* (F1 Respondent). Although the group acknowledged that the Student Council was involved in positive projects such as organising school trips, yet they felt excluded from its activities : *"You only go on a trip if you're good like...you have to be in with all these Student Councillors to go on these trips..."* (F1 Respondent).

They perceived themselves as having certain advantages in terms of life experience, however:

- *"The Posh Ones are going to end up thick like 'cause we're working, we're trying to work for something we don't have like and they've got it and they don't care like".*

- *"They're like 'I still got money!' but there's going to be time when they're not going to have it".*

- *"They won't understand the concept of working for money like"*

(F1 Respondents)

The group's overall analysis of their school life and the interaction of its peer groups led them to a firm and positive conclusion: *"We manage all right though, I think"* and *"We do manage."* (F1 Respondents)

A number of the respondents in a rural area (F4) had known each other from primary school and maintained their friendships through post-primary level, although they also made new friends. They saw themselves as retaining these friends after finishing school.

The perception of these young women was that the social interaction went beyond peer groups and included positive relationships with teachers.

- *"The teachers are sound, but I hate school still"*
- *"You can talk to them and they have more time for you. If you have a problem they are there for you."*
- *"If you're given a bit of leeway you know when to stop then, you know what I mean?"*

(F4 Respondents)

Male Findings – Social Interaction

M1 (average age 14.75, urban), M2 (average age 15, urban), M3 (average age 12, rural) and M4 (average age 16.5, rural)

The younger respondents already attending second level in different schools focused on the activities of older males within the school population. They recounted incidents of older males opening emergency exits on buses, and 'messing' in school (M3).

The young males' view of 'mitching' in secondary school was that it was futile, as a role call was taken in every class throughout the day and the school immediately telephoned the home of anyone reported missing. According to the young males, one group of older girls had tried to skip classes, but got caught and were suspended (M3).

Quite a lot of their discussion concentrated on **bullying**, where certain individuals had been picked on, and where the respondents themselves had participated in the bullying of these individuals. However a teacher had intervened and the young males were reprimanded for their involvement. One case of bullying recalled by the respondents involved a young male who, although talented and ambitious, gave up Irish dancing as *"...Yeah, they were all callin' him faggot an' queer"* (F3 Respondent).

The negative aspects of school for some respondents focused upon their relationships with the teaching staff, rather than on the amount of homework or study that was required. Some of the negative encounters involved verbal abuse, and one respondent stated that a teacher called him a *"retard"* (M2 Respondent) in front of the class. These negative relationships tended to continue outside school, and could lead to aggressive behaviour such as *"egging his* (the teacher's) *house"* (M2 Respondent).

One respondent (M2) who had experienced various degrees of criticism by teachers since he was quite young was discovered to be dyslexic late in his school career. The school apologised to the young man, but at the age of fifteen he left school with no qualification.

In contrast to the generally positive opinions that female participants expressed about a particular rural school, their male counterparts' views (M4) were quite negative, and focussed on the strictness with which rules were applied within the school. For example, *"If you go down town you are suspended for a day, if you are caught smoking you are suspended for a day."* (M4 Respondent). Generally they thought that there were too many rules and found them confusing and frustrating.

One young male gave an account of his career in the school, which contained a positive observation among a list of negatives. *"Well, in First Year I got in so much trouble, and then in Second Year it got a bit worse and I got suspended a couple of times, and put on report a couple of times; and Third Year it was pretty much the same. This year I suppose it's after getting a bit better, I'm not in so much trouble. It's still crap though, it's like a prison. Only certain times you can go to the toilet, can't do certain things..."* Their perception of teachers' was that they are *"... always telling us that we should be acting mature, and then they treat us like children"* (M4 Respondent).

5.3.4 Examination Year and Non-Examination Year

Female Findings

F1 (average age 14.5, urban), F2 (average age 15, urban) and F4 (average age 16.5, rural)

The general lack of enthusiasm for school was qualified by the opinion that 1st and 2nd years were less stressful and therefore more enjoyable. *"If you didn't have to do homework, I wouldn't mind"* (F1 Respondent). However this attitude underwent a change during examination years across all the post-primary schools, as illustrated by the following quotations.

- *"The horrible thing is the teachers on your back saying 'Study! Study! Study!"* (F1 Respondent).

- *"And it's going around in your head, and just like, I'd love to go up and hit one those teachers, like. All they're saying is 'Study for your Junior Cert, study for your Junior Cert. It's terrible, it is. I don't like it now."* (F2 Respondent)

The group thought that continuous assessment was *"really better, but you just know it's just no exams"* (F4 Respondent). These students were doing an LCVP course, where continuous assessment was based on projects and work experience done during the year.

Male Findings

M1 (average age 14.75, urban), M2 (average age 15, urban) and M4 (average age 16.5, rural)

In general the first and second year in post-primary school were considered positively but school got *"worse and worse"* as the years went on (M4 respondent). However the same stress levels were not as apparent as in the female focus groups. Some respondents at the time of the interview were preparing to sit their Leaving Certificate, but did not appear optimistic about their prospects in the examinations.

5.3.5 Transition Year, Leaving Certificate Applied and Leaving Certificate Vocational Programmes

Female Findings

F1 (average age 14.5, urban), F2 (average age 15, urban), F4 (average age 16.5, rural)

In schools where these options were available, the respondents were enthusiastic about their effectiveness and relevance, in particular their emphasis on continuous assessment that required report writing. The reports were produced in a format that was provided by their supervising teacher, and support was given on a continuous basis. The programmes were considered *"fun"* (F2 Respondent)

The Leaving Certificate Applied Programme involved project work and work placements with different businesses. In general the inclusion of work experience was viewed positively, but the participants recounted a number of incidents where, in their opinion, the businesses had not fulfilled their responsibilities to the trainees: *"You kind of have to do all their dirty jobs like"* (F2 Respondent). In one case the school had to intervene, and the young person's work experience placement was changed.

Male Findings

M1 (average age 14.75 urban), M2 (average age 15, urban) and M4 (average age 16.5, rural)

The young males had mixed reaction to these programmes; they enjoyed some of the work experience, but still felt *"you spend too much time in class rooms anyway"* (M4 Respondent). Others clarified this point by stating: *"They just explain things to you like. If they actually showed us things like. They'd show us bits alright in the Practical. In Theory, if they brought us out of school like and actually showed us it would be a lot better"* (M4 Respondent). In one location a young male had obtained work experience in car spraying, an area that he wished to pursue after school, and really appreciated the opportunity to experience the work before he left school.

Subjects such as woodwork and metalwork were seen as male domains, and women teachers in these areas were unwelcome by young males (M4).

5.3.6 School Size and Identity

Female Findings

F1 (average age 14.5, urban), F2 (average age 15, urban), F3 (average age 13 rural) and F4 (average age 16.5, rural)

At primary level the school's size and identity were not raised as an issue, but the young girls were looking forward to their eventual transfer to secondary school. However at post primary level some respondents felt their school was too big. This was linked by the respondents to their transition from primary to secondary school. In primary school *"...all the teachers knew your name, you knew everybody nearly in it...But when you go into this school there's so many teachers, you don't...you don't know the teachers names"* (F1 Respondent).

Rural isolation did not appear to be a significant problem to students from another geographical area, where the school's catchment area included a rural hinterland. Here the distance between homes was not seen as presenting obstacles for the young people in maintaining their friendships, *"Well, she just comes out to my house at the weekends and we see each other in school and we used to live in the housing estate, so if I want to go and see my friends I just walk down"* (F4 Respondent).

However the journey to and from school was disliked by those who had to use school buses. The bus picked some up at seven-thirty in the morning and returned them to their drop off point at four-thirty, from where they had to walk home. Obviously the day doesn't end for young people at this point, as *"...then you have to do house work as well"* and *"Yeah, and then you have to do homework."* (F4 Respondents)

The school that these young people (F4) attended was comparatively small, and the teachers and other staff are on first name terms with all the students. The respondents were able to identify approachable teachers, and one respondent stated: *"I used to be in a different school and I didn't like it, and I left school for a year and I was working and then I came here and it's brilliant. I just find everyone is just happier and more at ease or whatever, and the teachers are much nicer"* (F4 Respondent). So this respondent left school early, but later returned to full-time education. In general the young women in this group (F4) felt that the teachers knew them as individuals and acknowledged their identity.

A regular and (from their perspective) positive activity within a large school was "mitching" or truancy, which was viewed with amusement by members of F1. Their school has a large student population and a large staff, so the easiest method of *"mitching"* was simply to walk the corridors of the school. As the group explained: *"The teachers meets you – "And where are you supposed to be now?" – "Oh I'm going to get my book out of my locker"* (F1 Respondent). and confirmed within the group: *"That's it! And then you just hope you don't meet them again"* (F1 Respondent).

Male Findings

No male groups offered observations on School Size and Identity.

5.3.7 Extra Curricular Activities and Services with School

Female Findings

F1 (average age 14.5, urban), F2 (average age 15, urban), F3 (average age 12.5, rural) and F4 (average age 16.5, rural)

All the schools that were attended by participants provided a varying range of extra curricular activities and services, including Stay in School programmes, sports, self defence classes, access to gymnasiums, health and fitness programmes, performance and dance, library management, young entrepreneur schemes, debating and school councils.

One group (F1) questioned the effectiveness of the School Council as a way of involving young people in decision making in the school. In the first place, the 'Posh Ones' monopolised the council – *"They kind of think they're too good for us like"*, and this group self-excluded; secondly, they had a negative view of the power of the School Council to influence decision-making within the school: *"They want it; they ask for it; they don't get it though"* (F1 Respondents).

In contrast a decision-making mechanism which operated in another school was viewed more positively. This school had recently introduced a subsidised canteen that provided breakfast and lunches as part of their Stay-in-School programme. As this group explained, *"You get surveys of what you want in the canteen. It's deadly like. It's cool when we can get a choice, so it's fair for the teachers and the students"* (F4 Respondent). The students appreciated the opportunities presented to them to participate in decision-making which placed them on an equal footing with staff: *"Actually a lad came to talk to us about it…they took two people out of every class and they asked us 'What do you think of our funding?'"* (F4 Respondent). Although they regarded this event positively, the young people were unclear about the role or identity of this visitor.

Male Findings

M1 (average age 14.75, urban), M2 (average age 15, urban), M3 (average age 12, rural) and M4 (average age 16.5, rural)

The main extra curricular activities and services identified by the male respondents were **sports** and **counsellors**.

Sports on offer to these participants ranged from basketball to football, soccer and swimming, and school facilities were largely approved of. They viewed school as the principle forum for young people to become involved in sporting activities, especially team sports.

Attitudes among male students to counselling services provided in their schools were generally negative. One respondent in a secondary school had an ambivalent attitude to a teacher who had helped him through counselling: *"You'd go up to her and she would be a real help, but she'd be a real ignorant teacher"* (M3 Respondent). Another dismissed the service in his school as *"stupid"* (M1 Respondent).

5.3.8 Future Plans

Female Findings

F1 (average age 14.5, urban), F2 (average age 15, urban) and F4 (average age 16.5, rural)

A range of ideas were offered by respondents in one group (F1) regarding future plans, including working in a clothes shop, in the leisure industry, becoming an accountant, a hairdresser, a veterinarian. Only two participants stated they wished to go to college, and the prospective veterinarian was not among them, suggesting a lack of awareness on her part of the educational requirements involved.

However most who had sights on a particular career appeared to have a good knowledge of options open to them subsequent to completing school. These included PLC courses, training programmes and third level colleges. The majority of older respondents had a definite idea of what career they wanted to pursue.

Male Findings

M1 (average age 14.75, urban), M2 (average age 15, urban) and M4 (average age 16.5, rural)

None of the participants in one group (M2) expressed a wish to continue their education beyond secondary school, one stating that the minute he was sixteen he was going to leave regardless of whether he had employment or not, as school was *"dirt"* (M2 Respondent). Some of the younger participants in this group wanted to be soccer professionals *"like David Beckham"*, but also had contingency plans such as *'training as a mechanic'* (M2 Respondent).

The majority of the respondents in another location considered the differences between college and apprenticeship, opting in favour of an apprenticeship, as *" If you go to college it takes three or four years to get qualified, and with an apprenticeship, you're making money as well"*. This was confirmed within the group when another individual stated *"Most people that I know, the way I look at it you know, you're better off doing an apprenticeship than going to college"* (M4 Respondents).

The school population in this town drew from a large rural hinterland and this was reflected in the choice of future career paths offered, with one participant intending to go to an agriculture college where others chose apprenticeships. The first explained his preference: *"Depends what you're doing in college like. If you're a farm manager you get two fifty (Euros) a week while you're in training, so it's not too bad like"*(M4 Respondent).

5.3.9 Alternative Education

Female Findings

F3 (average age 12.5 rural)

The youngest female respondents identified a crèche and playschool in their area. Older female respondents did not identify any alternative education programmes.

Male Findings

M1 (average age 14.75, urban), M2 (average age 15, urban), M3 (average age 12, rural) and M4 (average age 16.5, rural)

One participant (M2) had been asked to leave the secondary school that he had attended through first and second year. He believed that he was getting blamed in school for things that he had not done. He now attended a Traveller Training Centre approximately twenty-five miles from his home, which focused on a vocational curriculum. This centre offered him the opportunity to develop his woodworking skills further than had been possible at his secondary school. However given the choice, he would prefer to return to his previous school, as his friends all went there.

Another participant attended an alternative education programme and was in receipt of a weekly payment. The young man stated the staff were *"ultimately nice"* and continued : *"They give us all these lessons – 'Don't Do Drugs' and all – 'cause we left school, and that's what I don't like...It's just like... it's just like they're baby-sitting."* (M1 Respondent), suggesting the young person viewed the alternative programme as patronising.

5.4 Youth Services

5.4.1 Introduction

This section focuses on Youth Services, which the respondents identified as provided by the private sector, the community and voluntary sectors and through self-organised activities. These services are considered under the headings of

- Awareness,
- Appropriateness of Service and
- Development of Services.

5.4.2 Awareness

The focus groups divided services into three broad areas – those provided by commercial interests and local authorities, those provided by the voluntary and community sector, and self organised activities. In some cases groups identified services that were available in distant towns, while other groups failed to identify services that operated in their own immediate areas. Hence, the identification of any service by a group should not be interpreted as implying a use of that service by group members.

The groups' identification of services available to young people in the county is displayed in the following table:

Table 5.5 – Identified Youth Services

Female Focus Groups		Male Focus Groups	
Private Sector Youth Services	Focus Groups	**Private Sector Youth Services**	Focus Groups
• Cinema	• All	• Cinema	• All
• Gaming Hall	• F2	• Pool Halls	• M1 M2
• Pool Hall	• F1 F2	• Swimming Pool	• All
• Swimming Pool	• All	• Nightclubs	• M4
• Roadshow Discos	• F2	• Gymnasium	• M4
• Library	• F2	• Park	• M1
• Nightclubs	• F4		
Female Focus Groups		**Male Focus Groups**	
Private Sector Youth Services	Focus Groups	**Private Sector Youth Services**	Focus Groups
• Scouts	• F3	• Youth Clubs	• All
• Girls Scouts (Guides)	• F3 F2	• Youth Project	• M1 M3
• Bridgins	• F2	• SAFE	• M1
• Irish Dancing	• All	• GAA Club	• All
• Athletics	• F2	o Hurling	• All
• Outdoor Pursuits Centre	• F3	o Football	• All
• Youth Clubs	• All	• Soccer Club	• All
• Youth Project	• F1 F2		
• Youth Info	• F2		
• Gymnastics	• F2		
Self-Organised		**Self-Organised**	
• Hugga Bugga (Street Rugby)	• F2	• Bicycles	• M1 M3
• Soccer	• F2	• Skateboarding	• M1
• Football	• F4	• Motor Bikes	• M3 M1
• Hide-and-go-seek	• F3	• Driving Cars	• M4
• Driving Cars	• F1	• Hot Rods	• M3 M4
		• Soccer	• All
		• Hurling	• All
		• Football	• All
		• Climbing buildings	• M3 M1
		• Wrestling	• M3
		• Hitting Golf Balls	• M3

Female Findings

F1 (average age 14.5, urban), F2 (average age 15, urban), F3 (average age, 12.5 rural) and F4 (average age 16.5, rural)

Each focus group could list a range of what they saw as youth services within in their own area or which they could access by arranging transport. The commercial and local authority services identified were pool halls, cinemas, discos, swimming pools and libraries.

The community and voluntary sector provided an outdoor pursuit centre, youth clubs, youth projects, an Information Point, and organised activities such as Boy and Girl Scouts, Bridgins, gymnastics, Irish dancing and athletics.

The general perception was nevertheless that most areas lacked facilities and amenities for young people, and the opinion of the females was that there appeared to be more activities for their male counterparts.

Self-organised activities included hide-and-go-seek (among younger respondents), soccer, football and *"hugga bugga"* (F2 respondent) a form of street rugby, played with mixed teams of boys and girls.

Male Findings

M1 (average age 14.75, urban), M2 (average age 15, urban), M3 (average age 12, rural) and M4 (average age 16.5, rural)

The male respondents identified similar services, but with more emphasis on sporting activities. However the range of self-organised activities was quite extensive – 'playing around' for the younger respondents (digging, chasing, wrestling, hitting golf balls, etc.), cycling, skateboarding, playing football and soccer, and driving motorbikes and cars.

5.4.3 Appropriateness of Services

Female Findings

F1 (average age 14.5, urban), F2 (average age 15, urban), F3 (average age 12.5, rural) and F4 (average age 16.5, rural)

Judgement of the appropriateness of service was based on personal experience, or having contact with someone that had used a service. For example, *"My cousin goes to the Girl Scouts and they go up to Dublin to climb mountains an'all. That's really good."* (F3 Respondent) This group (F3) believed their area lacked facilities and their main proposal was to have teenage discos provided.

In the older age groups the respondents had used numerous services at primary school age, but the appeal of these services waned on their entering secondary school. A junior disco that ran in a local premises had been used by one group at a younger age, but they now considered it inappropriate, as *"Everyone kind of stopped going to it 'cause it was all children going to it."* (F2 Respondent)

Involvement in a youth club was considered to be inappropriate for young people of their age (15 years), as was quickly identified within the group: *"In all fairness, if they had a youth club you'd come up once and then you'd forget about it"* (F2 Respondent)

However in another location the young women enjoyed using the youth club that had operated from two school premises. *"We used to have it in the Gym here, and we could play anything we wanted, or else we could go upstairs and listen to music. People would bring in CDs or whatever. And then when we were in the other school, it was basically the same thing, but just kinda bigger, and then there was table tennis tables."* They used to attended regularly; *"...every Friday night – half-seven 'til half-ten or something like that"* (F4 Respondent). This youth club was recently closed down, and their perception was that this decision was made by the adult in charge.

These young women thought that the establishment of another youth club would be a good idea. *"And not just on Friday nights; it should be a couple of nights a week or whatever, 'cos not a lot of people are going to be sitting in all night, and doin' nothing"* (F4 Respondent).

The young women considered that this service should also involve those younger than themselves: *"And it's not just for us, it's for younger people – twelve, thirteen and fourteen – who would love to do it too. I mean if they found more interest in that, they'll put their best into it"* (F4 Respondent). However there was also evidence of a wish to have a selection policy in operation: *"I'd say there's no doubt about people wanting to join, unless you have a few messers, but sure we can easily kick them out"* (F4 Respondent).

In another focus group discussion (F1) the participants identified only one youth service for their group. They believed that this service operated an open door policy – i.e. that anyone could in theory use it. However the group associated 'ownership' of this particular project with a rival peer group, and as they preferred to avoid this rival group, they self-excluded from the service.

Their statements regarding the youth service were quite negative, stating *"all they do is sit around and smoke"* and that it was *"stupid"* (F1 Respondents). However within the group this was challenged on the basis that it was better than sitting on the streets, which was the location for much of their own activity. The respondents stated that the centre closed at six o'clock in the evening, so after this time young people still had only the streets to use. Therefore from a young person's perception the service was inappropriately scheduled.

Availability of facilities and amenities is not a guarantee that young people will or indeed can use them. The swimming pool was seen as a summer activity. They chose not to frequent the library. A pool hall had *"barred"* (F2 Respondent) some of the participants from its premises, but the young people did not always understand the reason for their exclusion. The cinema was rarely visited, and one participant (F2) stated that she had never been to her local multi-screen venue. A commercial disco that ran infrequently was popular with participants who considered it expensive but worth the money. A youth information point in one town had been visited by only one participants of a group from the area who went once only, and the purpose of this service seemed unclear to the group. These facilities were all generally within walking distance for the respondents.

In another area a mobile cinema that used a local hall to show films as a private venture had failed. The young women (F1) denigrated this service, although visiting a multiscreen would involve time and transport costs for this group.

Male Findings

M1 (average age 14.75, urban), M2 (average age 15, urban), M3 (average age 12, rural) and M4 (average age 16.5, rural)

There appeared to be a contrast in the way male groups considered appropriateness of services. The older participants' initial response was that their area lacked amenities and services for young people, especially those under the age of seventeen, but their opinion was: *"Doesn't really matter now 'cos we are nearly seventeen, and we'll be starting to drive. If you're under the age of seventeen like, there's nothing really to do"* (M4 Respondent).

In general younger respondents (13-14 years) were more enthusiastic about youth services available to them. The voluntary and community based youth programmes were generally viewed in a positive way. The young people particularly liked the *"small numbers"* (M2 Respondent) of participants that availed of the services, providing them with a sense of ownership. The younger respondents often used their local park or playground, but also considered it a valuable amenity for younger children.

An older respondent (15 years) was *"barred"* (M2 Respondent) from a local youth project. He thought this was unfair, but did not supply an explanation or reasons. His best friend declined to use the service in a show of solidarity, and neither has returned to the project.

All the respondents in one area (M1) were attached to a particular service, which they had been involved with for some time and which they intended to continue to use. They knew that the centre was open to all young people in the area, but acknowledged that they were the main group involved. Recently a younger mostly male group had started attending, but its members were regarded as *"a pain"* (M1 Respondent) by these respondents.

The respondents were mainly positive about the service, but felt that its hours should be extended to include late-night and week-end openings. The young people stated that the particular strength of the service was that it was a place where *"you can just sit down and chill out"* (M1 Respondent).

5.4.4 Development of Youth Services

Female Findings

F1 (average age 14.5, urban), F2 (average age 15, urban), F3 (average age 12.5, rural) and F4 (average age 16.5, rural)

The young women thought it was important that young people should be involved in the establishment of a service for themselves. They wanted somewhere to hang out, and also wanted to be given responsibility in running services, but felt that they never had a real opportunity: *"Give us a chance to prove ourselves"* (F2 Respondent). They did not want constant adult supervision, but acknowledged that they might need at least one adult to be available, but *"...not like our ma's"* (F2 Respondent). They should be able to access such a facility when they wanted, and insisted that opening hours would need to be liberal.

Young women in a different location had a similar view; they felt they should be involved in the running of a low-maintenance facility. They did not want constant adult intervention in its day-to-day management. A sense of ownership was important to the group, as was access at all hours, *"you know, like the same Sarah McCoy kinda drop-in centre on Home and Away"* (F1 Respondent).

The importance of a service providing a sense of freedom for those that use it was critical: *"Yeah, but still it's not being at home, and you can talk about whatever you want to talk about."* (F4 Respondent)

Male Findings

M1 (average age 14.75, urban), M2 (average age 15, urban), M3 (average age, 12 rural) and M4 (average age 16.5, rural)

The development of services was not considered as deeply by males. In one location young men (M3) had a negative experience in the past when an adult in the community had tried to establish a club, but this had fallen through. They seemed to feel disillusioned about adults promising services and amenities, and made no real suggestions for development of services for their area.

The majority of male respondents were sports-oriented, either through self-organised activities or in sports clubs. A local development that some were keen on promoting was the erection of goalposts in green areas where they lived as, when they put up their own posts, they would be removed by the local authority or by vandals (M1 and M3).

In one focus group respondents appeared quite cynical about the motives of those involved in developing youth services for young people, stating *"it doesn't cost them anything."* (M1 Respondent) However as the discussion developed, it became obvious that they thought the youth service that they were using at present was appropriate, but needed to be expanded.

The development of services for youth was seen by another group (M4) as work that deserved payment, like any other job, rather than as a voluntary activity. They identified under-seventeens as the main user-group of any proposed service.

5.5 Justice

5.5.1 Introduction

The Justice findings are presented under two main headings, Perceptions of Illegal Activities and Knowledge of the Justice System. An initial table presents illegal activities identified through the focus group discussions. Those activities seen as acceptable behaviour within particular female and male peer groups are then outlined. The respondents' knowledge of the Justice system is presented under the headings of Gardai, Court Sentences and Identified Services.

5.5.2 Perceptions of Illegal Activity

Personal experience, either through contact with people who had been involved in illegal activity or through crime that occurred in their area, led respondents to identify the illegal activities presented in the following table.

Table 5.6 Illegal Activities Identified by Female and Male Respondents

Females Focus Groups		Male Focus Groups	
Illegal Activity	Focus Group	Illegal Activity	Focus Group
• Vandalism	• All	• Vandalism	• All
• Breaking and entering	• F3 F1	• Breaking and entering	• All
• Arson	• F3	• Arson	• M3
• Theft	• All	• Theft	• All
• Grievous bodily Harm	• F3	• Theft of motor vehicle	• M3
• Consumption of alcohol in a public place	• All	• Consumption of alcohol in a public place	• All
• Underage sexual activity	• F1,2, 4	• Use of illegal substances	• All
• Use of illegal substances	• All	• Underage sexual activity	• M1,2,4
• Supply of illegal substances	• F1	• Use of illegal substances	• All
• Common assault	• All	• Engaging the service of a prostitute	• M1
• Petty larceny (e.g. shoplifting)	• F1		
• Damaging property (e.g. breaking windows)	• F1	• Damaging property (e.g. 'egging' houses, cars)	• M1
• Driving without a license	• F1	• Driving without a license	• M1 M4
• Assault (i.e. fighting)	• F1	• Drunk Driving	• M4

Perceptions of Illegal Activity

Female Findings

F1 (average age 14.5, urban), F2 (average age 15, urban), F3 (average age 12.5, rural) and F4 (average age 16.5, rural)

Vandalism / Damaging Property As the table illustrates, all female respondents identified vandalism as an illegal activity. Some admitted to participating in group activities such as breaking windows, 'nick-knock' (knocking on someone's door and running away) and shoplifting, and saw these as ways of relieving *"boredom"* (F1 Respondent). However the groups had a negative view of mores serious offences against property such as breaking and entering, and this type of behaviour would appear to be generally unacceptable in their peer groups.

Discussion on this point demonstrated analysis by young people of peer group influence on behaviours. Speaking about a friend who had affiliated to their peer group at the time of the research, one respondent offered: *"I think it was just the people, you know; you hang around with people, you get in trouble."* (F1 Respondent). This group felt they had positively influenced his behaviour: *"He got in trouble with them, then he started to hang around with us, and he actually didn't get in trouble, like"* (F1 Respondent).

Breaking and Entering/ Arson Another group outlined a case involving young males who had entered and subsequently set fire to a building the members of the group all used. This was seen as a dramatic event by the participants. Although they thought the incident was terrible, they also appreciated the resulting benefits to themselves: *"All new furniture an'all, it's really nice"* (F3 Respondent).

Petty Larceny Shoplifting of sweets and small, inexpensive items was viewed as acceptable by one focus group, and seen by them as a normal activity for younger teenagers: *"Everyone goes through stages of shoplifting; then they'll get over it"* (F1 Respondent), the only constraint being *"they'll get caught."* (F1 Respondent). None of this group had got caught during their shoplifting *'phase'* (F1 Respondent), which they had now left behind. No other group identified themselves with this activity.

Participants' families were seen as setting boundaries, and they generally felt that, if they were *"caught"*, their families would be disappointed in them.

Underage Driving According to one female focus group, this was an occasional activity that would occur when one male friend had access to a family car while his father was away. The young person had experience of driving tractors, and the group appeared proud that the he was *"able to drive, he doesn't be driving into bushes or anything like that"* (F1 Respondent). However they weren't involved in racing with other cars; this was considered too risky.

Violence One group (F1) recounted an incident that happened at a local disco, where girls from a neighbouring area with which a tradition of rivalry apparently existed, stole an item of headgear from one of the group. This led to a disturbance, which came to blows between the respondent and another girls and both were ejected and barred from the disco. The other members of the respondent's peer group decided to leave in solidarity with their friend.

Sexual Activity Some young women were aware that a legal age of consent existed, but felt the law regarding this was rarely if ever enforced.

Perceptions of Illegal Activity

Male Findings

M1 (average age 14.75, urban), M2 (average age 15, urban), M3 (average age 12, rural) and M4 (average age 16.5, rural)

Arson / Under Age Driving One of the respondents (M3) along with other people he knew was questioned by the Gardai in relation to the burning of two cars in the area. The young man knew he was being accused in the wrong and suspected older teenagers were responsible for the burning of the vehicles. However the incident was not seen as particularly serious and the group suggested that these older youths *"were just messin' around like"* (M3 Respondent). The cars were behind a building, suggesting that they may have been previously abandoned.

A common pastime for young males in the area (M3) is the driving of motor cars and bikes in fields. Although this may not be an illegal activity, no clarification of how the vehicles got into the fields was given. However in another area the driving of uninsured vehicles, under age driving and driving while drunk were seen as common practices among young people (M4).

Illegal Substances The majority of young people misusing drugs knew that the activity was illegal, but this did not persuade them against the practice. A number of incidents were recalled by participants (M1) who believed they were being constantly stopped and searched by the Gardai for possession of drugs.

5.5.3 Knowledge of the Justice System

Female Findings

F1 (average age 14.5, urban), F2 (average age 15, urban), F3 (average age 12.5, rural) and F4 (average age 16.5, rural)

Gardai The knowledge of the Justice System by female participants appeared quite limited, and discussion tended to concentrate upon the Gardai. The younger respondents were quite neutral, but one young person believed that the Gardai avoided a particular location where fights had regularly taken place *"...because they were afraid to go near them in case they get the bottles"* (F3 Respondent).

The majority of older participants felt that the relationship between young people and the Gardai was negative. One observation in relation to young males they knew, was that the

Gardai would *"arrest people for nothing .... 'cause they were walking down the street"*. (F2 Respondent)

In expanding on their views, this group (F2) explained their negative view of the Gardai by identifying perceived Gardai prejudices against some of their male friends: *"... 'cause they could have brothers, some of them could have brothers like, that the Gardai don't like, so they just pick them up just to get them"* (F2 Respondent). In another area Gardai moved young people on from public spaces, and the group felt this was unfair, as *"...there's nowhere else to go...When we're sitting there, like, were not annoying anybody like."* (F1 Respondent)

One of the respondents expressed the belief that the Gardai were there to help, but finished this analysis with *"...but other times they can be whatever, like"* (F2 Respondent). This point was illustrated in other locations were it was felt that attitudes to young people varied among Gardai, leading to inconsistencies in the way young people felt they were treated; for example, some peers of one group (F1) had been fined by Gardai for drinking alcohol in public places, whereas others were simply moved on. They (F1) also felt that some Gardai abused their position, for example by driving with no seat belt, while prosecuting members of the public for the same offence.

Male Findings

M1 (average age 14.75 urban), M2 (average age 15, urban), M3 (average age 12, rural) and M4 (average age 16.5, rural)

Gardai The participants' knowledge of the Gardai was based on personal experience of being *"moved on"* from a public area and of reported Gardai intervention when they *"get on to people for doin' stuff like drinkin"* (M3 Respondent). One young male said he had been *"searched every week...Yeah, for nothing. Just for fucking walking around...I was only 15 like; they didn't even ask my parents' consent"* (M1 Respondent).

The young people are generally aware that as minors, their parents should be informed if the Gardai wish to search them or take them into custody. A number of respondents in one group (M1) had been taken to the Garda Barracks, but were not always aware of the reason why, or if their parents had been informed.

5.5.4 Court Sentences

(n.b. Focus Group F1 was the only group to offer views on this topic.)

Female Findings

F1 (average age 14.5, urban)

Again personal experience formed the basis for knowledge regarding the courts and sentencing policy. One participant (F1) told of being in a Garda station when a young male was bought into the station in handcuffs. She stated that this youth looked *"cool"* (F1 Respondent) and the image she described of the Garda buying food for the young person and then having to bring it to him was considered "really cool" by the others in the group (F1 Respondent).

In relation to a friend's custodial sentence it was stated: *"... like, they put him away, and when he goes away like, he's just going to come back out, and he's going to be worse again, like"* (F1 Respondent). But the group viewed the young person's behaviour in the context of his family's criminal behaviour: *"His family, like, have been in as well, so it's not just him"* (F1 Respondent).

They felt his custodial sentence for theft was severe, when compared with other cases they knew of, in particular one involving a person they understood to be a known dealer (*"...deals drugs to everyone..."*). They concluded that sentencing policy was *"unfair"* – *"Yeah, four months for robbing a stereo, and then this big druggie gets four months for dealing drugs."* (F1 Respondents)

Another comparison involved a local person they considered to have psychological problems, who was sentenced to a treatment centre rather than to jail. The group felt that *"...he's more of a threat to society than P is, and P gets 18 months for sweet fuck all like".*(F1 Respondent).

5.5.5 Identified Services

Female Findings

F1 (average age 14.5, urban)

Only one group identified (F1) additional support systems for young offenders such as social workers and Social Care delivered by the Health Board. But they were unclear regarding the role of these in the Justice system.

None of the groups identified the JLO programme, Crime Diversion Projects or the Probation and Welfare Service at any stage.

5.6 Independence

5.6.1 Introduction

This section presents findings reflecting Hill's (1973) Pyschosocial Model of Adolescent Development. (See: Literature Review) regarding Independence, and is presented under the following subheadings:

- the Family,
- Peer Groups,
- Relationships and
- Employment.

5.6.2 Family

Monetary and Practical Supports

Female Findings

F1 (average age 14.5, urban), F2 (average age 15, urban), F3 (average age 12.5, rural) and F4 (average age 16.5, rural)

The majority of the participants were currently unemployed, but attending school. Therefore they relied upon the family for income and often had to *"scrounge"* (F1 Respondents) money from their parents or did *"babysitting."* (F1 and F2 Respondents)

Generally young women who lived in the family home relied on the family for practical day-to-day supports such as meals and laundry, and acknowledged that *"...you don't realise how easy you've got it, 'cause everything is done for you"* (F1 Respondent).

The amounts of pocket money or allowances given was not indicated by any of the respondents, but one stated that her family bought her *"credit"* (F3 Respondent) for her telephone as a payment in kind for minding her younger brothers and sisters.

A minority of respondents had part-time employment and therefore did not rely totally upon the family for monetary supports – *"Yeah, I've been working there now* (a beauty salon) *for four year"* (F4 Respondent). Another older respondent stated: *"Yeah, I never take any money"* (F4 Respondent). However these young women did provide examples of when the family might assist with larger outlays of money (e.g. for school trips, holidays, etc.)

Male Findings

M1 (average age 14.75 urban), M2 (average age 15, urban), M3 (average age 12, rural) and M4 (average age 16.5, rural)

As a group the younger males (M3) were particularly aware of monetary support from the family. This support often paid for leisure activities where the parents accompanied them, such as swimming or golf *"That's the only time you'd get to go, but it's kinda expensive to get in as well. "* (M3 Respondent)

The majority of older male participants (M1, M2 and M4) had some form of independent income, either through part-time employment, full-time employment during the summer, or a training allowance. Therefore monetary support from the family was reduced or eliminated.

Parental Boundaries

Female Findings

F1 (average age, 14.5, urban), F2 (average age, 15, urban), F3 (average age, 12.5 rural) and F4 (average age 16.5, rural)

Among younger respondents (F3), where resources were available to the family, respondents saw their parents as encouraging them to become involved in supervised activities (music lessons, horse-riding, etc.) Others stated that they mostly stayed in and watched television. No one in the group exhibited evidence of non-compliance with their parents' wishes, although the group did provide examples of other young people of their own age who they believed behaved badly and caused disappointment to their families.

Older respondents conceded they were involved in various activities that would be regarded by their parents as undesirable behaviours. However this knowledge did not prevent them from participating in these activities. The fear of being 'caught' focused on the possible negative reaction of the parents, rather than on actions of the Gardai or teachers.

The young people recognised that family-set boundaries were a positive influence on them: *"I don't know, 'cause like, if you, if you were allowed to do whatever you wanted, you'd be a little terror, you'd be doing like"* (F1 Respondent).

However, when families responded to non-compliance with set boundaries, usually by setting curfews or *'grounding'* (F1 Respondent), the reported reaction from the young people could be quite dramatic, for example by threatening to *"run away"* (F1 Respondent).

Male Findings

M1 (average age 14.75, urban), M2 (average age 15, urban) M3 (average age 12, rural) and M4 (average age 16.5, rural)

The younger male participants seemed to spend a lot of their free time playing and hanging around the area where they lived. In some cases *"going down town"* (M2 Respondent) was prohibited by parents. The only references made to parental intervention by one group (M3) was when their activities became boisterous, and household property got damaged. For example, when a bed was broken, one mother did *"...nothin', she just gave out to me"* (M3 Respondent). In contrast another participant who lived with his mother, stated that she was *"rarely at home"* (M2 Respondent) and that he preferred to stay at his friend's house.

Family boundaries still applied to older male respondents who lived at home, but for them the appeal was evident of being *"... out on your own, you sorta make your own rules, there's no more house rules."* (M4 Respondent).

Family Conflict

Female Findings

F1(average age 14.5, urban), F2 (average age 15, urban), F3 (average age 12.5, rural) and F4 (average age 16.5, rural)

One younger respondent stated that arguments occurred frequently in her family, but asked *"Do you think that people who fight love each other more?"* (F3 Respondent) This question was evidently of concern for her in her struggle to make sense of the relationships around her at home.

The relationships that these young people had with their families were important to them. One group (F2) were quite open about their parents' relationships, one stating *"Well, my ma and da don't live together, but it's better like"* (F2 Respondent). The majority of parents of this focus group had separated, and the young people seemed to have adapted. They were able to identify benefits, for example, *"When you have fights with your ma, you can go live with your da, and when you have fights with your da, you can do the opposite"* (F2 Respondent). This tactic was confirmed in another focus group where a young woman declared her intention *" to move in with me Dad"*, even though in house she was generally *"...made clear up the whole place..."* (F1 Respondent).

However negative experiences and emotions were also identified in their relationships with their parents. One issue raised was where the separated parent at home started dating *"... 'cause they could get, they could start going with someone you don't like or something. And you get in trouble if you say anything to them like, and you feel like boxing the head off them"* (F2 Respondent).

Even those who offered no negative comments on their own family did acknowledge that *"...there are lots of families that are always fighting and all like"*, indicating an awareness of family conflict as a feature of the society they live in (F2 Respondent).

The general perception of the young women, negative comments notwithstanding, was that they had positive relationships within their family.

Male Findings

M1 (average age 14.75, urban), M2 (average age 15, urban), M3 (average age 12, rural) and M4 (average age 16.5, rural)

Focus groups had mixed feelings about their families, and the majority stated that their home life was sometimes *"crap"*. A variety of reasons were cited as the cause of this feeling, including separation, parents having extramarital affairs, and lack of money and resources.

Discussion of family conflict generally focused on the role of the parents; for example: *"...especially when you're in trouble in the house, and then your mama goes to your dad: 'If it's not he's going, I'm going!' That's queer bad then."* (M1 Respondent)

Although the majority of participants in older groups expressed negative views, one dissented : *"Yeah, but sure, still you say that all like, but if anything happened to them...I don't see why everyone goes on about 'And I hate this' and all. Of course you don't hate them, like. You always say that stuff anyway, though like you're still going to love them at the end of the day."* (M1 Respondent)

Out of Home

Female Findings

F1(average age 14.5, urban), F2 (average age 15, urban), F3 (average age 12.5, rural) and F4 (average age 16.5, rural)

One participant, aged 15 years, had moved out of the family home since the researchers' first meeting her during the initial data collection stage, to live with a sister living in the same street. The young women stated that her move was *"...grand, but they always come up and annoy me like"*, (F2 Respondent), but this was said with humour indicating that her parents are still in positive contact with her.

Male Findings

M1(average age 14.75, urban), M2 (average age 15, urban) M3 (average age 12, rural) and M4 (average age 16.5, rural)

The conversation regarding family conflicts led to some stating that they sometimes left home for a few days to stay with friends (i.e. "sofa surfing" – See: Literature Review 3.3.3). One respondent described the respite care organised through his social worker, where he could stay in a *"nice"* place every couple of weeks to give him a break from his family situation (M1 Respondent).

Others generally agreed that experiencing family conflict was very difficult, but one young person dealt with what he saw as negative family conflict by telling his parents to *"fuck off"*. (M1 Respondent) He was also one of those who spoke of staying with friends when he felt it necessary.

Siblings and Extended Family

Female Findings

F1 (average age 14.5, urban), F2 (average age 15, urban), F3 (average age 12.5, rural) and F4 (average age 16.5, rural)

All the female respondents spoke about their siblings in a positive way. They made observations on facilities needed by their younger brothers and sisters (e.g. a playground), and older siblings were looked up to and admired, particularly by younger respondents.

Male Findings

M1 (average age 14.75, urban), M2 (average age 15, urban), M3 (average age 12, rural) and M4 (average age 16.5, rural)

Those who spoke about their siblings and extended family did so positively. Older siblings were admired, and one specific extended family member, a godfather, was considered particularly "cool", (M3 Respondent) as he owned several high performance motorbikes.

5.6.3 Peer groups

Female Findings

F1(average age 14.5, urban), F2 (average age 15, urban), F3 (average age 12.5 rural) and F4 (average age 16.5, rural)

In the younger age group (F3) the respondents stated that they liked almost everyone in their class, except for one or two. A specific peer groups did not appear to have importance for this particular group at this time.

In the older age groups, peer groups were important to the young women as offering social interaction *"to have a bit of fun with, to go out with and all"* (F1, F2 and F4 Respondents). The rural location of some did not appear to be a problem as their parents would drive them in the car. They knew their friendships were strong, but were aware that the future might bring changes: *"Unless anybody is moving away to work or something, it'll probably be a bit different when we go to college alright, certain people will go to college and make new friends and change"* (F4 respondent).

In one location all the participants knew each other from childhood and saw peers groups within their area as hierarchical, as illustrated by the following quotes: *"It's kind of like the generations, like. People – all the boys that use to hang around on the corner like – don't anymore, so now we does it like"* (F2 Respondent). *"And before that there was other boys, and before that there was other boys like"* (F2 Respondent). The hierarchy of peer groups within their area was understood and accepted by them as the norm, and they believed the pattern would be repeated by succeeding groups.

Generally the older-aged focus groups were unambiguous regarding their peer group identity, and selective about other peer groups that they associated with. Those that they chose not to associate with they stereotyped and viewed as rivals. Young people who had switched from a rival peer group went to great lengths to illustrate their loyalty to their 'new' group. This involved denying membership of the other group or belittling their current activities.

However membership of a peer group did not prevent individuals from having different opinions. Peer groups were seen as an environment where members could feel safe, and "trust" and "loyalty" were highly valued and expected.

Male Findings

M1 (average age 14.75, urban), M2 (average age 15, urban), M3 (average age 12, rural) and M4 (average age 16.5, rural)

Males tended to hang out in peer groups from an early age. In some areas younger males were not bothered by older males, but bullying was a feature in one location: *"... you'd be playin' and you'd be grand, and these (older) lads would come and take the ball off ya and drive it away"* (M3 Respondent)

Older male groups would challenge the younger males in the area to perform dangerous feats, such as climbing high buildings: *"They would climb up on the roofs and then they'd tell you to do it, like"* although *"you'd be afraid of heights"*. The younger males felt pressure to meet these challenges although conscious of the danger (M3 Respondents).

The focus groups were unambiguous regarding their peer group identity, and were selective about other peer groups that they chose to associate with, and often stereotyped rival groups, labelling them as *"arrogant"* (M1 Respondent) or *"trouble-makers"* (M4 Respondent).

5.6.4 Relationships

One to one Relationships – Heterosexual

Female Findings

F1 (average age 14.5, urban), F2 (average age 15, urban) and F4 (average age 16.5, rural)

{N.B. Core questions regarding relationships were excluded for Focus Group F3, on age grounds}

The majority of participants at the time of the focus group had a boyfriend. Their interest in obtaining boyfriends began when they first started to attend discos, *"about three or four years ago like"* (F2 Respondent) and had got their friends to approach someone that they were interested in.

The association with male peer groups led in some cases to individual relationships; *"… like, we hung around with them before we got with them anyway, so…"* (F1 Respondent). For this focus group the mobile phone is identified as a tool used for flirting, and for establishing and monitoring relationships.

The consequences of being without a mobile phone were clear: *"You wouldn't get a lad really as much, wouldn't you not?"* (F1 Respondent). Another comment supported this: *"You wouldn't, 'cause that's how you get with them, by texting them"* (F1 Respondent). The majority of the participants in this group (F1) thought it was acceptable to have relations with more than one partner at a time, but a minority thought this was inappropriate.

Male Findings

M1 (average age 14.75, urban), M2 (average age 15, urban), M3 (average age, 12 rural) and M4 (average age 16.5, rural)

{N.B. Core questions regarding relationships were excluded for Focus Group M3}

During discussion of another topic, the participants of focus group M3 stated that none of them had girlfriends, although one of the participants *"nearly"* did, but this was treated humorously by the group. No other information was given by this group concerning one-to-one relationships.

One of the older groups (M1) used sexual connotations constantly during their conversation and their comments were frequently derogatory to women. In a discussion on one-to-one relationships, the main focus was around sex. At the time of the interview a few of the participants were in a 'long-term relationship' (e.g. 5 months), and two males in this situation said they saw their girlfriends every day in school, but choose not to interact with them in that setting. Instead they would "text" them during the week and usually go to the cinema at the week-end (M1 Respondents). In all areas individuals saw relationships with girlfriends as *"weekend activities"* (M1, M2, M4 Respondents).

One to One Relationships – Gay and Bi-sexual

Female Findings

F1 (average age 14.5, urban), F2 (average age 15, urban) and F4 (average age 16.5, rural)

Some young women stereotyped male gays positively *"They're always good looking."* (F2 Respondent). There were mixed views within the groups regarding lesbian relationships, some stating such relationships were *"disgusting"* (F1 Respondent) whereas others *"...don't care; whatever they want themselves"* (F1 Respondent). None of the respondents indicated a personal homosexual or bi-sexual preference.

Male Findings

M1 (average age 14.75 urban), M2 (average age 15 urban) and M4 (average age 16.5 rural)

All older male respondents spoke negatively about male gays. Those that they knew socially were considered alright, but they did not wish to be associated with them. In contrast the idea of lesbianism appealed to some males in a voyeuristic sense.

None of the respondents indicated a personal homosexual or bi-sexual preference.

Community Relationships

Female Findings

F1 (average age 14.5, urban), F2 (average age 15, urban), F3 (average age 12.5, rural) and F4 (average age 16.5, rural)

In both rural and urban settings all respondents felt safe living within their communities

Some focus group felt that adults living outside their community viewed them negatively. From their point of view, although other young people might want to mix with them, mothers of teenagers perpetuated prejudices against their area : *"You could ask people to come up to the street like and their ma's won't let them"* (F2 Respondent).

Their explanation for this attitude by mothers was *"... 'cause they think they're better than everyone else"* (F2 Respondent) and they recognised that adults from outside were not separating the individuals from the area they lived in: *"It could be the street that they don't like, but sure why are the stopping them hanging around with us like?"* (F2 Respondent).

The young people were aware that the wider community also viewed other parts of town negatively. When asked did they care what people thought of their area they stated: *"No, we don't care of what people think of us, but it's not right, that"* (F2 Respondent).

Another focus group offered a similar analysis to the way their area was considered by the wider community: *"All the posh knobs and everything... But we were, I don't care like, we were brought up in the council houses. But we were brought up better, because they're all too posh and spoilt to know right from wrong like, but we do, 'cause we were brought up like that"* (F1 Respondent).

The peer groups that used the street as a social space acknowledged that this had led to friction with adults within the community: *"Everyone* (adults) *like mouthing about us"*, which they felt was unfair, as *"...they don't let us...we sit in the car park and the Gardai come up and give out to us for sitting there, but we've nowhere else to go "* (F1 Respondent).

A specific incident cited by participants (F2) illustrates how these frictions can sometimes lead to confrontation. A local shopkeeper *"came out with a brush after her and me one night."* This act was seen as mildly threatening, if also comical, by the group: *"Yeah, one night she came out and she smacked it off the ground and she broke it in half and everyone just started laughing."* (F2 Respondent).

At times they self-organised games of football in existing facilities, *"...and we didn't have permission to play football in the hall like, so we had to get out"* (F1 Respondent). But their efforts are often opposed; for example, when a group gathers in a car park at evening time, *"...yeah, and we bring down a football and lads play football, and we sit there watching them, and then they* (Gardai) *come down and say they don't have permission, so we've to get out"* (F1 Respondent).

Male Findings

M1(average age 14.75, urban), M2 (average age 15, urban), M3 (average age 12, rural) and M4 (average age 16.5, rural)

The majority of participants felt safe in their communities, although in one area the young males did refer to *"a shooting"* (M2) that had recently occurred in their estate. However, this appeared to be offered more as an illustration of how tough the area could be, as it was also stated by this group that normally, nothing much happened in the area (M2 Respondents).

Community relationships with members of the wider adult community appeared to be negative in most areas. Adults appeared to be a source of aggravation: *"We all have to sit on P's wall, and we were all there one day and this woman came and started givin' out"* (M3 Respondent). This was connected by the young people to the image of their area; *"you get a name in this town"* (M1 Respondent). The arrival of local adults into the young people's space was invariably viewed negatively: *"And then if you are havin' a bit of fun then, the big nosy SOB's come out after ya"* (M3 Respondent)

A new housing development in one area was resented, as the respondents associated it with *"rich people"*. *"It's a private housing estate; you see they are going to have everything there, if they pay for it"*. When asked to define *'everything'*, the reply was: *"everything we were wanting"* (M3 Respondents) The young males here identified themselves as disadvantaged.

As this was explored further, the participants recalled a number of incidents where community groups had made promises to them when then they were younger: *"They promised swings and slides an' all that, down in the place."* *"Sure, we're just saying this, we don't want it anymore... well we do want it like, but the little lads will want it more anyway."* *"An' now if they promise little children, they'll be lookin' forward to it, an then just disappoint them all"* (M3 Respondents). Clearly, community initiatives in the past in this area have not met the expectations of young people.

5.6.5 Employment

Sources of Income

Female Findings

F1 (average age 14.5, urban), F2 (average age 15, urban), F3 (average age 12.5, rural) and F4 (average age 16.5, rural)

None of the younger participants (F3) had ever been formally employed and their only source of income was from the family. However older respondents in some cases were also dependent on the family for their income. In another location (F2) high unemployment within their community discouraged the young people from seeking work, and their future plans were uncertain.

In another location (F1) the group felt it was difficult for young people to gain suitable part-time employment that would enable them both to earn money and to continue attending school. Only one of the participants at the time of interview had a part-time job, as a waitress.

Male Findings

M1 (average age 14.75, urban), M2 (average age 15, urban), M3 (average age 12, rural) and M4 (average age 16.5, rural)

For most participants income was usually associated with employment, and families were not identified as an income source (except in the case of a Confirmation Day). In one geographical location (M2) none of the participants were employed, but one received a training allowance and another had received a once-off payment for work experience. The group believed their chances of gaining employment were slim.

A number of young people in another focus group (M1) had part-time employment and some were employed full-time. Jobs were mainly in the catering industry and retail sector, often obtained after leaving school early. Those working in catering agreed that it was *"hard work"* (M1 Respondent) and managers in the retail sector were viewed as *"a pack of wankers"* (M1 Respondent).

The majority of older young males in rural areas (M4) obtained summer jobs in the construction industry, mainly in labouring. They found it quite easy to find employment which was often secured through family connections.

Perception of Barriers to Securing Employment

Female Findings

F1 (average age 14.5, urban), F2 (average age 15, urban), F3 (average age 12.5, rural) and F4 (average age 16.5, rural)

Barriers identified by the group to securing employment were age, lack of experience, availability of foreign workers, and lack of available jobs. A minority of the group stated that they were too young, illustrating an awareness of employment legislation for young people. Lack of experience was also a problem, as some employers *"...want people with experience. But how are you supposed to get experience if they won't give you a job?"* (F1 Respondent)

A minority of the group believed the lack of jobs was due to foreigners, *"... 'cause they've taken over all the jobs, you can't get a job then"* (F1 Respondent). However this point was challenged within the group: *"No... the only reason they're getting a job is because you* (i.e. employers) *can pay them cheap, because you can't pay us like"* (F1 Respondent). This analysis did not change the minority's opinion, as their same point was raised later in the interview under a different topic (See: Culture 5.7.5).

Male groups made no observations on perceived barriers to employment.

Previous Employment

Female Findings

F1 (average age 14.5, urban), F2 (average age 15, urban), F3 (average age 12.5 rural) and F4 (average age16.5, rural)

Those who had offered an analysis regarding accessing employment had all previously worked in part-time positions, usually during the summer months. All those in one group (F1) had worked in the catering industry, mainly in fast food outlets, and some also in shops. Their experiences of work, both positive and negative, appeared to be linked more to relationships with other staff than with the work itself (e.g. *"I didn't like the chef."* (F1 Respondent)).

In another group (F4), some had part-time jobs, which provided money to go out at week ends and for shopping. These young women rarely had to accept money from their families, although their jobs were often secured through family connections.

Male groups made no observations on previous employment.

5.7 Culture

5.7.1 Introduction

Young people are seen as key customers in today's global economy, and contemporary Teenage Culture seeks to transcend ethnic, geographical and class differences (See : Literature Review, 3.1.1.3). The way in which adolescence is experienced is also embedded in social contexts, specific to the family and community in which the young person grows up. This section presents Culture Findings under the headings of Information and Communications Technologies, Media, Community, Different Backgrounds and Arts and Leisure Activities and Religion.

5.7.2 Information and Communications Technologies

Female Findings

F1 (average age 14.5, urban), F2 (average age 15, urban), F3 (average age 12.5 rural) and F4 (average age 16.5, rural)

PC's and the Internet The most obvious use of ICT's by younger participants was the use of personal computers and the Internet. The use of computers is promoted via the school curriculum and some have access to computers at home. Primary school students used the Internet to obtain information for themselves and for school assignments (F3).

Mobile Telephone Among younger participants access to and use of mobile telephones was restricted by parents, and one participant was not allowed a unit at all, as " *My mammy won't let me get one 'cause she said they are bad for your ears"* (F3 Respondent). Another member of the same group was bought *"credit"* for her mobile telephone for work done in the house.

Mobile telephones were prized possessions among some of the older respondents, as they serve many useful purposes for young people. Self-organising among the peer group is quick and simple – short calls are made to plan activities, to locate friends, to meet up in pairs or larger clusters, and to arrange a central meeting place for the whole group.

Text messages are used to initiate contact with a potential partner, and subsequently to establish and monitor the relationship: *"If you have a fella and he's texting a one like, you can find out like if his doing the dirt, from the messages like"* (F1 Respondent). Mobile phones also offer a cheap source of entertainment: *"If you have no money, keep your phone charged and you play the games on it"* (F1 Respondent).

One group (F2) offered no evidence of using this communication tool regularly, and their few references to its use involved texting.

Male Findings

M1 (average age 14.75 urban), M2 (average age 15, urban), M3 (average age 12, rural) and M4 (average age 16.5, rural)

Technology and Entertainment Although no references were made to the use of the Internet or e-mail, it is perhaps unsafe to draw inferences from this fact, as most of the participants would have been introduced to these on school computers.

Some males identified the use of computer games as a daily activity, which involved going to each others houses, sharing games and competing with each other. Watching DVD's and videos was also cited as an important leisure activity.

Mobile telephones These were used to make arrangements with peers, text girlfriends and order drugs (See: Health Section 5.2.2).

5.7.3 Media

All Groups

Media - The perception of the participants of the media across all groups focused mainly on television and music, with limited reference to the print media.

Television

Female Findings

F1 (average age 14.5, urban), F2 (average age 15, urban), F3 (average age 12.5, rural) and F4 (average age 16.5, rural)

The younger girls said they spend a lot of time watching television, and recounted plots and characters from soap operas, listing their favourites as *"Family Affairs, Home and Away, Emmerdale, Coronation Street, and Fair City"* (F3 Participants). A television programme particular admired and identified by the majority of respondents was 'Pop Stars'. The participants often illustrated and added depth to their discussion of an issue or concept by citing examples from familiar television programmes and films. In visualising a suitable youth facility for their area for example, one participant suggested *"...like the same Sarah McCoy kinda drop-in centre on Home and Away."* (F1Respondent)

Male Findings

M1 (average age 14.75, urban), M2 (average age 15, urban), M3 (average age 12, rural) and M4 (average age 16.5, rural)

There appeared to be a gender difference in the preferred viewing of television programmes. These participants watched sports programmes: *"I tell ya, Wrestling City!"* Their favourite fighters were *"...The Rock, Hollywood Cobra and Triple H."* (M3 Respondents). One respondent described the evidence of his enthusiasm: his bedroom contained *"...two WWF belts, the roof is covered with posters, every tape (video) we have is taped over with wrestlin'."* This young male dismissed female wrestling *"... 'cos they make it look so fake."* (M3 Respondent)

Others identified sports as particularly important to them, and admired media celebrities, such as David Beckham (M1 Respondent).

Music

Female Findings

F1 (average age 14.5, urban), F2 (average age 15, urban), F3 (average age, 12.5 rural) and F4 (average age 16.5, rural)

The younger participants (F3) identified pop stars like Six and Gareth Gates, but older respondents emphasised the role of music in their lives: *"Yeah, you can sing along or whatever, and I think that in itself is enough to relax you and it's your own time"* (F4) and *"It's deadly in the night clubs."* (F4)

Male Findings

M1 (average age 14.75, urban), M2 (average age 15, urban), M3 (average age 12, rural) and M4 (average age 16.5, rural)

Some older respondents (M4) preferred listening to music, especially CD's, rather than watching television, and obtained information about new bands mainly from music programmes on TV. Their choice of music sometimes caused conflict in the family, with one respondent stating : *"My parents just hate my music, just drives them off"* (M4 Respondent) In other cases however, the parents shared the participants' tastes in music.

Print Media

Female Findings

F1 (average age 14.5, urban), F2 (average age 15, urban), F3 (average age 12.5, rural) and F4 (average age 16.5, rural)

One group (F3) was critical of the way local newspapers had reported an incident that had brought unwanted attention to their area: *"Sometimes whatever happens, it's written in the newspaper"* and *"Yeah, some people get a different story altogether, and they think it's really bad."* (F3 Respondents). The older respondents (F1, F2 and F4) were less critical, reading the local newspaper for the *"court reports"* (F1 Respondent) and magazines for fashion (F2 and F4).

Fashion During a discussion on eating disorders, the influence of the print media and fashion on young women's self-image was raised. Their perception was that females tend to *"... see other girls thin, and you just envy them. You'd say 'Oh, look at the figure on her and look what she can wear when you're that thin', and like 'I wish I was like that', you know what I mean?"* (F4 Respondent).

These girls stated they wanted an individual look, but also that they tried to fit in with what was currently in fashion. They felt that *"There is some competition with girls though; you would even notice it now"* and *"you can't go out the same weekend with the same top...You could maybe wear the same trousers"* (F4 Respondent).

Male Findings

M3 (average age 12, rural)

On the topic of local newspapers, references were made to the coverage of a recent event in the area that got a lot of publicity (M3). The participants described the details of the story with great enthusiasm. Coverage of the same story was criticised by the females from the same area.

Other male groups made no reference to print media.

5.7.4 Community

Female Findings

F1 (average age 14.5, urban), F2 (average age 15, urban), F3 (average age 12.5, rural) and F4 (average age 16.5, rural)

The majority of respondents had a sense of identity with their community. In one rural area (F3) a particular teacher promoted local folklore and history through the school, which the respondents seemed to find very interesting: *" He loves history. He has everything in history. He brings in all things, old stuff from the old ages."* (F3 Respondent)

In another group the perception of the young women was that their sense of identity was being eroded by the rapid urban expansion of the area, largely to accommodate commuters, which had transformed the town. The young people's sense of community has been threatened, leading the participants to feel *"bad"* (F1 Respondent) and *"it's not a community, like"* (F1 Respondent) and "you don't know who's in your own town." (F1 Respondent). This rapid change is leading to segregation among the population, as those who have recently moved into the area *"...don't mix either. It's the same people that were here all the time are still mixing"* (F1 Respondent).

Male Findings

M1 (average age 14.75, urban), M2 (average age 15, urban), M3 (average age 12, rural) and M4 (average age 16.5, rural)

The younger respondents (M3) knew everyone in their locality, but felt that their relationships with adults, especially women, were generally negative. One respondent recalled a clearly harassed neighbour shouting at him: *"Would ye get outa there! Some people are tryin' to sleep!"* (M3).

It was evident from their discussions that the older respondents in a rural community (M4) knew almost everyone in their locality. They constantly referred to going away – for work, for leisure activities, for further education etc. – but most intended returning to live in the area. Their sense of identity was strongly linked to their 'home' area.

5.7.5 Different Backgrounds

Female Findings

F1 (average age 14.5, urban), F2 (average age 15, urban), F3 (average age 12.5, rural) and F4 (average age 16.5, rural)

The perception of different backgrounds varied slightly. The younger respondents did not really identify "difference", but the older respondents spoke extensively on the topic. The respondents from one area which has a busy tourist season were quite clear about their dislike for people from Dublin who have recently moved to the area in large numbers, *"...because they come down in the summer as if they own* (the area) *like; and then they move here, they mouth about us: 'Bogger Land'"* (F1 Respondent).

Another respondent in this focus group stated *"People don't like different religions"*, and later revealed: *"I don't like foreigners...'cause they've taken over all the jobs"* (See also 5.6.5). This attitude was challenged in the group and the majority disagreed, feeling that they don't object *"...to anyone else, it's just Dubliners, the way they think they own the place"* (F1 Respondent).

The issue of racism was discussed quite extensively by one focus group (F2) who criticised all forms of prejudice and discrimination against those with different skin colour or ethnic background. They thought it was mainly *"...Irish people that are starting the fights"*, as they *"...only think of themselves and not other people. They don't care about other people's feelings, only themselves"* (F2 respondent).

The group went on to explore some other possible causes of hostile behaviour against foreigners. They were aware of the deportation of asylum seekers, which they viewed negatively, but they also commented on what they viewed as the favourable treatment that some immigrants were receiving, stating: *"They don't have to go out and work like, for money; they just go to the clinic and they're getting money every week like."*

Male Findings

M1 (average age 14.75, urban), M2 (average age 15, urban), M3 (average age 12, rural) and M4 (average age 16.5, rural)

The only reference made to people from different backgrounds in one area was regarding the young males from a rival area that they viewed as *"trouble makers"* (M4). In another area where a housing development was taking place, the different background identified was of *"rich people"* (M3).

A number of nationalities were listed by an older group as living locally in one area, and the ethnic group most clearly identified by this focus group was Russians. The only associated comment offered was from one young male who thought a Russian girl attending his school was a *"fine thing"*. (M1)

Two respondents provided an example of a teacher's racist comments in their class with a young person of African origin in the room. The young African did not say anything at the time, nor did the respondents, but they thought it was *"...really bad."* (M1)

5.7.6 Arts and Leisure Activities

Female Findings

F1 (average age 14.5, urban), F2 (average age 15, urban), F3 (average age 12.5 rural) and F4 (average age 16.5, rural)

Some parents, with available resources encouraged participants to become involved in additional activities such as music lessons and pony riding, which provided opportunities to make new friends outside the immediate locality. However equivalent options were not reported by the majority of respondents.

At national school all respondents had participated in plays and stage performances, but when they reached post-primary level there was less evidence of their being involved in these activities.

Particular people, ('posh ones') (F1 Respondent) were associated with these productions, and it was felt they were chosen because they would have had attended singing and dancing classes. The respondents viewed these privileges as offering the others *"an advantage"* (F1 Respondent) over them. However, when asked how they felt about this, they said they didn't care. Although a number of the focus group participants were confident that they could sing and dance well, they expressed uncertainty about being able to memorise lines of script.

Older respondents (F4) went to nightclubs each weekend as their main leisure activity.

Male Findings

M1 (average age 14.75, urban), M2 (average age 15, urban), M3 (average age 12, rural) and M4 (average age 16.5, rural)

Males across the age ranges tended to identify more Arts and Leisure activities than female respondents. The perception of all age groups was that most males played **sports**. While some were affiliated to clubs and trained regularly, others would self-organise football and soccer games on the green areas in their communities.

Skateboarding was also an important pastime for some of these young males, and the older participants would often leave their immediate neighbourhood and go downtown to join up with other skaters, including older males and even some *"professionals"* (M2).

Some young males seemed particularly enthusiastic about **motorbikes and cars**, and appeared to have occasional access to motorbikes and hotrods through adults and older adolescent males in the area. Constructing and playing with imitation hotrods was described by one of the group who converted an old sit-on toy tractor which he had had since childhood: *"Well, I got the seat off and I put holes in it and ripped the seat along and turned it into a hotrod"* (M3).

Variety Concerts were occasionally organised in the community as a way of raising funds for youth activities. Some of the respondents were meant to be in a **performance**, which had been called off. One of the respondents enjoyed singing in public when younger: *" I used to sing at my cousin's concerts"* (M3 Respondent). This group also spoke about a teenager they knew who had been involved in Irish dancing and singing who became a target for bullying by others, and as result eventually gave up these activities.

Commercial music and rock concerts were particular appreciated by older respondents, although there was limited access to live music in their area. Some travelled with groups of friends to large open air concerts by minibus. They were aware of the commercialism of the music industry, but their attitude was one of acceptance: *"What's the matter, sure? Like, everything is. Someone has to do that sort of stuff"* (F4)

5.7.7 Religion

Only one group made a reference to practicing a religion

Male Findings

M2 (average age 15, urban)

The reference to religion regarded a participant's upcoming Confirmation, which he clearly felt was an important family day. Preparation was quite extensive, and he was now looking forward to eating out with his family, and spending his confirmation money on clothes for himself, and on presents for his mum and dad (M2 respondent).

5.8 Political Involvement

5.8.1 Introduction

The participation of young people in matters that affect them as promoted by the National Children's Strategy (2000) seeks to develop political awareness and participation through involvement in decision-making (See: Literature Review). The findings in this section are presented under two headings: Perceptions of Current Involvement in Decision-making and Decision-making and Development of Services.

5.8.2 Perceptions of Current Involvement in Decision-making

Female Findings

F1 (average age 14.5, urban), F2 (average age 15, urban), F3 (average age 12.5, rural) and F4 (average age 16.5, rural)

Generally respondents felt they had few opportunities to become involved in decision-making. In two groups (F2 and F3) the respondents stated they had never previously been asked by adults for their opinions on issues and topics that affected them. The majority of respondents felt that the approach adopted by the researchers in coming to speak to them was a good idea, and if approached in the same way they would participate again. This validates, at least to a degree, the approach chosen by the research team.

The school provided a context for involvement in decision-making for two groups (F1 and F4). One offered a School Council, and the other a Stay-in-School programme which offered a number of initiatives requiring consultation with students. None of the participants from the first group had ever been involved in the School Council and saw it as belonging to the *"posh ones"* (See: Education Findings). Their perception of the School Council as a mechanism for authentic participation by young people was negative, as the students seemed to have little real influence on school policy: *"They want it, they ask for it, they don't get though"* (F1 Respondent)

A decision-making process that was regarded positively related to a Stay-in-School programme. *"Actually a lad came to talk to us about it...they took two people out of every class and they asked us 'What do you think of our funding?"*. (F4 Respondent). Young people and teachers are still involved in a weekly survey to compile the canteen lunch menu as part of this initiative.

Mainstream Politics was mentioned by one focus group in connection with canvassing for the recent General Election. The participants weren't really interested in politics and were put off by the approach of some campaigners : *"And they say "Are you voting?" an'all, and "You know who to look after", that's what they say"* (F4 Respondent).

Male Findings

M1 (average age 14.75, urban), M2 (average age 15, urban), M3 (average age 12, rural) and M4 (average age 16.5, rural)

The younger male respondents (M3) were aware of community initiatives that involved local participation, although they were not directly involved themselves. However, they associated such community initiatives with adults who often failed to deliver what they promised. *"They promised swings and slides an'all that down in the place; they were after puttin' the cement down and goals and that, so they promised us that they'd get us slides an swings." "And every time someone said it to them they said they'd have it some other time. They never had it"* (M3 respondents)

The male participants who attended the schools where decision–making processes were identified by female focus groups (i.e. School Council and Stay-in-School Programme) did not identify these services.

In general, these young males felt they had little power in the school system, and their general perception was that young people were rarely asked their opinions. Some respondents who had chosen to access a service believed their involvement in decision-making in that service was tokenistic, and the real decisions were made by the adults. Although the majority stated it was a good idea to ask young people their opinions, as a group they were sceptical that this would occur, or if it did, that it would have any substance *"It's pointless though"* (M1 Respondent).

5.8.3 Decision Making and the Development of Services

Female Findings

F1 (average age 14.5, urban), F2 (average age 15, urban), F3 (average age, 12.5 rural) and F4 (average age 16.5, rural)

When respondents were asked did they think young people should be asked for their opinions and be involved in decisions regarding youth provisions and services, they all agreed it was a good idea.

Participants recruited from one area revealed that in preparing for the focus group, they had discussed issue and topics, indicating their interest in the process. Nevertheless they still expressed anxiety about being involved in the focus group discussion, despite the time spent by the researchers building relationships with them: *"We were afraid to come up here, but since we started talking an' all, we're all right like"* (F2 Respondent).

The idea of young people being involved in the development of services in areas such as Health was questioned by participants of a different group: *"The old ones should kind of, you know, from their experience, tell us before we go up"* (F1 Respondents). But their reluctance might be due to lack of information: *"We never heard much about it to get involved"* (F1 Respondent). They would make up their own minds *"...and then if we're interested we'd get involved"* (F1 Respondent).

The participants' greatest difficulty in responding to this issue appeared to be that they had no clear understanding of what involvement actually meant, and found it difficult to visualise a situation where their ideas and experiences would be valued and incorporated in the development of new services. Their life experiences had not persuaded them that such a concept was either realistic or likely.

In relation to youth services they were more than willing to participate in and take responsibility for the management of a facility appropriate to their needs (F2, F3 and F4). *"Give us a chance to prove ourselves"* (F2 Respondent). One group (F4) thought that fourteen year-olds would be too young to accept responsibility for participating in the management of a service, whereas they themselves, at 17, felt competent to do so. However they believed that younger teenagers should be consulted and involved in decision-making in such a service, using a peer management approach.

Male Findings

M1 (average age 14.75, urban), M2 (average age 15, urban), M3 (average age 12, rural) and M4 (average age 16.5, rural)

Generally young males thought it was a good idea to involve young people in decision making, but the opportunities for involvement in decision-making must be genuine and authentic.

5.9 Engagement Strategies

5.9.1 Introduction

This section details the researchers' experiences and observations of the engagement strategies used during the research process. Their views do not necessarily match those of the young people engaged with, which are included in the previous section on Political Involvement.

The research was designed to explore two types of engagement strategy in working with young people – detached and thematic. The first section presents the findings regarding the two methods of engagement under the following headings:

- Young People Engaged With
- Locations Used
- Quality of Interaction
- Advantages
- Disadvantages

The second section summarises the information gained relating to practice for workers in this field, and compares the researchers' observations to published material. Finally the researchers' own conclusions on engagement strategies are offered.

5.9.2 Detached Method

The definition of detached work for the purpose of this study was adapted from the Welsh Youth Agency (2001) and reads as follows:

> *"Detached work" is a broad term used to describe an approach to engage with young people, who may be or may not be accessing existing youth provisions. The researchers will initially engage with young people on the streets, those who use public spaces such as parks or other public facilities. These young people may have become "detached" from conventional youth provision, either because they reject these services, are excluded from them, or are unaware of them.*
>
> *(Wales Youth Agency, 2001: p4)*

This broad approach enabled the researchers to literally approach any young person in a public space and ask to speak to them.

Prior to carrying out this fieldwork, area visits were conducted by the researchers, which enabled them to map and 'get a feel' for each area. This information enabled the researchers to plan their engagement visits to maximise their opportunities to meet young people.

5.9.2.1 Young People Engaged With – Detached Method

The researchers have met young people from a wide variety of backgrounds, including many subsequently identified to them by service providers as being exposed to a number of risk factors. These include:

- young people with special needs
- ethnic minorities
- young people who have recently moved into the area
- young people in care
- young people who have been dealt with by the justice system
- young people whose parents have separated
- lone parents
- early school leavers
- young people in part-time employment
- young people who have been involved in petty crime
- young people who use illegal substances
- young people with few resources
- young people with erratic school attendance records

5.9.2.2 Locations Used – Detached Method

The researchers usually met young people at night between 7.00 and 11.00pm. The public spaces used by young people were generally associated with their age. It appears that younger people (9–11 years approximately) tend to gather in the early evening in public spaces in their immediate locality, such as the green area on their estate or the street or road where they live.

Older adolescents (12 – 18 years approximately) on the other hand appear to frequent both green spaces and streets near home after dark. However as they get older, they tend to venture further, and have been engaged with through detached methods in the following areas:

- alleyways
- car parks
- benches on streets and in parks
- pool halls
- takeaways/cafes
- outside off-licences

- shopping areas
- school grounds
- public parks
- sitting on walls
- behind buildings
- bus stops
- around sealed-up buildings

Though groups can be composed of both genders, males are more evident in these areas, and also appear to be more territorial. In maintaining the gender balance required by the project however, the researchers endeavoured to engage with equal numbers of males and females.

During the mapping stage, local gatekeepers were asked to identify places that had a reputation locally as 'risky', and where they themselves would be reluctant to go after dark. The researchers referred to these places as 'no-go areas'.

'No-go areas' (cemeteries, handball alleys, derelict buildings, fields, riverbanks, etc.) were visited on a regular basis by the researchers, but young people were never found there. However, on two separate nights the researchers were invited by young people to their own 'no-go areas', areas they frequented but which also had a certain local notoriety, particularly after dark.

The young people did not display any anxiety in these locations. As they had invited the researchers, the young people displayed no signs of nervousness in their presence, nor did they seem threatened in any way by their surroundings. They were on their own territory, and in control. Any anxieties that the researchers might have felt in these circumstances were quickly allayed by the reassuring comments and attitude of the young people, who were always friendly and polite. We were their guests and were treated at all times with courtesy and made to feel welcome.

5.9.2.3 Quality of Interaction – Detached Method

The response from the young people towards the researchers has been generally positive. There appears to be a slight difference in the way age groups commit to an interaction. Generally, younger people (9–13 years approximately) would enter into a general conversation immediately when approached. In only one area did young people under the age of twelve go to a nearby adult on being approached by the researchers. The adult then spoke to the researchers to establish why we were there.

In contrast, those aged thirteen and over tended to first establish the reasons for the researchers' presence. Once this was clarified, they committed to the interaction in almost every case.

Throughout the research process using the detached method, no young person, whether male or female, refused to speak to the researchers once initial introductions had been made. On two separate occasions however, individual young males over thirteen peeled away from the group they were with as they saw the researchers approaching.

5.9.2.4 Interaction and Parents – Detached Method

Interaction of the researchers with parents occurred after the initial building of relationships with the young people. As parental consent was required for anyone under fifteen to take part in a focus group, volunteers in this age group were asked by the researchers for permission to call to their home. An activity day which took participants outside their immediate area also required parental consent, regardless of the age of the participants.

The reception from parents varied. Although all parents seemed quite happy to meet and speak with the researchers, parental consent was not given for two young females who initially wanted to participate in a focus group. No clear reasons were given in these cases.

5.9.2.5 Advantages of Detached Method

As an engagement strategy, the detached method provided opportunities for young people to participate in matters that affect them, and to have their ideas listened to. Perhaps most importantly, this method gives the young people control of the process, and they can make a free choice in the way they participate, or decline the offer if they so wish.

Detached work offers a method of engaging with young people without the need for large amounts of equipment. However costs such as insurance cover and payment of staff cannot be overlooked.

Young people were more than willing to offer their ideas and opinions to adults when approached in this way. This suggests that as an initial engagement method, detached work can be very effective.

The method is also very flexible and can be adapted to suit a variety of purposes. It can be used for example to provide information and raise awareness among young people about existing services. It also offers organisations opportunities to develop progression routes into existing or proposed services. Or it can be developed into a sustainable method of working with those young people who prefer not to attach to any specific service.

It would appear that the introduction of a replacement researcher in the middle of the project presented few problems to the process, and positive contact with groups was re-established within a relatively short time. Again the free choice to work with the new researcher remained with the young people, indicating the flexibility and adaptability of the detached method.

5.9.2.6 Disadvantages of Detached Method

The detached method requires a significant amount of time to build up a picture of a young person's background and issues. The relative significance of this fact depends upon the purpose for which the method is being used.

The need for good team-work and honesty between researchers is important; they must provide support for each other as the work involves unsociable hours and can be uncomfortable, demoralising and exhausting when pacing empty streets on cold winter nights.

People with appropriate core skills may be difficult to attract and retain for this work.

The relatively unstructured nature of the work means that sometimes no engagements are made, and arrangements and appointments previously committed to cannot be guaranteed. The approach does not lend itself to measurements of productivity that focus on quotas of individual contacts.

Therefore detached interventions should be used only as one strategy in a more comprehensive work plan.

5.9.3 Thematic Entry Points

The young people contacted through thematic entry points were already identified as being 'at risk' by the referring service. The initial contact process was quite formally structured, originating with a recommendation from the 'gatekeeper'. The researchers then contacted each potential participant at their home address, and a follow-up letter (Appendix Four) containing details of proposed sessions was delivered to them.

5.9.3.1 Young People Engaged With – Thematic Entry Point

The young people initially contacted through thematic entry points included:

- young people who had been detained by the Justice system
- potential early school leavers
- lone parents
- young people in part-time employment
- young people who had been involved in petty crime
- young people from the Traveller Community

5.9.3.2 Location Used – Thematic Entry Point

The contact process was more formal than with the detached method and developing regular contact with individuals proved difficult. Some of the potential participants were rarely to be found at home, although appointments had been previously arranged with the parents.

The young people themselves decided upon the location of the follow-up sessions and the activities that they wished to do. Although young people were facilitated to make decisions regarding the activity sessions, those initially most difficult to contact attended irregularly, and in general they appeared less enthusiastic about the research process.

When asked by the researchers to recommend opportunities for developing more contacts (as 'snowballing' into other groups was required by the research), the participants suggested places rather than individual names. Once the researchers commenced work in these locations, they were able to establish that the suggestions offered were valid and helpful.

This 'snowballing' into other areas also increased the range of young people from different backgrounds who could be included in the development of the Topic Guide for the study. The backgrounds of these new contacts were similar to those described previously under the section on Detached Methods (5.9.2.1).

5.9.3.4 Quality of Interaction – Thematic Entry Point

The need to form a group for the project meant that young people were drawn from different peer groups, although the majority would seem to have been loosely acquainted already. This mixing led to a degree of internal conflict and negative interaction which appeared to inhibit 'openness' in the group.

The perceived lack of 'openness' could also be explained by the fact that a majority of the participants were referrals from a service that monitored their everyday activities. Their previous involvement in secretive behaviours and their experiences of being 'caught' by the authorities in these behaviours may have led to their more guarded approach, either to this particular project, or to adults in general.

Their need to avoid being identified as an 'informer' or 'snitch' among their peers may also account for their offer of areas rather than of direct names in the snowballing process.

The number of issues identified by these young people was limited compared with those obtained through detached methods.

5.9.3. 5 Interaction with Parents – Thematic Entry Points

At the introductory stage the parents were immediately involved. Their reactions to the researchers were mixed, and at the outset four referrals preferred not to have their son or daughter participate in the research process.

In one case a potential respondent whom the researchers did not meet in person was a source of concern for the parents. The individual had undergone a particularly bad experience, and the parents stated that promised access to services had never materialised.

The parents liaised with their child on behalf of the researchers. In the follow-up contact the parents informed the researchers that the young person had declined to participate.

The fact that services had previously been sought but had not materialised for this young person, for whatever reason, may have had some influence on the person's decision not to participate. It also indicates that services are not always readily available when required by individuals or their carers.

Those parents that gave their consent were positive towards the research and the activities involved, and parents commonly expressed the view that there weren't a lot of constructive activities available for these young people.

5.9.3.6 Advantages of Thematic Entry Points

Individual gatekeepers were nominated by representatives of Service providers to enable the researchers to access the target population who were already identified as exhibiting characteristics of 'risk' from a professional perspective. Therefore it is a quick and efficient method of identification. Information on background and on support services currently accessed by the participants is readily available. The involvement of the parents from the beginning means that they are aware of the research process.

5.9.3.7 Disadvantages of Thematic Entry Points

At the introductory stage, the young person, although chosen at random from a sample, has already been identified through the recommendation of an adult working within a service. A power inequality may exist in the relationship between child and adult, and this could influence the motivation and attitude of the young person towards the project.

The involvement of the parent at the beginning could also be viewed as a disadvantage. For example, if the parent and the young person have opposing opinions regarding participation, the choice of the young person can be taken from them, and could result in their disempowerment and/or pseudo-participation.

Where thematic entry points were involved, significant amounts of time and resources were used by the researchers to try to establish trust with potential participants. Although this appeared to be effective in some areas, in one location the young people became disruptive and withdrew from the focus group, stating that they did not trust the process. However some of the respondents of this group agreed to individual interviews, which were used to supplement the data collected up to the point of withdrawal.

When the researchers went to areas recommended to them by thematic entry point participants, they changed to the detached method, talking directly with young people in these areas. This appeared to increase the number of youth-raised issues, and improved the quality of interaction between researchers and young people.

This suggests that speaking to young people 'on their own turf' and in their own peer groups is more productive than working through a constructed group session with participants drawn from different peer groups.

5.9.4 Informing Practice

The study of different engagement strategies provided valuable information for the researchers, which can be utilised and adapted by practitioners across a range of service provision.

The focus group structure, when employed as a method of ascertaining young people's perceptions of current services and of identifying their needs, provided significant amounts of useful data.

The investigation of engagement strategies has revealed significant findings for practice. This information includes:

- young people gather mainly after dark
- young people, given the choice, will interact with adults in a positive way
- young people will provide information on their own terms
- young people gather in particular areas or territories that are readily identifiable by other young people
- young people can respond to a change in personnel in a positive way (but this may be connected to their having a free choice whether to reject or accept the new person).
- purposive sampling of peer groups, rather than of individuals in peer groups, means that trust already exists within the group and people are more likely to participate
- the numbers of young people in public places fell during bad weather; however a core number of both males and females used public spaces in all weathers, and tended to use the warmer options like cafes when necessary
- those who used public spaces in all weathers would openly speak to researchers on the streets, but preferred not to participate in focus groups.

The information provided here will seem "common sense" to those working with adolescents, and published reports of the activities of young people generally contain similar evidence. For example:

- Gardai report juvenile offending as at its highest between 8pm and 10pm. (See: Literature Review 3.3.3).
- That young people make themselves visible on the streets has been documented in various texts as an expression of youth culture (See: Literature Review 3.1.1.3).
- The ability of young people to recognise other peer groups through dress, behaviours and areas where they congregate has been comprehensively documented (ibid.).
- The importance of peer groups cannot be underestimated when working with young people, as is acknowledged in various texts (ibid.).

5.9.5 Researchers' Perspective

The purpose of any intervention, whether assessment, prevention, treatment, development, raising awareness, or a combination of these, needs to be clearly identified and understood by workers prior to accessing any groups of young people.

As researchers with different experiences of working with young people (i.e. Education and Youth Work respectively), we could identify advantages and disadvantages in both methods of engagement.

However, if authentic access to and participation of young people are regarded as priorities in the research, the detached method of engagement offers many advantages over thematic entry points, as the participants have a free choice in becoming involved or not.

The Detached Method as an approach has the potential to be adapted across a range of services as detailed above. It offers a style of intervention more appropriate to young people who are reluctant to enter official buildings, as they have a sense of ownership of the streets and public areas where they hang out.

In contrast the use of a Thematic Entry Point for this project involved engaging with young people who were already defined as 'at risk' from an agency perspective, and the target group immediately associated the researchers with the referral service. While this association can be either positive or negative depending upon the experience of the young person, expectations are nevertheless unconsciously established from the outset for both parties involved in the interaction.

The researchers' perspective is that detached methods of engagement have the potential to deliver more positive experiences for both workers and young people than thematic entry.

5. 10 Summary of Findings

This section presents a summary of the main findings of each of the topics discussed in focus groups.

5.10.1 Risk and Resilience

The findings illustrated that younger female respondents (i.e. those under 14 years) do not view themselves as 'at risk' or 'taking risks'. In contrast young males of a similar age identify bullying and peer pressure as both influencing the risks that they are prepared to take and placing them generally 'at risk'.

Older respondents, both female and male, acknowledge that they participate in risk behaviours although they are aware of the possible dangers.

Young males view someone that cannot be trusted as placing them 'at risk', and identified the need for trust and confidentiality as key principles in any engagement that seeks to meaningfully involve them.

Those who projected a positive self-image to the researchers through their attitude and language were generally able to illustrate positive experiences in other contexts too, evidencing resilient qualities in coping with negative situations.

5.10.2 Health

Significant amounts of information were gained providing insights into behaviours that may impact significantly on the short and long term health of these people's lives.

A difference in their behaviours is very evident between younger and older adolescents. Those under fourteen years of age (to use a rough approximation) do not generally drink alcohol, use drugs or get involved in one-to-one relationships, whereas these behaviours are considered "normal" by those over fourteen.

In general young people's knowledge of current Health Service provision is limited, with females identifying more services that males. However both females and males believe that they are responsible for their own health care (albeit with parental supports), and only seek services when necessary. Therefore health issues for most young people concern cure rather than prevention.

Young people are aware of their own health needs and of ways of meeting those needs, and they can make a positive contribution to the development of Health Services targeted at their age group.

5.10.3 Education

The attitudes towards school of students at both primary and post-primary levels were generally positive, and they identified their school as a key area of social interaction in their lives. This social interaction mainly involved other students. Relationships with staff were viewed more positively by females than males.

The size of the school population appears to influence the way young people relate to their school, and how they identify themselves and others within the school. This can result in peer-group rivalries that cause some to self-exclude from activities and services available through the school.

Examination years were identified as particularly stressful, and alternative programmes, a transition year, work experience and continuous assessment were highlighted as more positive experiences by the older students. Some students in the Leaving Certificate cycle appeared to lack accurate information on educational requirements for prospective careers.

Those who were attending alternative education facilities and services said they would prefer to be attached to the mainstream system.

5.10.4 Youth Services

The general perception of the participants was that youth services, whether provided by the private, statutory or community/voluntary sectors, were insufficient to meet the needs of the young people in their area.

Young people are capable of self-organising group activities. Young males were able to identify more activities available to them than young females.

Those who use services were able to highlight factors they associated with successful facilities. These include:

- maintaining small numbers of participants,
- creating a relaxed, informal atmosphere,

- providing a 'chill out' area where people can chat, listen to music or just sit and do nothing, and
- ensuring that the participants have a sense of ownership of the service.

Current methods of working with young people were generally approved of. Suggestions for improving existing youth and voluntary services included having personnel from outside the locality to supervise clubs and projects, and extending opening times to include evenings and week-ends.

Female participants identified the need for a low maintenance 'drop-in' facility, which would involve young people in its day-to-day management, with minimum adult intervention. Liberal opening hours and a sense of freedom and ownership for its users were key elements of their proposals.

Young males expressed more cynical views about services, citing failed projects and broken promises, and believed there was a general reluctance to allocate sufficient funds to develop adequate youth services.

5.10.5 Justice

All the older respondents (i.e. fourteen years or over) were able to identify activities they were involved in that they knew to be illegal, but this knowledge did not prevent them from maintaining their involvement. Likely parental reactions to getting caught represented the most powerful inhibiting influence, but ultimately the peer group set the boundaries for 'acceptable' activity.

Their knowledge of the justice system is limited and they appear hostile to it, viewing its operations as inconsistent and unfair. The majority see their relationship with the Gardai as negative. This was attributed by many to being moved on or being stopped and searched, but even those who had no direct experience of such interventions seemed to have adopted a negative perspective to the Gardai anyway.

5.10.6 Independence

There was a clear difference in the degrees of independence demonstrated by those under fourteen years of age and their older counterparts. Younger adolescents were clearly attached to their immediate family and had not begun to challenge parental boundaries, unlike their older counterparts who evidenced various ways in which they were increasingly detaching from the family unit.

Family conflicts were cited by both younger and older respondents, and sources of conflict including lack of adequate resources, family separation and reconstituted families. Some young people move regularly between the homes of their separated parents, and others sleep temporarily at the houses of relatives or friends to avoid conflict at home.

Sexual relationships are accepted as normal among teenagers. All respondents who identified their sexuality claimed a heterosexual preference, but young females were more tolerant of 'gays' than young males. Nevertheless 'coming out' in such a culture would be an intimidating prospect for any young person.

Peer groups are extremely important to young people. They offer emotional and moral support, and interact in an elaborate prescribed social hierarchy.

The majority of respondents had a strong identity with their communities where they feel safe and which provides them with a sense of confidence. However some highlighted the erosion of their communities through rapid urban expansion. Other communities suffer from labelling by the wider community based on social class.

Many older respondents in rural areas had part-time jobs, which were usually secured through family connections. In urban areas a smaller proportion had jobs, usually in fast food restaurants or supermarkets. Young people generally felt it was difficult to obtain suitable employment that fitted easily with their school hours. Most young people relied on their families for money, until they could earn enough to cover their needs independently.

5.10.7 Culture

The use of Information and Communications Technologies by young people demonstrates the fluid nature of youth culture. The younger respondents constantly referred to mobiles, the Internet, computer games and DVD's. The older respondents in contrast used less jargon and fewer references to ICTs. The essential piece of equipment for both however, is the mobile phone, which they use for a variety of tasks: to make arrangements within peer groups; to initiate, maintain, and monitor one-to-one relationships; to order illegal drugs; and to pass the time playing games on its screen.

Only one group showed little interest in mobile phones, but more research would be required to explain this anomaly within the findings.

The mass media play a significant role in shaping youth culture. References to popular television programmes were regularly used to illustrate and add meaning to points made in discussions. There also appeared to be a gender difference regarding viewing preferences, with females preferring soaps and males opting for sports programmes, particularly soccer and wrestling.

The commercialism of the music industry was seen as inescapable, and again preferences changed with age, from media-promoted pop groups for younger respondents to alternative and more individualised styles among older teenagers. Music features in young people's lives privately at home, socially where it is used to help define peer identities, and in larger crowds at nightclubs and concerts.

The print media appear to be the least used form of modern communication among young people. Magazines are read for entertainment and for information on current tastes in fashion, and newspapers are reviewed for local court reports.

Young people, when judging Difference of Background, read it in relation to their own locality, and identify anyone as 'different' who is from outside their immediate area, whether from a different social class, a different town, city or country. But tolerance of difference is a feature of much of their discourse and of the values they express, and a young person's judging someone as 'different' should not be read as implying a value judgement.

Art and Leisure activities were invariably appreciated and participated in by the younger respondents, regardless of who else was involved. However older respondents tended to feel that activities they had participated in as children were no longer appropriate. They also identified drama and arts as the reserve of exclusive groups they often choose not to mix with. As a result, it is much more difficult for older teenagers without significant resources to become involved in art and leisure activities, even when they are provided locally.

Sport plays a significant role in the lives of young males, and males who enjoy sport have access to a range of well organised and funded leisure activities. Females are significantly less provided for, as are males who choose not to participate in sport.

5.10.8 Political Involvement

It is evident that few opportunities exist currently for young people to become involved in decision-making in matters that affect them. Participatory decision-making structures within schools and clubs are seen by young people as largely ineffective, as the power remains with the adults in the system. Those structures that do offer consultative roles to young people can be claimed by a particular peer group, or offer what is perceived as token participation only. One initiative that was seen as effective by respondents gave teachers and students an equal voice in deciding on a weekly school menu. Affirmation and acknowledgement were identified as outcomes of this process by its supporters (all females). Perhaps significantly, males of the same age attending the same schools failed to identify this decision-making process as being of any significance for them.

Chapter Six
Research Analysis

6. Introduction

The information summarised in the previous Findings chapter (Ch 5) is analysed here under the following headings:

6.1 Risk and Resilience first explores the gap between the Risk Factors identified by agencies and organisations and those identified by young people themselves. The following section on Resilience looks at different responses to multiple factors of risk by individuals and groups encountered during the project.

6.2 Health discusses Associated Behaviours before exploring young people's perceptions of Current Health Services, their levels of Awareness of these services, issues of Access and the Development of Services required by young people.

6. 3 Education explores a range of themes relating to school-based programmes and activities, and also looks at young people's Attitudes to school, Third Level Education and Future Plans

6.4 Youth Service looks at the perceptions of young people regarding the delivery of youth services under the categories of Private and Statutory Providers, the Community and Voluntary Sector and Self Organised Activities.

6.5 Justice explores the limited Knowledge that young people have of the Justice system and their Relationship with the Gardai.

6.6 Independence examines adolescents' views and experiences of their relationships with the Family, their One-to-One Relationships, and their social connections with Peer Groups, the wider Community and through Employment.

6.7 Culture investigates everyday environments, activities, services and products that were identified by young people as valued by them. It explores their concepts of Community, of Different Backgrounds and Arts and Leisure Activities.

6.8 Political Involvement explores the level of Involvement in decision making currently available to young people, and their attitudes to Political Involvement.

6.9 Engagement Strategies argues for developing appropriate processes and practices in working with young people who exhibit multiple factors of vulnerability in their lives.

6.1 Risk and Resilience Analysis

6.1.1 Introduction

This section is presented in two parts. We first explore the gap that exists between risk factors identified by those working with or for young people on the one hand and young people's own perceptions of risk on the other. Successfully bridging this gap is seen to be achievable only through authentic participation by young people in the development of effective services for them. The subsequent section explores the theory of Resilience (See: Literature Review 3.4), which is then related to participants in the project whose lives may share similar characteristics of risk, and yet who appear to have very different attitudes to their own situations and sense of well-being.

6.1.2 Risk

Everyone is exposed to various risks in today's society, and in our everyday lives we constantly make decisions based upon our evaluation of these risks (See: Literature Review 3.2). Young people are generally regarded as more vulnerable than adults, and according to Bell (1995), their exposure to risk is embedded in individual, family and environmental factors (See: Literature Review 3.2). Agencies that work with young people have identified a range of these factors. Any increase in the number of risk factors in a person's situation is seen to dramatically increase their level of vulnerability (ibid.).

In the focus group discussions, participants across the age range cited all but one of the agency-identified risk factors, either through direct personal experience or through contact with others who had experienced them. The one exception was "working in prostitution" (although involvement with prostitutes was recorded).

However it emerged clearly that young people did not necessarily perceive all the agency-identified factors as actual 'risks', or that being exposed to these factors necessarily placed them 'at risk'. When asked what they considered to be 'risky' for young people, the participants offered a variety of responses.

6.1.3 Young People's Perceptions of Risk

Some young people obviously exposed to agency-defined risk characteristics stated that they weren't involved in anything risky, and never saw themselves as in any way 'at risk' (F1).

Other respondents referred to immediate physical risk, in activities such as unprotected sex, drug misuse, climbing and driving. (All Focus Groups of average age 13 and over). But knowing that such practices involved risk, and were in some cases perhaps illegal or dangerous and even life-threatening, did not prevent them from risk-taking for what they saw as the immediate benefits offered by such activities.

This indicates that risk often exists only in the present moment for young people, and possible long-term consequences are minimised, as also observed in research on risk taking among adolescents. (See: Literature Review 3.3)

Perhaps more interestingly, some young people stated that they saw themselves as mainly 'at risk' from people they could not trust. Their issues of trust related both to adults and to other young people. The identification of trust and risk by young people illustrates cognitive powers that are perhaps underestimated by adults when working with young people. Trust and risk are intertwined (See: Literature Review 3.2) at the access point where the young person decides between the likely gains and losses of the interaction to be risked.

Currently young people who attempt to access services they do not trust are taking a significant risk, especially if they are involved in illegal activities. Yet traditionally services have been organised in the expectation that young people will choose to enter the domain of the adult. The power relationship between an adult supported by an organisation and a young person coming through the door generally favours the adult. Therefore an inequality often exists even prior to access.

Service providers working with youth "at risk" can feel disappointed and demoralised when their clients choose not to avail of services and supports offered. This does not mean that the service is necessarily irrelevant or of no potential benefit to the young person; it may mean that the young person has no reason to trust the service, and that they reject it because the risk they take in accessing the service is considered by them as too great.

This indicates that from the outset there is a gap between the young people's perceptions of risk, (i.e. their need to trust the people they connect with), and those of professionals and volunteers who work for and with them. It's clear that in order to bridge this gap, the delivery of services to young people requires 'trust' as a core underpinning principle.

As discussed in the Literature Review (3.3), adults constantly place their trust in 'abstract systems' (e.g. air and road travel, medicine, banking etc.,) that are managed and operated by experts with specialist knowledge. Within our everyday lives we all learn to rely on these services, even though we do not necessarily have complete confidence in them.

The possessors of 'expert knowledge' in the context of youth needs are young people themselves. The expressed aim of the National Children's Strategy (2000) to give young people *"a voice in matters which affect them"* (ibid.) provides services with a framework to gain this 'expert' knowledge.

The promotion of authentic participation by young people in matters that affect them is critical to identifying their needs, and to developing appropriate services to meet those needs. However this can not be achieved without developing trust between young people and the services and organisations that work with them, at the access point where trust and risk are intertwined.

6.1. 4. Resilience

Resilience can be defined as *"the healing potential that may lie naturally within children, in their normal daily experience or their social networks"* (Gilligan, 2000). The literature indicates that resilient children exhibit particular personal characteristics and find supports in the family context and from the wider community (See: Literature Review 3.4).

Working through both detached and thematic entry points, the researchers on this project have engaged with many young people whose situations reflected a wide variety of risk characteristics. Considerable time was invested in the observation of groups to identify characteristics of 'risk', as defined by both the service providers and by the young people themselves.

This process also enabled the researchers to identify resilient factors shown in varying degrees by different participants.

One group of females (F1) exhibited most of the risk characteristics identified in the literature, and availed only of services that were compulsory for them (e.g. school). Yet these young women displayed considerable resilience in the management of their lives.

Through the group discussion they were able to identify positive factors both in themselves and in their relationships with family and community. They appeared to have positive relationships with their families and were trusted to self-manage within boundaries set by parents. Although they identified many negative aspects of their contacts with the wider community, social interaction – particularly with peers – was very important to them.

In contrast other respondents, both male and female, who participated in similar activities and exhibited similar risk behaviours, appeared to focus more on negative factors in their life situations. Some of these individuals were attached to far more services than the 'resilient' young women.

Some respondents described negative family relationships, and poor relationships in general with adults in the wider community. Membership of a peer group was seen as very important by these participants also, as it could provide supports that were lacking in other areas of their lives.

Respondents who used services often identified a positive relationship with a particular individual attached to a service, rather than expressing a positive attitude to that service as a whole. Gilligan (2001) refers to the crucial "turning point" that such relationships can sometimes bring about in young people's lives (See: Literature Review 3.4.3).

As service providers we must recognise that we do not have all the answers. Young people who choose to remain detached from services and who exhibit multiple characteristics of risk can be capable of finding alternative resources in their own lives that offer adequate forms of support. Those who lack these resilience factors are the most vulnerable among the youth population, and are most at risk of not reaching their full potential.

6.2 Health

6.2.1. Introduction

This section explores those associated behaviours which are considered to have short and long term negative effects on the health of young people, including misuse of alcohol, drugs and substances and other health issues, and goes on to analyse their perceptions of current health services, including awareness and access, and services they would like to see developed.

6.2.2 Associated Behaviours

The data supplied by the focus groups illustrates a marked difference in behaviours between those at Primary and Post-Primary levels in regard to participation in risk associated with alcohol consumption and drug and substance misuse.

6.2.2.1 Alcohol

The respondents at Primary level stated that they did not consume alcohol. However a case was identified of a young male introducing alcohol to a school setting, indicating that some young people at this level are using alcohol. The fact that young people are introduced to public houses by family members, together with their attitude to soft drinks as *"not a proper drink"*, suggests that the encouragement of children by adults and older teenagers to drink alcohol begins an early age.

A review of the focus group findings for the older respondents (those aged 14 and over) reveals that consumption of alcohol is considered a normal social activity among teenagers. Considering the customary introduction of young people to a "drink culture" at a much earlier age, should this attitude surprise us?

Spending power influences the types and amounts of alcohol drunk by young people. In some areas inexpensive beers were cited as the most popular drink, and this was usually among those who did not have access to paid part-time employment.

In other areas where young people had money either from part-time employment or through family support, more expensive beers and spirits (particularly alco-pops and shots) were cited as the most popular drinks. The fact that participants are able to obtain alcohol without difficulty, and that they prefer to diminish or ignore the risks involved although they are aware of them, suggests that, in the prevailing Irish context, a realistic alternative to the "drink culture" would be difficult to promote to young people.

6.2.2.2 Drugs and Substance Misuse

The younger respondents had limited knowledge regarding drug and substance misuse. However this age group suspected older teenagers were 'using' and some had witnessed the sourcing of drugs by older teenagers.

The secretive behaviour of older teenagers around drug use due to its illegal nature, suggests that the exposure of younger children to their sourcing of drugs is unintentional, but it also suggests that older teenagers often underestimate the understanding that younger siblings and neighbours have of their activities.

Therefore younger children have little control regarding their exposure to drug use (as also applies to many other issues) in their communities. The perception of old teenagers that peer group behaviour is hierarchical (See: Independence Findings, 5.6.3) implies that some young people will inevitably become absorbed into the drug culture.

Older respondents were able to accurately analyse drug misuse in their area. One focus group had labelled another in the same town as *"druggies"*, and members of this second group did acknowledge that they had used illegal substances, with a minority stating that they believed drugs should be legalised.

However, in examining the view that Youth Society is divided between those that clearly use drugs and those that claim not to, the *"druggies"* own analysis proposed that many peer groups declaring themselves as non-users were often simply more secretive, but that in fact they also used illegal substances. This analysis was unintentionally confirmed by the focus group that first labelled the druggies, when they rationalised the misuse of specific drugs among their own peer group as acceptable.

This illustrates that young people are capable of accurate critical analysis. But the analysis of drug use by these two groups focused on male misusers only. However in other geographical locations, the use of drugs was seen as involving both males and females, confirming that illegal drug use has perforated Youth Culture in Wexford, regardless of gender or social background.

The fact that young women can be been seen to socially construct drug misuse as acceptable behaviour among their male peers means that misuse by females could be constructed in a similar way. The perceived barriers to seeking assistance by adult women drug users (See: Literature Review 3.3.2), and the likelihood that in the majority of cases these adult women would have begun 'using' at a younger age, indicate that existing and potential services in this field must respond to the needs of younger women who may be less forthcoming than their male peers in seeking assistance.

Statistics in both the quantitative and literature review illustrate that more males than females are accessing addiction support services from both the Health Board and the Cornmarket Project in Wexford town.

However a reported increase of young females accessing and using the Cornmarket Project (See: Quantitative Chapter, 2.12.2) may indicate that young women users perceive fewer barriers to accessing services than their adult counterparts. Nevertheless, it seems that drug misuse among young women in County Wexford is more prevalent than previously thought by service providers and by society generally.

The identification of drug misuse as normal behaviour and the increasing numbers of both young females and males accessing current services through the Health Boards and the community and voluntary sector indicates that more service will be required in the future in the area of addiction counselling.

Smoking cigarettes was also seen as a everyday activity of young people, with females stating that more girls than boys smoked. The initiation into smoking for some young people occurred in primary school. Although a number of respondents smoked during focus group interviews, only one group identified smoking as a long-term health risk.

The use of solvents and aerosols was not identified by any group. This may suggest that misuse of these substances is not considered appropriate behaviour within these peer groups. The fact that information was freely supplied regarding the use of illegal substances would seem to support this analysis.

6.2.2.3. Sexual Activity and Health

This topic was considered inappropriate for younger respondents in the research, and any data regarding related issues gathered from this age group was offered by them unprompted by the researchers.

The younger female respondents made no reference to sexual development. The young males generally viewed girls and adult women as nuisances who interfered with their fun, although one expressed an interest in having a girlfriend. In Hill's model of Psychosocial Development (See: Literature Review, 3.1.1.4) these groups correspond to the pre-adolescent stage.

As illustrated by the focus group findings, sexual attraction and relationships gained in significance with age. Formation of sexual identity is seen as one of the key elements of adolescent development (ibid.). In both male and female groups, language laced with sexual innuendo was frequently used to describe various situations, but in the oldest male focus group the use of this type of language predominated throughout, and was often very derogatory to women.

Heterosexual Relationships

All respondents who commented on this topic expressed heterosexual preferences.

Female Perspective - In the female groups, sexual activity was acknowledged as a common activity that for some commenced at twelve or thirteen years of age. The young women stated that their knowledge regarding sexual health was obtained from various sources, e.g. friends, family, the street and school. As young people they felt that their sexual education was fragmented and inconsistent, and they suggested a review of sex education programmes provided for teenagers.

The need for contraception was linked to the general perception that this was the responsibility of both partners, but males were generally viewed as irresponsible, and unwanted pregnancy was seen as a real risk in young people's lives. This perspective increases the likelihood that they rely on methods such as the contraceptive pill, rather than trusting their partner to use condoms. The young women viewed early pregnancy as an undesirable option for themselves, but the female respondents (F1,F2 and F4) all personally knew young mothers who had given birth at or before fifteen years of age. The total number of teenage mothers thus identified by groups was seven.

The South Eastern Health Board has a higher rate of teenage pregnancies than the national average (See: Quantitative Chapter 2.9.2) and young women are aware that their male partners are as unsure as they themselves are about safe sexual practise.

The twin challenges of motherhood and attending school are difficult to balance. As a result young mothers often opt out of school, due to the inadequate supply of practical supports such as child care and crèches. As identified elsewhere, (See: Quantitative Chapter 2.13.1) those who leave the education system early often face a life-time of intermittent low paid employment and poverty.

A limited awareness of sexually transmitted infections coupled with views among some that having multiple partners is acceptable, and the association of condoms with pregnancy prevention rather than with protection against infection suggests that the numbers attending the Waterford STI clinic (See: Literature Review 3.3.2) will continue to increase.

Only one group (F4) described a sex education programme delivered by a visitor to their school that focused on contraception. This suggests that not all schools avail of this particular service. It seems unlikely that those participants advocating such programmes in their own school may have missed them due to "mitching" or being absent, as they did identify sex education programmes delivered by teachers which they regarded as inadequate.

The reliance on the school as the sole context for delivering sex education programmes means those who attend irregularly or who have left the system may never get this information. Many in this category are identified with lower socio-economic backgrounds and are likely to be already exposed to various other risk factors (See: Literature Review 3.3.1).

The Health Promotion Units (See: Quantitative Chapter 2.6.4) were established in 1987 and further expanded in 1993 to provide supports and advice to community-based health initiatives and to promote health programmes in schools. But community-based health initiatives were not readily identified by young people (See: 6.2.5) and this suggests that some young people already out of school will never access accurate information regarding sexual health.

Male Perspective - In male groups, sexual activity was acknowledged as a common activity, although the threshold age for sexual relations was not disclosed. None of the male respondents stated that they were fathers, but they did admit taking risks by having unprotected sex under the influence of alcohol or drugs.

The general consensus was that being involved with more than one partner was acceptable. Participants also acknowledged that they often ignored the need to use condoms, particularly when alcohol was involved. Males also view pregnancy prevention as greater priority than protection against Sexually Transmitted Infections. One seventeen-year-old admitted that he had used the services of a prostitute on a number of occasions, suggesting he is exposing both himself and subsequent partners to a higher risk of STIs. Given all this, it seems likely that recent increase in attendance at STI clinics will continue.

Homosexual relationships - There was a marked difference between the attitudes of females and males toward homosexuality. In general females were more accepting of gay relationships and stereotyped gay males as "fun, and usually good looking". The attitude of a majority of the young women to lesbian relationships was one of tolerance – "as long as they don't bother me, it's okay".

In contrast, males were openly aggressive and negative to gay males, and would choose to distance themselves from people that they knew were gay. Some of the groups had obtained information about gay, lesbian and bisexual relationships through TV and cinema so it could be argued that their knowledge was at least partly based on abstract contexts. However the open aggression expressed towards gay males and their exclusion in the local context indicates the difficulties encountered by young gay Irish males and females in 'coming out' to their families and friends. Therefore a confidential service for young gay people would act as an important support.

6.2 3 Other Health Issues

Mental Health - The younger respondents were quite open about emotional problems experienced by young people. They would normally speak to their friends about such issues, but also felt confident that they could approach a *"nice"* teacher if they needed to.

Generally the older respondents expressed negative views about the counsellors available through the school system and said they wouldn't use them. This suggests that teachers who provide counselling within the secondary school system are not always appreciated by their clients, and that school is perhaps not the most appropriate context to offer such a service.

Among older respondents there was little difference between female and male attitudes to mental health. On occasion the majority of young people had felt "down" but would usually speak to friends, as they could be *"trusted"*.

However the availability of friends was not enough in some case. A young male participant who had previously attempted suicide, felt ambivalent about the way he was treated within the medical system. An individual doctor prevented his admission to a mental institution, and this he believed *"saved me"*. Young males from both rural and urban settings discussed suicide more openly and more deeply than female respondents. This reflects the current research view that para-suicide and suicide is pre-dominantly a male issue (See: Literature Review 3.3.3). It could be argued that the media has influenced young men in their attitude towards suicide, but this does not detract from the fact that for some young people suicide is a real risk.

This particular young man was referred on to other services within the health system, where again, the individuals he worked with helped him. He now has a positive, if qualified, attitude towards the services that he accessed. But could earlier intervention have been more beneficial to him?

Eating Disorders - The global youth culture has created sophisticated and persuasive selling techniques that promote "cool" and "sexy" stereotypes to define and idealise physical beauty (See: Literature Review 3.3.1). Females and males both argued that eating disorders were mainly a female issue. Young females associating "being thin" with the influence of magazines and the media generally and also with peer pressure. Males thought that comments on a person's size could often influence someone in trying to lose weight. The participants' reactions to someone with an eating disorder ranged from empathy to ridicule. But it's clear that some young women who already exhibit multi-factors of vulnerability are at risk of becoming victims of bulimia and anorexia.

6.2.5 Perceptions of Current Health Services

Arriving at a definition of services required discussion within the focus groups to clarify what the term 'Services' actually meant. From a young persons perspective these were segregated broadly into private or consumer services and those provided by the faceless "they". "They" were the public services, including Health, Education, Justice, Councils and Corporations, and the Community/ Voluntary sector.

In general young women were able to identify more health services than males, but overall knowledge of services was limited. This could be a reflection of the traditional view that within society women are normally associated with being 'carers', and from their involvement in socialisation systems, the young people have acquired a gender perspective that sees health services as mainly concerned with family supports and baby clinics.

Both females and males thought their health was their own responsibility (with the support of their family), and accessed services only when required. However the young women's view of these services contained no assessment of quality of delivery; they were seen as merely available, to be used when necessary. Their use of health services is above all, pragmatic.

In contrast, young males recalled services that they had personally experienced and which they generally viewed positively. Their positive attitudes were linked to individuals within the system that had, from their perspective, treated them well, rather than to the organisation that provided the service. Therefore dealing with an individual member of staff rather than a faceless "they" proved beneficial when the individual had entered the health system.

The findings illustrate that young people's awareness of the range of services is limited, and so it was not possible to ascertain their perceptions on the wide range of services that do exist as they are unaware of them.

6.2.6 Awareness of Current Health Service

Increasing the awareness of appropriate services among young people is essential. They need to be aware not only of the existence of these services, but also of the procedures involved in accessing them. As previously stated, females are more aware of supports, particularly child and family supports. Most young females appear to obtain their information about health issues and agencies through leaflets picked up in chemist shops and Health Centres.

In today's changing society, where new family structures are emerging (See: Independence Findings 5.6.2) separated and reconstituted families provide significant supports for some children and adolescents, while others find such arrangements extremely stressful. The traditional allocation of the role of carer of children to females, especially mothers, should no longer be taken for granted, as young people often choose to live with their fathers, or move between parents. Others "sofa surf" for short periods or leave home entirely. The responsibility of "carer" can often be shared among different family members or involve people outside of the immediate family. In any case, the carer, whoever they may be, should be able to access family support as required.

Therefore information regarding the availability of and access to the full range of statutory health services must be promoted to both female and males.

Health initiatives and programmes are also provided in other contexts such as school and the community and voluntary sector. Seven of the eight focus groups identified school counsellors as a service, but were negative about this service. Only two focus groups, both rural, identified community based-services (a day care centre for elderly people, an addiction service, CURA and SMART). This indicates that the Community/ Voluntary sector's input into health initiatives is almost invisible to most young people.

Yet the Community and Voluntary Sector does offer many health based initiatives, including addiction services, counselling service, health and fitness programmes and information services to clients under the age of eighteen. But young people clearly associate health issues with the statutory Health Board system, and not as available through the Community and Voluntary sector.

6.2.7 Access

The fact that young people only access health services as a "cure", generally with parental support, coupled with their lack of knowledge regarding the range of services available in their community, suggests that a gap exists in provision by the Health Boards between implementing preventative strategies and responding to illness.

In order to address the perceived gap between preventative strategies and the treatment of illness, a locally-based service which is accessible, professionally staffed and easily identifiable by young people prior to their entering the statutory health system or other community and voluntary based initiatives could powerfully influence their overall perception of the health service, and could also link them to the service most appropriate to meet an identified health need. As stated previously (See: Risk and Resilience Analysis 6.2), the interface of services with clients is where first impressions are formed, and where the decision to trust is initiated.

The Department of Health and Children has a statutory responsible for children up the age of eighteen years, and at least some young people appreciate the services that they have successfully accessed. But these services will be withdrawn when they reach eighteen. One 17 year-old respondent seemed unaware that the service he appreciated and valued would be withdrawn from him within the next ten months. A "gap" may then exist between services for those under eighteen and older teenagers. To encourage independence among young people, it would prove more empowering to facilitate them to negotiate their own arrangements for leaving the care system by extending provision of the existing aftercare services.

6.2.8 Services Suggested by Young People

The older respondents had four proposals for the development of health services for young people:

- A specific medical service for young women
- A comprehensive Sex Education Programme
- A walk-in Crisis Service
- A confidential help line

The specific medical service for young women staffed by female personnel was suggested by one female focus group (F1) as a model that young women would access more readily than the current service available to them. In some areas Women's Clinics have already been established, and perhaps this service could be expanded to target younger women.

Comprehensive Sex Education Programmes need to be delivered within the school system (but could also be adapted to suit other contexts such as youth work). This initiative was seen by female respondents (F1) as a positive measure to promote sexual health among both males and females.

Perceived inconsistencies in the content and delivery of Personal Development Courses suggest that, from a young person's perspective, teachers are not always suitable for delivering these courses, and those most at risk, who have probably already left the school system or attend irregularly, do not benefit from them in any case (See: Literature Review 3.3.1).

The SEHB region has a higher rate of teenage pregnancy than the national average (See Quantitative Chapter, 2.9.2). In the focus group sessions young women stated that early motherhood is not a preferred option for them, but they know that contraception is not always reliable or even practised. The young females are aware of a gap in their knowledge regarding information about safe sexual practices, but see current education on this issue through schools as ineffective. They recommend a revision both of course content and methods of delivery to supplement the information (most probably inaccurate) gained on a continuous basis on the streets.

A local walk-in service available to young people who are perhaps experiencing a crisis and even contemplating suicide, was suggested by an older male focus group (M1). Young males' knowledge is limited regarding existing health services, including psychological and psychiatric services and how to access them. Waiting lists for such services, which can vary from one Health Board to another, can also cause existing service to appear ineffectual to a young person requiring immediate support.

Although school counsellors can be seen to offer an instant support service, young males are often alienated within the school system, and can see school counsellors as inappropriate to their needs. A walk-in service available locally could provide an immediate response to a young person's needs, and could facilitate the young person to explore further options available to him or her.

The 'gap' already identified in services provided for those under and over eighteen years and the need for an expanded aftercare service, could both be met by a walk-in service. This type of service could provide a practical way of addressing the immediate needs of a young person in crisis, and could also offer additional aftercare services to individuals adjusting to the withdrawal of services that had been available to them up to the age of eighteen.

A Confidential Telephone Line suggested in one area (F4) as a possible service, appears to be based upon the Childline concept but would operate on a local basis.

The findings indicate that young people are capable of accurately identifying their own needs. However young people currently have little influence or control over services put in place to meet their needs. The young people involved in this project have proposed services based on their own identified needs, which reflect issues that are of concern for health service providers. The National Children's Strategy (2000) insists that *"children will receive quality supports and services to promote all aspects of their development"*; for this to be achieved, the information gathered here from the young people themselves can hopefully provide information to influence the provision of services which they will accept and use to meet their needs.

6.3 Education

6.3.1 Introduction

The Department of Education and Science has a statutory responsibility for providing compulsory education for young people. Young people spend a significant proportion of their lives in an educational setting which constitutes a major element of their social reality. This section explores their perceptions of education under the headings of Attitudes to school, Transition Year and Leaving Certificate Vocational Programmes, Alternative Education Programmes, Third Level Education and Future Plans, and Extra-Curricular Activities.

6.3.2 Attitudes to school

All the focus group participants (regardless of age) expressed one common attitude – that given the choice they would prefer to attend school. However this did not necessarily mean that all the respondents attended school on a regular basis, and this factor is explored in the following sections.

Primary School - The respondents who attended primary school, both female and male, were generally positive about school. Individuals were able to identify particular teachers and subjects that they especially liked, suggesting that at primary school young people are generally able to identify aspects of their school experiences that they enjoy and that are relevant to their needs.

Their future transition from primary to post-primary school was viewed by most of the respondents as offering potential benefits. The majority of those transferring had older siblings in the post-primary school to which they were moving. None of the respondents acknowledged the existence of any induction programmes to ease their transition from primary to secondary level however. This suggests either that the young people were unaware of them, or that they were unavailable within their schools.

Secondary School - All the respondents cited the importance of the social interaction that took place within the school context. This does not mean that the social activities were always viewed positively, but even those respondents who recounted negative experiences still attended school (albeit irregularly), suggesting that at least some of their needs were being met.

Young people in school whose student population was largely urban-based were acutely aware of inequalities within the school system. This reflects the social constructionist theory that selection of pupils for particular roles is based on their social background (See: Literature Review 3.1.1.3).

This assigning of roles could be offered as an explanation for those experiencing a 'loss of identity' – that the education system is failing to offer meaningful roles to many young people or is allotting them unacceptable roles, leading to internal and external conflict for individuals and a consequent 'mismatch' of expectations and needs.

Young people's ability to critically analyse the school system, seeing its inequalities as established and regarding themselves as potentially challenging perceived inequalities, may influence the way they choose to participate in the school system. The behaviours described in the findings indicate that these young peoples' responses reflect a combination of simultaneously rejecting and challenging the system.

Some of the young people prefer to "mitch" classes, placing themselves at risk of falling behind their more compliant peers. This activity was cited mainly by young females and seen as a conscious choice. Direct confrontation with teachers by others, particularly young males, illustrates negative relationships with staff. Such views are also reported by early school leavers in the WAP (1998) research report.

Therefore these young people can be viewed as 'at risk' of becoming early school leavers. It could be argued that young people who exhibit behaviours such as rejection and/or challenge are unconsciously colluding in their own disempowerment. Usually the consequences of these behaviours are exclusion and alienation from the system, with the predictable outcome for some of leaving school with few or no qualifications.

In rural areas, where schools had a smaller population and friendships were maintained from primary school, the loss of identity was not seen as a significant issue by respondents. In contrast young people felt that they were known as individuals and that the teachers were helpful in general.

6.3.3 Transition Year and Leaving Certificate Vocational Programmes

Transition Year and Leaving Certificate Vocational Programmes were viewed mainly as positive experiences, suggesting that these initiatives are meeting the needs of some young people who might previously have become detached from the education system.

However these programmes were not without criticism. Male participants wanted more practical work and work experience. The females cited cases where work experience placements had involved inappropriate or meaningless tasks for students, suggesting that a possible mismatch can develop between work placement requirements and the needs of young people, leading students to becoming dissatisfied with a programme which they initially viewed positively.

Constant monitoring of these programmes is important, especially regarding placements, to ensure that placement tasks are appropriate. (In the case cited above, the school intervened to reorganise the placement.) Work placements have the potential to offer significant benefits for potential employers and students alike.

6.3.4 Alternative Education Programmes

A number of participants did not attend mainstream education, but instead attended alternative education programmes such as YouthReach and Traveller Training Centres, either through recommendation or through having felt excluded from their original school.

Although the participants consistently attended these alternative programmes and appreciated the weekly allowance involved, their perception of the curricula and methods of delivery were generally negative. The referral of these young people from the mainstream to alternative education programmes indicates that a mismatch had occurred between what the school has to offer and what the participants required.

However it appears that mismatches are also occurring in alternative education programmes, which are specifically targeted responses. For some individuals, involvement in these programmes adds to their feelings of exclusion, isolation and rejection.

Given a choice, the respondents would prefer to attend mainstream education and remain with their friends. This again indicates the importance of peer groups and of the social interaction that occurs in the school context.

While from a school perspective a student may be regarded as disruptive or anti-social, and an alternative programme and centre seen as the only option, it appears that the positive support a young person experiences through social interaction within the school context is of great importance to their identity and sense of wellbeing.

Therefore removal from the mainstream is a critical decision, and may not be the most appropriate intervention.

6.3.5 Third Level Education and Future Plans

The majority of male participants did not indicate any ambition to attend third level. Females on the other hand did, but their understanding of the educational requirement for their career of choice was often vague and unstructured. Current statistics (See: Quantitative Chapter 2.13.2) illustrate than in County Wexford young females are more likely to complete second level education than males, but have low transfer rates to third level.

The fact that County Wexford did not have any third level facility until recently, and that it has one of the highest proportions of early school leavers nationally (See: Quantitative Chapter 2.13.2.3), suggests that expectations of preventing early school leaving and of increased transfers to third level are based on unreliable foundations.

The Education (Welfare) Bill 1999 offers the potential for schools to develop and implement programmes at local level to tackle non-attendance and early school leaving. Many Wexford schools are currently implementing various measures to encourage and support students with specific needs and their families, but the effectiveness of these programmes will not be visible for some time.

In one school attended by focus group participants a Stay-in-School programme had been in operation for nearly two years. The female respondents that attended the school spoke about the programme enthusiastically. In contrast the males never mentioned the programme, other than to criticise the rules that prevented "mitching". The opposing female and male views of the programme are quite stark, but as in general males did not associate their future plans with third level, therefore a Stay-in-School programme may not have the same appeal for them as for females who had ambitions to go on to further education.

However the availability of other training options available to school leavers, such as PLC courses and YouthTrain, FAS and CERT courses, etc., were only identified by one focus group (F4). This may be due to the fact that respondents did not think of them at the time of the interview, but it could also mean that they were unaware of such opportunities.

Therefore a gap may exist between encouraging young people to remain in school to complete the secondary cycle and offering clear options to them after they leave school, whether further education, training or employment.

6.3.6 Extra Curricular Activities

All schools offered additional activities such as sports, debating, drama, etc, but the majority of respondents did not participate in these, mainly because respondents did not mix with peer groups associated with the activities.

No respondents mentioned the home-school liaison service, either because none had personal experience of this service or because they lacked knowledge of the role of the home school liaison person in their school.

The respondents who were aware of school counsellors generally believed them to be ineffective. This suggests that the role of teachers as counsellors needs to be assessed, and that school may not be the most appropriate context for offering such a service.

6.4 Youth Services

6.4.1. Introduction

It is clearly illustrated by the findings that young people do not differentiate between activities, entertainment and youth work. Initially the concept of Youth Services needed to be discussed within the focus groups to clarify what the term actually meant (See: Youth Service Findings 5.4.2). Youth services are explored under the headings of private sector services, public sector and self-organised activities. The young people's awareness of services and their views on their appropriateness are outlined, and finally the development of services they proposed to meet their needs is analysed.

6.4.2 Private Sector Services

As the findings illustrate most young people are aware of privately owned and commercial services that young people access and use within their area. These ranged from pool halls and arcades to cinemas, cafes and pubs.

The quality of these services varied. A private service that had been unsuccessful in one area for example was a cinema with a portable screen which was used occasionally in a local venue. This facility was viewed negatively by the group as the films shown were considered to be out of date and the equipment was sometimes faulty.

The global media industry promotes high quality services to the public and targets youth as a profitable customer base, setting high expectations of cinema services. (See: Literature Review 3.1.1.3). If young people are offered private services in response to a perceived gap or need, it is clear that they demand high quality in these services. Private services that do not meet the high expectations of young consumers will rarely succeed.

A major barrier to accessing services was the issue of travel, as public transport was often inadequate, parents were often either unable or unwilling to assist, and taxi fares were seen as extremely expensive.

However in one location, participants in their early and mid-teens lived within walking distance of a local cinema used regularly by other teenagers, but they rarely went there, and one respondent stated that she had never gone. Their reasons for not using such a convenient and popular service were not made clear.

The findings illustrate that some female participants in both urban and rural settings are barred from some private services. Because they operate a business, commercial services providers don't tolerate behaviour they consider inappropriate, but this applies to their adult customers too.

In one incident a respondent thought her barring from a private service was unfair as she had done nothing wrong. But other members of her peer group had previously been barred from the same premises because of their behaviour. The probability is that she was judged guilty by association, reflecting the process of labelling (See: Literature Review 3.1.1.3).

Although this instance of barring was not based on racial discrimination, during the fieldwork certain cases of discrimination against ethnic minorities were cited by participants.

A privately run non-alcoholic Road Show Disco, which visited one area four times a year, was considered expensive by its customers who nevertheless regarded it as good value. The security people prevented access to anyone under the influence of alcohol or drugs and any threats of violence were quickly controlled. It also appears that parents trusted the event organisers, as evidenced by the large numbers of young people who attended each event.

6.4.3 Community and Voluntary Sector Services

Younger Respondents - It appears that younger respondents do access and enjoy available public and community/voluntary based services, without discriminating on the basis of peer group ownership. As the findings illustrate, they are also concerned about the development of amenities for the younger children in their community.

Attachment to the family unit is stronger for pre-adolescents than for adolescents (See: Independence Findings 5.6.2). Their concern for younger children could be a reflection of this, in that they still relate to the needs of this age group, and younger siblings are important in their relationships.

However young people of this age group are not without criticism of the community/voluntary sector. For example one group told of how local adults had tried to establish a youth club, but the local hall committee had blocked the use of their premises. The young people's perception of the situation was that the adults had generally let them down, when they had been willing to play their part in fundraising and participating.

The adults' perceptions of what occurred may be completely different, but the outcome for the young people who had been encouraged to look forward to this positive development was a sense of disempowerment. (It is highly probable that at least some of the adults involved also felt disempowered.)

This example provides an insight into how young people can become disillusioned, not specifically with youth services, but with adults who raise expectations which are left unmet. Therefore eliciting and acknowledging the views of young people in the establishment and maintenance of youth services is very important, especially in the light of the recently enacted Youth Work Act (2001) where local Vocational Education Committees have a statutory obligation to co-ordinate and manage youth services within their jurisdiction.

This policy proposes that one fifth of the membership of the advisory Youth Councils must be under the age of twenty. If young people are to be included in this decision-making structure, it is important that authentic representation and consultation is made real, if the voices of those hitherto marginalised is to be heard.

Older Respondents - Services for younger children such as Irish Dancing, Scouts, Brigins, community-based discos, etc., lose their appeal for the majority of teenagers as they grow older, and gradually come to be considered inappropriate.

Awareness - Initially the older teenagers' knowledge of youth services seemed quite limited. However through the group interaction, information offered indicated that young people are accessing some youth services, but are often not consciously aware that they are doing so.

Therefore youth services which may pay considerable attention to the purposes of their intervention in their reports and documentation, appear not to transfer the same meanings to their clients. It may be that this information is relayed in a way that is not understood by the young people, or that some projects at practice level do not provide this information, or perhaps that young people do not differentiate between private and community/voluntary organisations, and so do not view this information as particularly important to them.

Some respondents were not aware of youth services available to them within their area, and this suggests the need to raise young people's awareness of facilities and activities they can access. In other areas, services that once existed had been closed down, again according to young people, because of decisions made by one or more adults. The fact that young people have been seen to employ accurate critical analysis in other areas (e.g. Health and Education Findings) suggests that their citing of adults as responsible for these closures is not unreasonable.

Where groups are aware of youth services, they sometimes associate their ownership with peer groups who they choose not to mix with, and so decline to use them. The stereotyping of services associated with particular peer groups is a difficulty for service providers, especially in areas with a small population.

Appropriateness of services - A particular youth project that was identified by its clients as positive has successfully targeted young people who from an agency perspective exhibit multiple risk factors. Those who used the service appreciated it, as some of their needs are being met there, and they recommended its expansion into other client groups. Therefore the project can be regarded as successful for the client group that use it.

However those that decline to use it self-exclude from this service because of its association with the peer group that attend regularly, but they also admit they would like to attach to a similar service, if it was available to them. The sense of ownership of a youth project or club is important, but to provide a specific service to every peer group or area would be impractical, unless it was delivered by a team of youth workers operating a mobile unit.

Services currently being used by older teenagers were generally considered positively, but came under criticism regarding opening times. Those involved in youth work circles are probably already aware that young people would like existing services expanded to include late evening and weekend opening times.

Traditionally youth services have depended heavily on a volunteer base, with paid workers employed both to support volunteers and to develop and manage special projects. Considerable resources would be required to expand services to provide adequate support to young people, volunteers and paid workers alike. The current Youth Work Act 2001 maintains the emphasis on volunteerism in Youth Work.

However the findings also illustrate that young people often prefer to have adults they do not know in another context to be involved in the direct running of their clubs and projects. Therefore community or volunteer initiatives which use the skills of willing adults from the local area may be under-appreciated by young people. While not suggesting that volunteerism should be dissolved, other roles could also be considered for volunteers, for example in the co-management of projects with the young people themselves. Many volunteers may also prefer behind-the-scene roles such as fundraising or administration to direct Youth Work.

During the entire research process only one young male stated that he had been barred from a community project, but the specific reason was not supplied. As an act of solidarity his best friend subsequently boycotted the service. However these young males also availed of a number of other services within their locality, which suggests that the possibility may exist for some young people of playing one service off against another.

6.4.4 Development of services

The findings illustrate that young people are quite clear regarding what they would like from youth services. In the younger age group their needs included play areas and football posts and that green areas would be regularly maintained and looked after.

Some young people have had negative experiences regarding the development of amenities and services within their area. Their own attempts to provide amenities for themselves such as erecting goals posts, are usually undone by adults or older teenagers. It is quite possible that their attempts are viewed as unsafe by adults, but the fact that they have initiated something themselves illustrates that they are willing to work at a project they are committed to.

Older respondents who were not attached to services appeared interested in becoming involved in the setting up and operating of youth centres for themselves. Females particularly offered strategies to operate a facility which would provide a low cost, low maintenance room or building where they could socialise, and which would be available to them until late at night and on weekends. They did not want continuous adult intervention, but saw adults more in the role of caretakers who would not judge them and who they could talk to if and when they wished to.

It would appear that a development of this type of service would be fraught with insurance and security difficulties, but private sector service providers operate open door services to young people in pool halls in many towns, with relatively small numbers of staff. But as previously stated, private services are profit driven and will exclude those they consider undesirable. This does not mean that a similar approach could not be adopted by a youth service however, as long the principle was accepted from the beginning that such a service existed to generally include rather than exclude young people.

Young people view peer groups as hierarchies whose traditions are accepted (See: Independence Findings 5.6.3). Yet the literature review points out that youth culture is not static but fluid, and that trends come and go. Detachment and gaining autonomy from the family is seen as natural element of adolescent development, and the findings verify that young people tend to attach to peer groups in order to compensate for this displacement. But because peer groups are hierarchical, the behaviours of younger teenagers are heavily influenced by what they see and learn from their older counterparts. This suggests that resources targeted at older teenagers, which provided positive experiences for them and influenced their behaviours, would also have a percolating effect on the younger teenagers' attitudes and behaviours. In this way, the traditions passed on to the next generation of peer groups can be positively influenced by service providers.

6.4.5 Self-organised activities

Both female and male participants proved very capable of self-organising. For younger girls more time is spent indoors than applies to their male counterparts; older females are present on the streets, but are considerably out-numbered by males.

Peer groups show adolescents' skills at self-organising and providing mutual support. Mobile phones are used to maintain contact and to arrange meeting times and places.

Males particularly like being outdoors, playing, climbing, cycling, skateboarding, and using motorbikes, hotrods and cars when the opportunity arises. All these activities have an element of risk attached and young people are not generally safety-conscious. Some activities which are self-organised can be regarded in certain situations as being dangerous and even life-threatening (See: Literature Review 3.3.3)

If these activities were offered by youth programmes on a regular basis, young people would be able to participate under supervision and under safe conditions while still enjoying important developmental risk opportunities. Young people reluctant to attach to services but who are already self organising these activities are likely to identify immediate positive benefits for themselves in such a context. Youth activities do not necessarily have to occur in or attached to a building

Young females also self-organise into groups on the streets (See: Literature Review 3.1.1.3). However in the focus groups they stated that if they had somewhere to go which they could call their own and where they were free from parental supervision, they would not spent so much time on the streets.

Although some activities that young females self-organise may be frowned on by parents or the wider community, such disapproval does not prevent them from engaging in these behaviours. The findings in this section illustrate that young people can both identify their own needs and propose ways of meeting these needs. Their expert knowledge is available to service providers who can turn their suggestions into practical projects.

6.5 Justice

6.5.1 Introduction

The findings of the section concerning the Justice System had two themes, the young people's perceptions of illegal activities and their knowledge of the Justice system. The following analysis explores issues raised in the findings under these two headings.

6.5.2 Perceptions of Illegal Activities

It would appear that both younger respondents (i.e. those under 13) and their older counterparts are able to identify a range of illegal activities engaged in by young people. However their perceptions of the boundaries between acceptable and unacceptable activities are quite different.

The younger female participants were able to list illegal activities, but did not want to be identified with any such activities. In contrast the younger male participants appeared to glamorise illegal activities that occurred in their area, particular those involving older males. Although they see themselves as involved in *"messin'"* they did not recognise any of their own activities as illegal.

The peer group constructs its own values and applies its own boundaries to the range of illegal activities its members might participate in and consider acceptable. However the high visibility of youth culture on the streets suggests that young people seek to assert their independence from adult society by their style rather than through criminal behaviour (See: Literature Review 3.1.1.3). Yet as the findings illustrate, these young people know their activities are illegal, but they nevertheless view them as acceptable among their peers, including some that can be quite serious and even life-threatening (e.g. drinking and driving).

In all areas except one, the young people had experienced being *"moved on"* by the Gardai. The majority of young people felt this was unfair as there was nowhere else for them to go. One of the focus groups suggested that the Gardai may simply be acting on requests by adult residents to move the teenagers out of the area.

The moving on of young people has a number of aspects. Are these adults concerned for the safety of these young people that they regard as "at risk" by being on the street? Or do the adults identify this manifestation of a youth sub-culture as a tangible threat that needs to be controlled? And to what extent do the young people themselves collude in this stereotyping? After all, "moral panics" can be induced in the public mind, and young people can present appropriate behaviours, in order to fulfil the image 'assigned' to them through labelling (See: Literature Review 3.1.1.3).

From either point of view, the moving on of young people from one location to another means neither that they are removed from any perceived risk nor that their sub-culture will disappear. Furthermore it continually brings young people and Gardai into negative contact with each other, and colours the young people's view of the Gardai as a result. If young people are continually moved on at the insistence either of the Gardai or of local residents, it can only confirm for some of them their already strong sense of exclusion.

6.5.3. Knowledge of the Justice System

In the all the focus groups the main topic of discussion regarding the Justice system was their relationship with the Gardai. Those in the younger age range in both female and male focus groups generally viewed the Gardai in a neutral way. In contrast the views of the older age groups were more negative.

One female focus group (F2) had a very negative view of the Gardai and believed that young people from their area were victimised by them. They believed that this prejudice was based either on the area they lived in (which they identified as being viewed negatively by the wider community in general), or on family association where older siblings may already be known to the Gardai.

Another female group (F1) had a more comprehensive knowledge of the Justice System, but they also regarded as unfair the different ways in which young people can be treated by the Justice System.

Respondents from this focus group had admitted to being involved in illegal activity, but had never been cautioned by the Gardai. However they were also aware of and participated in the labelling of other young people in the area who from time to time had been in trouble with the Gardai. This group managed to successfully avoid similar labelling and any consequent association with illegal activity.

This point was further illustrated by their account of a male who had previously been in trouble with the Gardai and affiliated to their peer group via a relationship with one of the girls. The participants believed his behaviour had been "better" while he was linked with their group. Although he was still involved in illegal activities during this time, he had not come to the attention of the Gardai as much as previously.

Although these young women managed to avoid being labelled themselves, they attached a certain glamour to young male offenders in custody.

In general the older males viewed their relationships with the Gardai as negative. This was particular apparent in the group labelled as the *"druggies"*, a label they themselves accepted. This group felt that the Gardai picked on members of their peer group. An alternative view would suggest that the Gardai were simply carrying out their duty when they stopped and searched these young people who regularly and openly misused illegal substances. However the young people were aware of their rights (e.g. that being under fifteen, their parents needed to be contacted), and they believed these rights were occasionally violated by the Gardai. So from their perspective they had been treated unfairly.

In their focus group, these young males either did not know of or else preferred not to consider other services offered to young people by the Justice System.

The statistics for juvenile offences clearly indicate that more young males than females are dealt with by the Juvenile Justice System (Quantitative Chapter, 2.15). This may either be due to the fact that they are involved in more illegal activities, or that criminal behaviour involving women is less 'visible', and so is not prosecuted as often.

Young people's perceptions of the Justice System are based on personal experience, as is the case with most other services, but in this case their relationship, if any, with the Gardai is usually formed in negative circumstances. Young people generally believe that the Gardai act out their role as they choose, and discriminate against those living in particular areas or involved with particular peer groups. The opportunities available to Gardai to develop positive relationships with young people seem limited by these factors.

The finding that young people did not readily identify or were not aware of the Probation and Welfare Service or the JLO Service may offer opportunities for the Justice System to promote a greater awareness of these alternative ways of working with adolescents, in order to develop a more positive and constructive context for its work with young people.

6.6 Independence

6.6.1 Introduction

According to Hill (See: Literature Review 3.1.1.4), adolescent development involves a complex combination of psychosocial themes. This section explores a number of these themes ('detachment-autonomy, sexuality, identity and self-definition' (ibid.)) under the following headings:

- Family
- Peer groups
- Community Relationships
- One-to-One Relationships
- Employment

6.6.2 Family

The research illustrates that attitudes towards Family varies between age groups. In general the younger age group (aged 13 and under), and particularly younger females, complied with the wishes of the parents. This suggests that these young people are pre-adolescent and that the desire to "detach" from their parents has not yet surfaced. (See: Literature Review 3.1.1.4)

In contrast the older respondents, although aware of the benefits of being within a family irrespective of its make-up, clearly challenge boundaries set by parents and the wider family. This can be seen as their attempt to detach from the family unit and to gain individual identity. Part of this process involves the young person 'taking risks'.

However this process of 'taking risks' is fraught with pitfalls for the individual, which may alienate them from their families and may occasionally place them in life-threatening situations.

Family Conflict - The findings show that across the age range of this research some young people have a negative view of their own relationships with their families. Young people's language is often laced with terms of aggression and physical abuse (e.g. fighting, boxing and slapping) when referring to family issues and situations that they find stressful.

The findings illustrate that some young people are identified by their parents as the source of conflict in the family. Developing a positive self-image and identity within such a family context can often prove difficult if not impossible.

The findings also indicate that some young people move between houses; some whose parents are separated move back and forth between the two, while others sometimes stay with friends or relatives as a method of temporarily avoiding the family home.

Is there a direct transfer from parents' criticism and blaming of children into young people's reactive risk taking? For example, is it always irresponsible of young people to remove themselves from the immediate family context and move temporarily to a friends' or relative's house (i.e. "sofa surf")? Or could these be seen as individual coping mechanism, providing young people under pressure with a temporary break from the family home, much like the respite care provided to another participant by the Health Board?

To remove oneself from an immediate family conflict by staying away may appear reactive, but it does provide an immediate if temporary solution to a difficult problem. However, those availing of Health Board respite care have the benefit of additional supports and a structured, negotiated approach to the management of their stay. On the other hand, when a young person uses sofa surfing as a way of coping with conflict, such additional supports are lacking, and it may be impossible to negotiate a return to the family home.

Obviously the level of risk involved varies with the individual and their situation, and so is difficult to assess accurately with a view to constructive intervention by service providers. However, moving between homes will persist as an invisible though relatively common practice among young people.

Positive Family Relationships - Most young people across the age range of the study illustrated that they had positive relationships with their families. They generally recognised that family boundaries were a positive influence on them, even though they might often challenge these imposed limits. It appeared also that young people were generally trusted by parents to self-manage without overt monitoring.

6.6.3 Peer Groups

Younger respondents - The females did not acknowledge membership of a particular peer group, but liked to socialise with a wide range of people. In contrast younger males tended to stay together in groups. However the importance of peer group increased with age, in keeping with typical patterns of adolescent development (See: Literature Review 3.1.1.4). Irrespective of the groups' membership, or of the defined boundaries that separated them from rivals, all peer groups exhibited similar behaviours.

Older Respondents

Similar behaviours - The general discourse among older focus groups accepts the consumption of alcohol, drug use and sexual activity as normal activities among their peers.

Peer groups use both public and private sites for these activities (e.g. fields, laneways, 'free' houses, etc.) but each peer group claims a particular "territory" over which they express a sense of 'ownership'. Territorial divisions were clearly maintained and reinforced by stereotyping of other groups, and by creating 'in' and 'out' groups either to ally with or to regard as rivals.

Although the general public may tend to view the activities and conventions of such groups negatively (See: Literature Review 3.1.1.3) the peer group structure offers important support for young people. The peer group is a forum that young people trust.

Influence of Peer Groups - Young people who had switched their allegiance from one peer group to a rival one generally went to great lengths to illustrate their loyalty to their 'new' group. This involved either denying their membership of the now despised former group or belittling its current activities.

In some areas older male peer groups applied pressure on younger males to participate in dangerous activities and bullied them.

Participants themselves were able to suggest that peer groups operate in a hierarchical structure that is understood, accepted and sustained across the full range of teenage years. One instance of prejudice against young people from a different geographical location (F1) indicates the strength of conventions within and between groups; the participant's attitude here was based on an inherited tradition and never questioned.

Considering the importance of peer groups, and the hierarchical structure that endows older groups with the power to influence younger ones, a seemingly logical approach by service providers would be to make resources available to work initially with older teenagers. However this approach presents its own difficulties which are discussed in detail in the section on Development of Youth Services.

6.6.4 Relationships

Community Relationships - In general, all the respondents felt safe living within their communities. However their perception of others, and of others' views of them, was dependant on considerations of age and class.

As young people they are aware that their presence on the streets and in public spaces causes friction between themselves and adults within the community. However they generally state that they have nowhere else to go.

This does not necessarily mean that services and amenities are not available locally, although some communities are clearly better provided for than others. Many young people lack the resources to access those amenities that are in or near their area. Also adults, either individually or collectively, can often limit or entirely prevent young people's access to facilities. And some services or locations are considered inappropriate, either by the parents of the young people, or by their own peer group who will self-exclude rather than associate with a rival group.

Young females are class conscious, and most participants were aware that their area was associated with a particular social class. Those that identified the reputation of their area in negative terms stated that they did not care what people thought of them, but they also thought such labelling was unfair. Young people's ability to analyse and identify issues for themselves is often underestimated, but can be sharp and accurate.

However, their ability to analyse issues does not mean that they try to change them. The unspoken acceptance of peer group conventions indicates the difficulty of challenging traditions or patterns of behaviour within an area, either for the young person or for an intervening adult.

One-to-one Relationships - The findings indicate that one-to-one relationships are initiated generally in the years between twelve and fourteen, and that by the age of fifteen many young people are involved in intimate relationships. The establishment of one's sexual identity is seen as a natural element of adolescent development (See: Literature Review 3.1.1.4). Older respondents (aged seventeen and over) chose not to speak about their one-to-one relationships.

In general young people believed that families had a negative view of teen pregnancy, but pregnancy outside marriage at a later stage would be acceptable. This mirrors the general attitude in Irish society towards marriage and parenthood. (See: Literature Review 3.3.2).

6.6.5 Employment

A personal income can prove crucial to a young person's achieving independence and autonomy. In particular parts of County Wexford high unemployment rates persist, despite the recent economic growth of the national economy (See: Quantitative Chapter 2.16).

The findings show that some young people in the county are apathetic about employment and believe that job opportunities for them simply do not exist. But little analysis was offered on the topic.

In contrast others suggested barriers that they perceived as preventing them from securing employment, including the presence in their area of foreign workers. Although the majority in one group rejected this view, some young people clearly hold racist views, which may warrant further research.

Many of the young people in full time employment worked in the catering industry, traditionally associated with low rates of pay for young workers. Early school leavers are more likely to work in low paid jobs (ibid.), but these young people were generally unaware of training programmes and accreditation systems within the catering industry. Indeed, participants generally seemed to have only the vaguest knowledge regarding the educational qualifications required for their career options (See: Education Findings 5.3.8).

In one particular rural area, most young males and females stated that they did not have any difficulty in obtaining employment, but their work was mainly gained through family connections. Young people from other rural areas also acknowledged their good fortune in having links into families that operated businesses.

Therefore family contacts and social networks may play a more significant part in securing work (particularly part-time or temporary work) for young people in rural areas.

6.7 Cultural Needs

6.7.1 Introduction

The social reality of young people's lives is embedded in their everyday activities. Through the research it was possible to identify prevailing cultural trends and these are analysed under the headings of Information and Communications Technologies, Media, Community, Different Backgrounds and Creative and Leisure Activities.

6.7.2 Information & Communications Technologies (ICTs)

The findings illustrate that ICTs are regarded differently by respondents of different ages. Younger respondents included the use of computers and the Internet in their general conversation, and also mention computer games, DVDs and mobile telephones. From comments made by those at the upper end of the age range, mobile telephones seem to be more important in the lives of older teenagers than either computer games or the Internet.

However in one focus group none of the respondents used a mobile phone, and their conversation rarely referred to text messaging or other uses of mobile phones.

This exception would seem to indicate a form of social disadvantage for these respondents, as other young people use mobile telephones regularly and for a variety of purposes – to initiate, establish and monitor relationships and to communicate and self-organise within the peer group. More research is needed to explain this anomaly in the findings.

In promoting a holistic approach to childhood development, the National Children's Strategy (2000) recommends the provision of widespread access to computers. The fact that younger respondents seem to be very familiar with the Internet offers service providers a powerful new method of involving and collaborating with young people.

International media enterprises dominate contemporary information exchange, and consumers who are able to connect with the prevailing 'global culture' via the Internet will inevitably be placed at an advantage over those who lack resources (See : Literature Review 3.3.1).

If ICTs are to be employed in promoting the inclusion of young people in matters that affect them, service providers must ensure that supports are put in place to enable *all* young people to have adequate access and training in these technologies.

Although all schools promote the use of ICTs in their curricula, provision of hardware and software is not distributed equally. Some schools acquire extra equipment through voucher schemes marketed by supermarkets and other commercial organisations. This method of equipping schools, based as it is on the purchasing power of parents, can only compound other aspects of inequality experienced by children from disadvantaged communities.

6.7.3 Media

All respondents made reference to television as a feature of their everyday lives. In the focus groups they frequently used examples from TV programmes to add colour and meaning to their descriptions of experiences and ideas.

This finding supports the argument that global media corporations have increasingly gained ownership of 'Youth Culture', and have transformed it into a commodity to be marketed to adolescent consumers (See Literature Review 3.1.1.3).

However not all the implications of this relationship are negative. In this case, the medium of television has helped young people to develop and clarify their own needs and preferences. The media used in this manner can literally provide a picture to young people of what is possible for them.

The types of programme younger teenagers prefer was seen to be divided by gender. Female respondents tended to watch soap operas and 'teenage' dramas such as *Sabrina the Teenage Witch*. In contrast, males preferred sports programmes, often those associated with 'macho' representations of maleness such as wrestling.

It can be argued that programmes targeted at young people contribute to and maintain stereotyping through their traditional representations of gender and social roles. It is perhaps inevitable that the role models and situations presented on TV will reflect the underpinning values of the system that produces and markets these programmes. Education services must develop critical competencies in young consumers, enabling them to 'read' and judge underlying assumptions in the products and services that help shape their culture.

The findings illustrate that young people are eager consumers of merchandise associated with programmes and films. In theory the opportunity to acquire these items is based purely on spending power, but young people do sometimes choose to subvert the established order through shoplifting (See: Justice Findings 5.5.2) and illegal copying of videos and software files and programmes.

Cinema is popular among young people. Almost all respondents from areas without a cinema listed this as a priority requirement for their community. Perhaps the most startling finding however concerned respondents from an estate, within walking distance of a popular cinema, who had rarely attended, with one respondent stating that she had never been to see a film there. These thirteen to fifteen year-olds gave no specific reasons why they didn't use the cinema.

Music was important to some. Respondents' choice ranged from heavy-metal, through nu-metal, dance and rave to pop groups like Six. The older respondents were aware of the commercialism of music, but accepted this as inevitable. This indicates how young people can willingly accept consumerism without questioning its construction. A minority of respondents played music, which they learned by attending music lesson (e.g. piano) or in the family context (e.g. violin), but these respondents also loved their own 'brand' of commercial music.

Printed media seem to have relatively little impact on youth culture. Local newspapers were referred to only in relation to their reporting of incidents in the young people's local areas; magazines were mentioned once, in connection with standard representations of physical attractiveness, in a discussion relating to eating disorders.

This suggests that these young people have comparatively little day-to-day contact with the print media, and visual news and entertainment predominates in their world.

6.7.4 Community

All the respondents felt safe where they lived and had a sense of belonging to their community, although two factors identified by different focus groups (F1 and M3) threatened to erode this sense of belonging: rapid population increase in towns within the Dublin commuter belt, and large private housing developments in small villages. Urban and rural difference and the perpetuation of social class difference were highlighted by another focus group (F2), illustrating that young people are quite willing to analyse their own situations, without necessarily desiring or knowing how to challenge established social relations.

Urban and Rural Differences - The findings highlight particular situations where rapid urban expansion can give rise to negative attitudes towards 'outsiders' taking up residence in the locality. In different areas these 'outsiders' are identified either by their origin (e.g. *"Dubliners"*), or by their status (e.g. *"rich people"*).

The perception of the young people in these locations is that their communities are becoming segregated and they no longer know their neighbours. Self-identity is important to adolescents, but in areas where rapid expansion is occurring, young people have no influence on that development, and their sense of belonging is threatened.

It is hardly surprising therefore when young people identify particular groups (e.g. *"Dubliners"*) with the disintegration of what they regard as 'their' community. A greater awareness of local government systems would help young people to understand the involvement of Planning Officers and the County Council in urban expansion (See also: Political Involvement Findings 5.8.2 and Analysis 6.8.2).

Social Class - The female respondents analysed social class differences more acutely than their male counterparts. This may suggest that females are more conscious of class hierarchies than males, but further research is needed here. However, participants frequently identified mature middle-class women as expressing and perpetuating negative attitudes towards specific residential areas and those who live there.

This creating of divisions between areas is seen by the young people to be based on social class. Its effects on those living in the denigrated areas is difficult to assess, as compensating positive factors within a community can often counteract such negative assessments (See: Literature Review 3.4).

This process of division may not be quite as deep-rooted and pervasive as the young people believe. But the experiences of social division they have identified are likely to be perpetuated unless effective methods of challenging such social exclusion are established.

6.7.5 Different Backgrounds

The younger age groups referred to people moving into and out of their locality and to people they had met on holiday abroad, but without making value judgements on observed ethnic or cultural differences. However older respondents expressed both positive and negative views about their encounters with people from various backgrounds.

This finding confirms that older adolescents have more opportunities to meet people from different backgrounds, as they begin to move outside their immediate area. Also as they mature, adolescents' cognitive abilities increase, enabling them to examine and analyse experiences and concepts more thoroughly (See: Literature Review 3.1.1.4).

The respondents' analysis of the backgrounds of groups different from their own focused on ethnic origins, urban and rural differences, and social class.

Ethnic minorities identified by respondents were mainly from East European countries. A majority of the young people indicated that they were anti-racist, and within the focus groups they directly challenged the negative racial comments of the minority. However in other contexts such as school, racial comments overheard had not generally been challenged by the participants.

The focus groups recruited for this project were based on peer groups, which offer a forum that young people can trust (See also: Independence Findings 5.6.3 and Analysis 6.6.3). Within these peer groups it was seen as acceptable to speak openly, to express personal opinions and to challenge others' views.

However, challenging opinions encountered outside the peer group, whether from adults or other young people, is not so easy. For young people who already feel alienated from many systems, openly challenging racism outside their peer group can prove difficult if not impossible. This does not mean that they refuse to combat racism, but that a gap exists between the values they hold and their willingness to publicly declare those values.

Interestingly none of the respondents identified Travellers as "different" or as having their own cultural identity. Yet throughout the fieldwork, young members of the Traveller Community related incidents of prejudice against them because of their ethnic identity.

As a minority group, Travellers who comprise 0.5% of the total national population (See: Quantitative Chapter 2.7.1) regularly come into contact with 'settled people' in a wide variety of contexts – schools, shops, church, etc. However the majority of settled people do not necessarily come into direct contact with Travellers every day, and so they can remain relatively invisible to mainstream society. Therefore some young people, while viewing travellers as a distinctive population within Irish society, may not regard them as comprising an ethnic group with its own culture and identity. Travellers are predominantly young, with 50% of the Traveller population under the age of fourteen (ibid.), and the Traveller Community suffers more discrimination than any other ethnic group living in the country (Task Force Report, 1995).

Adults working for and with young people have a clear responsibility to constantly question their own views and assumptions, and to guard against being seen to endorse opinions that promote prejudice and exclusion.

6.7.6 Creative and Leisure Activities

Younger Respondents - Opportunities to participate in organised creative activities (e.g. arts and crafts, drama and variety shows) were generally taken up by younger male and female respondents, who participated regardless of who else might be involved. In contrast, their older counterparts tended to regard facilities and locations as 'owned' by particular peer groups, and so self-excluded from many opportunities offered by service providers. This difference can be linked to the finding that peer group influence has less significance in the lives of younger adolescents (See: Independence Findings 5.6.3).

However there was a significant difference in the leisure activities preferred by females and males. Younger males spent more time outside the home, playing GAA and soccer (both self-organised and through clubs), cycling and skateboarding, driving motorbikes and cars, and playing with their friends in fields, lane-ways and open spaces.

Young females on the other hand seemed to spend much of their time indoors, watching TV and playing with siblings and/or friends, and when outside the home generally engaged in organised and supervised activities, in contrast to their male counterparts who would seem to have a far greater degree of freedom in organising their leisure time.

The prevalence of this tendency for girls to operate in domestic and controlled environments may be surprising, as we tend to expect that modern society no longer allots the conventional functions of home maker and carer exclusively to females. Yet it seems that gender differences and traditional roles still have a powerful influence on the behaviour of pre-adolescent females, and their compliance in fulfilling these stereotypes can often be encouraged by conventional images and messages conveyed by popular magazines, TV programmes and other media.

Older Respondents - Older adolescents had generally participated in similar activities until aged thirteen or fourteen, but after this their involvement with their peer group tended to take precedence (See: Youth Services Findings 5.4.1).

Sport - The main difference highlighted among young males was between those who played sport and those who did not. For some, sport can be experienced as an inclusive activity (See Literature Review 3.1.1.3), but inequalities around family and community resources relating to money, facilities, transport and coaching do exist and can cause exclusion for some. Even the cost of football boots and shin guards can sometimes be enough to discourage a young person from joining a football club.

Sports provides positive opportunities for talented participants, but those who have access to additional tuition and organised training have clear advantages over those who don't. While natural talent cannot be created through coaching, nevertheless confidence, ambition and skills can be developed and promoted.

Those who are less competitive or less athletic can also find themselves excluded from a wide variety of activities and opportunities accessed through sport. In every community, organised sport receives significant ongoing investment of volunteers' resources of time, abilities and funds; resources of capacity and commitment which potentially exist in every community, and which can transform the lives of young people at risk when harnessed effectively by organisations serving their needs.

Spiritual Beliefs - The National Children's Strategy (2000) states that a holistic approach towards children's development should include consideration of their spiritual and moral well-being. Only one respondent referred to organised religion, in connection with his Confirmation Day which was to be a big family occasion. Since no other specific mention of religion or spirituality was made in any of the other focus groups, it would be inappropriate to offer any analysis on this topic.

6.8 Political Involvement- Participation and Decision Making

6.8.1 Introduction

The National Children's Strategy (2000) provides a legislative framework for involving young people in matters that affect them. However as previously highlighted (Literature Review 3.6) young people have traditionally been excluded from decision-making. The next sections explore young people's perceptions of their involvement in decision-making, in mainstream politics and in the development of participation strategies which involve young people.

6.8.2 Perception of Involvement in Decision-Making

From the findings it is apparent that very few opportunities currently exist for young people to become involved at any level in decision-making processes on matters that affect them. Mechanisms that do exist such as School Councils were viewed cynically by focus group members, and regarded as the reserve of elite groups. Opportunities for participation were seen as tokenistic and lacking in any substantial influence. This is not to deny that those who do become involved in School Councils may derive significant benefits and acquire valuable skills from their participation, whether or not others reject them as inappropriate.

One positive reaction to participation was cited in another school in a different area, in regard to the consultative aspects of the Stay-in-School programme. What the participants saw as authentic participation and involvement evoked their enthusiastic support and identifiable results.

It could be argued that involvement here is at a low level, and that the real decisions of how the school is run remain with the adults. However this particular process included all students and staff, giving them equal input into the drawing up of the school cafeteria menu. It could be seen as a useful and imaginative first step in building capacities among young people to develop their decision-making and participation skills.

Maintenance of participants and ongoing motivation is important. Some focus group members had become disillusioned with a youth project in which they were involved to varying degrees, stating: *"It's pointless though"*. The young people's perception was that they don't in fact possess a lot of power, and ultimately the real decisions are made by the adults.

The fact that young people can analyse their own position in the wider context can provide a starting point to changing that position, if they so wish. Even the act of identifying oneself as "powerless" could be the necessary spark to begin the process of empowerment (See: Literature Review 3.6).

6.8.3 Political Parties and Elections

No participant expressed interest in organised politics. The traditional canvassing approach and electioneering in general failed to impress those focus group participants who encountered it.

6.8.4 Development of Participation Strategies to Involve Young People

Traditionally young people have been excluded from decision-making, and initiatives are now being promoted to encourage the participation of young people, "giving them a voice in matters that affect them" (National Children's Strategy, 2000). This development was supported in the findings where consultation with young people and their participation in decision-making was widely approved of by participants.

However it was clear that the process would have to be relevant to them, that it had to be a process that could be trusted, and that young people would not become involved just for the sake of it. Therefore participation, inclusion and decision-making must be underpinned by mutual trust, and must provide identifiable benefits for those involved.

Most respondents had experience of services and amenities that had either been promised and never materialised, or had operated successfully and then shut down for whatever reason. The view of the young people in each case was that "they", the service providers or adults, had broken faith. These young people were made more sceptical of the benefits of involvement as a result.

Therefore, if the inclusion of young people in matters that affect them is to be authentic, real consultation must inform the process, open exchange of information must be maintained, and clear and immediate benefits must be provided to the participants.

6.9 Engagement Strategies

This section is based on the researchers' perspective, and considers the engagement processes employed during the research. It considers both detached and thematic entry points and their use in the recruitment of focus groups.

As previously described (See: Findings, Engagement Strategies, 5.9.2.4) the researchers believe that the detached method of approaching young people better reflects the principles of equality, as the young people are provided with a free choice whether to participate or not.

As the findings illustrate the majority of respondents identified the detached method as a positive experience, and all stated that they would speak to adults who approached them in this way. The fact that young people are willing to give their opinions and ideas to adults, as illustrated in various sections of this report, indicates an enthusiasm for involvement that adults perhaps sometimes underestimate.

However the recruitment of volunteers for focus groups proved more challenging. One focus group (organised through thematic entry) was halted, as the respondents stated that they did not trust the process, and became disruptive. The information gathered to this point was subsequently supplemented by individual interviews.

These respondents had communicated openly with the researchers over several days during informal activity-based sessions prior to the focus group. But on the introduction of the more formal focus group structure (seating around a table, tape recorder, introduction of topics, etc.) they rejected the process, despite their earlier commitments to participate. This may indicate that young people will reject methods quickly and in an uncompromising way, if they feel uncomfortable.

In contrast those that had been approached via detached engagement methods experienced an initial nervousness regarding the focus group. But some had prepared for the interaction by discussing issues among themselves prior to the interview, and later stated that once the process had begun they were able to talk unselfconsciously and felt relaxed.

The initial lack of enthusiasm of young people to participate in focus groups could result from a variety of reasons. Particularly in thematic entry points, young people appeared to be concerned about being identified as a "snitch", and the participants initially associated the researchers with the service that had been used to gain access to them. Therefore speaking to researchers during a taped interview could be regarded as "snitching".

In detached areas where recruitment to focus groups proved challenging, the incentive of a day's activity was offered, providing an identifiable and immediate reward to participants.

Involvement in the process itself seemed to prove rewarding for the participants, as the respondents generally stated that they enjoyed the experience. However the promise of a positive experience alone appeared to be inadequate for most young people, perhaps because of their common perception that adults representing organisations frequently break their promises of services and amenities, and are in general not to be trusted.

Is it therefore realistic for us as service providers to expect young people to freely volunteer to participate in the running of what have traditionally been adult controlled services? To create quotas of seats for young people on decision-making committees is unlikely to provide a place at the conference table for those young people who don't attach to any service.

It is more likely that these places will be filled by those that have developed skills to promote their points of view (e.g. the *Posh Ones* of the School Council) leading to possible further disempowerment and isolation of excluded young people.

The "expert knowledge" gained from young people in this way may lead to the expansion, development and establishment of services that suit the needs of certain groups, but which would be inappropriate for the very groups that service providers are trying to target – those that display multiple characteristics of being "at risk". The mismatch of their needs and any services intended for them would remain unresolved.

The research has indicated that speaking to young people in their own social context, giving them a free choice to participate or not, and offering them immediate benefits provide a way of engaging with young people who would not usually participate in processes that involved adult interventions.

The National Children's Strategy (2000) states that all young people have the right to have their voices listened to. Appropriate methods need to be devised to encourage the meaningful inclusion of those young people who often find themselves excluded, for whatever reason, from services and supports available to other adolescents.

Chapter Seven
Research Conclusions

7 Introduction

From the outset, a holistic approach was adopted in this research project to investigate adolescents' perceptions of their own needs and the supports available to them in their environment. This holistic approach is based on the psycho-social themes of adolescent development identified by Hill, (i.e. detachment-autonomy; intimacy; sexuality; achievement; and identity), which he links with bio-psychosocial factors (e.g. puberty; cognition; self-definition) and contextual influences generated in the wider environment (gender; race-ethnicity and social class) (Adams et al, 1996: p2) (See also: Literature Review, 3.1.1.4).

The method employed in interviewing participants was Participatory Narrative Inquiry (See: 4.1.1), a process which facilitates young people in exploring and identifying issues and topics. The information provided in the engagements included the young people's own perceptions of risk, the supports and actions that they needed from services, and suggested ways of meeting those needs across a range of sectors and situations.

The Thematic Framework (See: 4.6.2), used both to organise and present the information yielded by the research, is based on the project's holistic perspective. The Conclusions which follow are presented in the same order of nine subsections as used in the Findings and Analysis chapters (See: Ch. 5 and 6). An Overall Conclusion closes the chapter.

7.1 Risk and Resilience

Risk - Vulnerable young people are often exposed to a multiplicity of risks, and an increase in the number of risk factors that apply in their behaviours and environment exponentially increases their level of vulnerability (See: Literature Review 3.3). But 'risk' behaviours and situations as defined by agencies and organisations are not always seen in the same way by young people, who in some cases treat such perceived 'risks' as normal and acceptable within their culture.

On the other hand, young people generally regard anyone who cannot be trusted, be they adult or peer, as a potential 'risk' to them, and feel that becoming involved with such a person places them 'at risk'.

Therefore a gap exists between the concept of risk as defined by agencies and by the young people themselves. If this gap is to be bridged through consultation and participation, it can only be done if the core principle of trust underpins all connections between young people and service providers. And points of contact are the interface where trust and risk become intertwined for these two groups.

Currently young people who attempt to access services they do not trust are taking a significant risk, especially if they are involved in illegal activities. Yet traditionally services have been organised in the expectation that young people will choose to enter the domain of the adult. The power relationship between an adult supported by an organisation and a young person (probably with few resources) coming through the door generally favours the adult. Young people's participation in the ensuing process will be further influenced by any indications they might interpret as implying a preconceived agenda.

On the other hand, if young people are not even aware of the existence of a service, then access is not the principal issue. If appropriate information of a service is not readily available to them, young people who either lack the skills to obtain information for themselves or who are alienated from existing systems, can often be excluded, regardless of how 'user-friendly' the service strives to be.

Problems of access to information can be eased, and the power relationship between adult and adolescent can be adjusted, through the adult approaching young people in their environment and on their terms. When such an adult becomes identifiable, visible and familiar in young people's everyday lives, the point of access to services is moved from the adult domain into the domain of the young person. Therefore the element of risk for the young person in becoming involved is reduced, as the interface is relocated. Within their own environment, young people are more likely to respond positively to any approach, as their community provides young people with a sense of identity and confidence, giving them a feeling of security they can lack in other contexts.

The risk is increased for the adult however, who must now trust the young person not to reject them. Therefore in some ways the power imbalance is redressed, and during the ensuing process of interaction between the young person and the adult, a new equilibrium is established.

Resilience - Resilience Theory centres on the observation that although many young people can be exposed to similar risk factors, some prove to be more successful in overcoming adversity than others, due mainly to personal characteristics and the supports available to them from their family, their personal networks and the wider community.

Those who display factors of resilient behaviour are able to identify positive qualities in themselves, and are able to develop successful coping mechanisms to meet the challenges they face. In contrast, those less resilient exhibit negative attitudes to their situations and appear less able to feel in control of their lives. The building of resilience can be encouraged and developed among vulnerable young people by strengthening the supports to them at individual, family and community levels.

It can be argued that the provision of such supports simply reinforces social inequality, and advocates an attitude of complacency and acceptance among those most already socially excluded. Encouraging vulnerable young people to merely cope with their situation will not help bring about the economic and social changes that are essential in providing them with meaningful opportunities to develop to their full potential.

However the possibility for any young person to achieve their potential is negligible if they are in a state of constant vulnerability or negativity, regardless of the opportunities provided.

Resilience theory argues the existence of a 'turning point' which can often cause a young person to fundamentally reassess their situation and the coping strategies they employ. Turning points can be provided by seemingly minor experiences or encounters, or can be the result of an incremental shift in perspective over time. The ripple effect of such turning points can have a profound effect on a growing person's life, and consequently, on the lives of those around them.

The turning point may result in the young person being able to cope more effectively with negative issues in their immediate situation, but may also enable them to make conscious choices to seek change through processes of participation and empowerment in the longer term. Provision and delivery of appropriate services that seek to build resilience can serve both to support the individual and to provide greater resources to the family, the immediate social environment and the wider community. Such initiatives can act as a catalyst for change.

7.2 Health

The Department of Health and Children is responsible for a wide range of services for young people. It has published a great deal of research regarding both behaviours associated with health risks among young people and the factors which can influence their vulnerability. This data has been used as a basis for providing Health Services to meet the needs of young people throughout the country.

The associated behaviours identified as increasing both short term and long term health risks include alcohol consumption, substance misuse, sexual activity, and reckless or drunk driving. Yet these activities are considered by the majority of adolescents involved in this research to be 'normal' youth behaviours within their culture. They participate regularly in such behaviours without necessarily considering the consequences of their actions. This suggests that the numbers of young people using confidential services as a consequence of being involved in these behaviours will continue to increase in the future.

Because adolescents still gain much of their information from 'the street' where these behaviours originate, and because younger children can be exposed to and tend to imitate the behaviours of their older peers, it is likely that such behaviours will be perpetuated into the next generation of adolescents.

But Irish youth are no different from their counterparts in other countries. Global youth culture has created a market in which products and services are marketed through the mass media using sophisticated and persuasive selling techniques that promote 'cool' and 'sexy' values and behaviours focused on immediate gratification. Young people are continuously presented with images and messages that define and idealise narrow stereotypes

– of physical beauty, of material comfort, of lifestyle, of sexual and emotional attachment, and of drug and alcohol consumption.

Against this backdrop it is inevitable that the majority of adolescents will find themselves exposed from time to time to various social pressures and risk situations. Those with low resilience and few supports are more likely to develop emotional and behavioural problems, leading in some cases to self- harm and even suicide.

Young people are pragmatic about the Health services available to them, and only attempt to access services when they are ill or in need of specific care (e.g. in pregnancy). Health services are regarded by these clients as existing to 'cure' rather than 'prevent' illness. The respondents in this project see services as available through the Department of Health and Children, and generally have little awareness of services provided through the Community and Voluntary Sector.

Yet the Community and Voluntary Sector offers many health-based initiatives, including addiction services, counselling services, health and fitness programmes and information services, which are more readily available to young people under eighteen than those offered through the Health Boards (although some community and voluntary initiatives do not work with under-eighteens).

Most young people access the health services with the assistance of their parents. This involvement of parents will naturally apply in most cases, but some children are inevitably unable to depend on such assistance. In extreme cases parents themselves can be the cause of the child's ill-health or injury.

The variety of family units emerging in today's society suggests additional forms of family support will be required in the future. Separated and reconstituted families provide significant support opportunities for some children and adolescents, while in contrast other young people find their new family arrangements very stressful.

The traditional allocation of the role of carer of children to females should no longer be taken for granted, as young people often choose to live with their fathers in separated families, or move between parents. Others 'sofa surf' for short periods or leave home entirely. The responsibility of 'carer' can fall on any family member, or indeed on someone outside the family altogether. In any case, the carer should be able to access established 'family' supports as required.

The Department of Health and Children has a statutory responsible for children up to the age of eighteen years. A young person 'in care' exposed to multi-factors of vulnerability during adolescence is likely to continue to need support after their eighteenth year. But unconditional ongoing support might encourage their dependence on the system. A balance could be achieved through extending provision of the current aftercare services to seek to promote independence and to empower the person over eighteen to make their own arrangements about leaving the care system.

The following specific needs were identified by the young people engaged with in this research:

- a comprehensive sex-education programme for all young people,*
- a Health service specifically for young women and staffed by female personnel,
- a 24-hour confidential walk-in counselling and crisis intervention service,
- a confidential telephone helpline specifically for young people.

[*The current delivery of sex-education programmes is provided through schools, which limits their effectiveness on two counts: the programmes are thought by the young people to be inconsistent and too dependant on the attitudes of the teachers assigned to teach them; also those that have chosen to leave school for whatever reason lose this access to information, although they have the same need for accurate information as their peers who remain behind.]

The Health Promotion Unit established in 1987 to disseminate information regarding health issues is seen by the Health Service as one part of an overall preventative strategy. However, the promotion of health and preventative measures is not an aspect of Health Service activity that is readily recognised by young people. Also the effect of information on the behaviour of young people is hard to measure. Although young people can recite accurate information about health risk factors, this does not prevent them from participating in "risky" behaviours. Taking risks is both inevitable for young people and a key element of their development.

In many case the scheduling and availability of services do not match the needs of young people trying to access them, either independently or with support. For most young people the lack of a personal contact for them within the system acts as an inhibiting factor in accessing services they might need.

As a response to young people's health needs, the mere putting in place of preventative and curative services is inadequate if crucial issues of awareness, access and appropriateness remain unaddressed.

To attempt to meet the health requirements of young people, a number of issues need to be considered:

- The traditional family unit is being augmented in society by a variety of alternative arrangements;
- Young people view the Health System as an amorphous, anonymous entity, represented by faceless and nameless agents referred to invariably as 'they';
- Young people do not view illness prevention as a significant aspect of Health service provision;
- Young people obtain their information on 'the street', and partial or incorrect information can expose them to health-damaging behaviours;

- Young people will inevitably take risks, some of which are of a serious or life threatening nature;
- Merely setting up additional services is an inadequate response to a perceived need – issues of awareness, independent access, appropriateness and availability also need to be addressed;
- Young people are able and willing to suggest appropriate responses to meet their needs.

7.3 Education

Educational attainment is highly valued by Irish society, and the Department of Education and Science allocates significant resources to the compulsory education of young people. However, inequalities that exist within the education system are well documented, and incidents of early school leaving and lower transfer rates to third level are seen to be more prevalent in County Wexford than in other parts of the country.

The views expressed by participants regarding both mainstream education and alternative programmes provide an insight into how young people regard the education system. One significant positive finding is that given the choice, young people would prefer to attend mainstream schools. This view is held by those in mainstream schooling and also those enrolled in alternative training facilities.

Social interaction is an element of school life that is viewed as extremely important for students at both primary and post-primary level.

From a female perspective, the structure of social interactions at post-primary level is very much governed by an established framework of peer groups based on social class. Middle class students tend to monopolise activities promoted by the official school culture. Those from other social and economic backgrounds often find themselves constructively excluded from such activities, as they choose not to associate with these peer groups. Nevertheless, young females remain generally positive about their school experience and believe that they manage adequately within the system.

On the other hand, young males are less prone to analysing school cultures based on social class, and instead identify attachment to peer groups through sporting activities, differentiating between those who participate and those who choose not to.

Social and cultural differences within schools are readily identified by young people, and young people are quick to notice inequalities in and between schools, and to base their actions and affiliations on such perceptions.

These actions and affiliations can also be influenced by young people's interpretations of the roles that the education system as a socialising mechanism allocates to its students. Some report a loss of identity in adjusting to the system, while others challenge and perhaps eventually reject the system. But whether by engaging in practices such as skipping classes and attending irregularly, or by involving themselves in persistent conflicts with teachers and school authorities, those who feel most marginalised can collude in their own stereotyping, and place themselves at risk of fulfilling others' expectations that they will leave school with few or no qualifications.

New initiatives have been introduced at second level to address the problem of early school leaving and to promote more consistent attendance among the most excluded students. Female students view the Stay-in-School programme positively, as they see its associated activities as encouraging participation and decision-making. But males have less regard for it. They tend to value more the practical experiences they gained through work placements in Transition Year, LCVP, and Applied Leaving Certificate programmes.

However those younger males who expressed no intention of remaining in school beyond 16 reject all these initiatives. Encouraging them to remain at school will remain a very difficult task, as their decisions are influenced largely by factors outside the remit of the school, primarily the opportunity to earn an income.

The schools attended by the young people involved in the research varied in population and available resources. Those who attended larger post-primary schools felt they were too big and impersonal and engendered a loss of identity, particularly for those entering first year. Smaller schools, where teachers knew all the students by name, tended to be viewed more positively.

Although some young people transferred from mainstream schools to alternative education programmes for a number of reasons, even here, given a meaningful choice, students would prefer to have remained in mainstream education. Those who already feel socially excluded appear conscious of a stigma attached to their participation in alternative education and training services, only serving to compound their sense of being marginalised.

The respondents did not identify additional support services such as the Home-School Liaison Officer. The school counselling service was found by many to be inappropriate, as the teacher's dual roles of authority figure and counsellor can confuse issues of trust and authority for students. It is also questionable as to whether school is always the most appropriate context for counselling, particularly for those students who already feel excluded from the official school culture.

Neither males nor females accurately linked educational qualifications to third level access, future training or employment prospects. The majority of participants in the research did not appear to want to pursue third level courses, but were more interested in securing apprenticeships or in getting employment directly on leaving school. A small number intended leaving school as soon as legally possible, even though they had no career plans. Their knowledge of available avenues to employment appeared extremely limited.

7.4 Youth Services

Young people see youth services as provided by the private, community and voluntary sectors. Where services are unavailable or irrelevant to their needs, they self-organise their activities. Young people need a variety of experiences in different contexts and are generally self-sufficient in providing for their own entertainment. They will maintain their commitment to any activity for only as long as they remain interested or perceive a definite benefit.

The distribution of services and types of activity vary considerably from area to area. Larger urban communities are serviced by both commercial interests and the community and voluntary sector. Services delivered by the community and voluntary sector include mainline youth clubs, targeted projects and crime diversion programmes. Those who use them do appreciate them, but their limited access for young people is a problem, as most close too early and are not available on weekends.

In smaller urban populations, services quickly become stereotyped with particular groups, leading to other groups refusing to become involved. In one area, those that had rejected a particular project sought a similar service for their own peer group, illustrating the strength of allegiance which peer groups demand, and which cannot be ignored when trying to establish youth services in a new area.

However those who use the services really value the freedom and space provided to them there, and recommend extending their opening hours to include late nights and weekends.

In areas where services and facilities are limited, the researchers often found a history of mistrust between adults and young people. Lack of facilities causes young people to congregate in public spaces and to engage in activities that adults frequently interpret as anti-social. As a result, certain individuals or groups can be denied access by adults to public facilities such as community halls and sports clubs. In these situations the opportunities for constructive engagement between adults and young people are further reduced, and mutual suspicion increases.

An advocate for young people in such a community could provide a link to negotiate their access to community facilities.

If young people are provided with the opportunity to operate youth centres for themselves with minimum adult supervision, 'ownership' of the centre becomes theirs, and participation and responsibility are encouraged and developed.

Access to available venues however will not cause young people to disappear completely from public spaces in their neighbourhood. Nor should this be their purpose. Young people playing in parks and hanging out on the streets provide a vibrancy and energy to the area that would surely be lacking if they were kept out of sight. Public facilities in open spaces can be improved by regular maintenance, and the provision of equipment such as goalposts, benches, playgrounds etc., would improve the local environment for all members of the community.

The ongoing recruitment of volunteers is a challenge for most organisations. Established approaches that seek to develop skills among the local population through training in community development have significant advantages, not least because such measures promote resilience factors within the community for vulnerable adolescents. But young people's stated preference for having people from outside the area as supervisors, as opposed to neighbours and family members, suggests that volunteer workers need to be augmented by more full-time personnel if services are to remain attractive to their clients.

A team of full-time workers providing a mobile service to areas at present lacking adequate provision could either be managed as a stand alone Youth Service initiative, or developed as part of an integrated programme involving a cluster of associated services.

The volunteer base that supports and informs so much valuable youth work needs to be retained, but if direct supervision of youth activities devolves more on professionals, as the young people suggest, then volunteer work could be extended to include other productive channels such as fund raising, strategic development, and co-management of projects with young people.

Other activities that young people self-organise may not be generally approved of by adults, and may often appear to them to involve unnecessary risk taking (e.g. motorbike riding, driving cars, climbing.) Some however might be incorporated into youth programmes which would thereby offer their adolescent clients the thrill of the experience while minimising the risk.

7.5 Justice

Many young people are frequently involved in illegal activities, but they tend to view these activities as mischief rather than as serious offences. Families and peer groups set the boundaries for acceptable behaviour, and the dread of being caught in these behaviours and bringing shame on the family is a major inhibiting factor.

Although young people's knowledge of the Justice System is limited, they regard the system as unfair. They view the treatment of young people by the Gardai as uneven, and the Courts as inconsistent in applying sentencing policies.

This negative view of the Gardai is based mainly on young people's negative personal experiences of being moved from favourite locations, and of being stopped and search without a specific reason being offered. For most, their only contact with the Department of Justice is the Gardai, who are required to perform a difficult role at the interface between young people and the service.

As with other sectors, the interface has been identified as the point where young people's perceptions of the overall service is formed. This suggests that creating opportunities for more positive experiences between Gardai and young people is crucial to providing adolescents with a better and more positive understanding of the Justice System. Investing now in establishing and developing positive connections with young people will ultimately bring benefits to the Gardai in their work with the wider community.

However the information that young people are largely unaware of (or at least did not identify) other justice services such as JLOS and Probation and Welfare Service provides an opportunity for the Justice System to improve young people's awareness of the services it provides and the variety of approaches it can take in dealing with its clients.

7.6 Independence

The adolescent years are principally concerned with personal development and gaining independence. This involves detachment from the family, engagement in one-to-one relationships, acquiring autonomy, and achieving monetary independence. The experience of adolescents varies, but is always embedded in contextual factors of gender, and social and economic background (Adams et al. 1996). The changes that take place for any individual occur in the context of policies and legislation that provide a framework within which service providers operate.

The Family -The fundamental unit of social support is the family. The majority of participants in the project spoke about their families with love and affection, but this did not imply that all respondents lived in a conflict-free home. Indeed some participants were seen as the principal source of hostility within their families and the focus of parental arguments.

One coping mechanism young people develop in this situation is to leave the family home for a time to stay with relatives or friends. While 'sofa surfing' may provide a short-term option for young people who wish to avoid stressful conflicts within their family, the route back into the family home can afterwards be difficult to establish. For young people in this situation, available supports may be scarce.

Other respondents who reported good relationships with their family relied on them for support and resources, but admitted they rarely acknowledged this openly. However, this implied if unspoken trust makes the negotiation of supports and resources less stressful than in families who do not share a similar understanding.

Peer groups are considered to operate through a natural hierarchical structure among young people, and it is an unwritten rule that the established order of precedence must be followed. The influence of older adolescents on the behaviour of their younger peers can be a powerful support to adults wishing to gain the acceptance of young people in a new area.

Peer groups provide forums for their members based on trust and loyalty, and members of peer groups look after each other. The ability of peer groups to self-organise is generally well developed. These positive attributes should also be appreciated by adults when working with young people in different contexts.

Relationships - The development of self-identity involves acknowledging one's sexual identity. None of the respondents stated that they were homosexual or bi-sexual, but it appears that young females are more tolerant of homosexuality than young males. In any case, the difficulties for gay young people to 'come out' to their peers in the predominant heterosexual culture are considerable.

Throughout their conversations, young people lace their comments with sexual innuendo. Workers engaged with young people must develop a tolerance of this form of exchange. In the Children First Guidelines (1999) the use of sexually explicit language by children is identified as a possible indicator of deeply rooted issues. Any overtly negative response from an adult could possibly close off a significant issue a young person might be trying to explore.

Community - In general young people are aware that their presence on the streets and in public areas is a source of antagonism and potential conflict with the adult community. Young people feel that they have little choice in where they congregate as they often have nowhere else to go. However the majority of young people feel safe in their own area, which provides them with a sense of identity and a degree of self-confidence.

The perception of some young females that negative views of their neighbourhood are perpetuated, particularly by mothers of teenagers from other areas, provides an interesting analysis of how social inequalities persist and are maintained. A similar class-based analysis of the social inequalities that apply within schools was offered by a different female focus group. In contrast, males did not offer any significant analysis of social inequality based on class.

Employment - Some communities have traditionally been identified as unemployment black spots. The recent decline in national unemployment rates has not been mirrored to the same extent throughout County Wexford. Good employment opportunities and associated economic independence are remote prospects for the majority of young people contacted during the research.

Those participants who were in employment often gained it through family contacts, particularly in rural areas. Others who left school early had taken up low paid positions in the catering and retail sectors. Those who were not employed relied on their families, whose resources in some cases appeared limited.

Neither males nor females accurately linked educational qualifications with future employment or training prospects, indicating a lack of knowledge or of real engagement with their future plans. Clearly for some, the progression from school to employment is not viewed as something concrete leading to independence, but as a transition more or less outside their control.

The predominant lack of understanding of educational requirements and opportunities for further training among young people in areas of traditionally high unemployment indicates that information on employment and training services needs to be actively promoted.

7.7 Culture

Young people's experience of youth culture is very much based on new technologies and visual media. Mobile telephones are highly valued as they play a significant role in communicating among peer groups, in organising activities, and in initiating, building and monitoring relationships.

Information and Communications Technologies offer young people the opportunity to connect with global media products and services. TV serials and films illustrate and add meaning to young people's concepts and arguments. The programmes they watch are to some extent gender-divided, with young females preferring soap operas and pop music shows, and young males opting for competitive sports programmes (e.g. soccer and wrestling).

Young people are eager to absorb information through this medium, and they accept the commercialism of TV, cinema and music without applying a critical analysis of the power relationships that control the mass media. As consumers they are heavily influenced by advertising, and seem to purchase the products of multinational corporations without any ethical or political consideration of the social and economic injustices that are often involved in their manufacture.

Young people tend to identify most with the communities where they grew up. Rapid urban expansion has recently occurred in some areas, and the intimacy that once existed for young people in their close-knit social network can vanish in the space of two or three years. It is difficult for young people to retain a sense of belonging when the structure of their community has changed so dramatically.

Young females readily acknowledge that particular areas and neighbourhoods are viewed negatively by sections of the wider community. They regard as unfair any negative judgement of an individual based on their address or family background, but some have personally experienced discrimination on this basis.

The integration of young people from different backgrounds appears not to be an issue for the majority of adolescents. However young people from the Traveller Community have a strong and justified sense of discrimination. The Travelling Community is not generally recognised by young people as a specific ethnic group, and unlike non-nationals, their culture is not seen as "different". Young Travellers are not seen as part of a distinct community by other young people who seem more or less indifferent to their social and economic conditions.

The culture of any society or group is often displayed through their creative and leisure activities. Pre-adolescents, both male and female, tend to participate in all activities within their areas, regardless of who else might attend. However this changes quite dramatically in the teenage years, when particular activities that were once considered desirable are now seen as either irrelevant or inappropriate.

This judgement is divided along lines of gender and social class. For example, young males are identified as "gay" and bullied if they express an interest in dancing, and stage performance in school is considered by young females as the preserve of the middle classes. Peer groups have a major influence on what is deemed appropriate or acceptable.

Consequently, young people can be forced to exclude themselves from participating in creative activities, despite having sufficient talent and personal interest.

7.8 Political Involvement

Recent national policies relating to services for young people appear to have shifted significantly towards a more inclusive approach, encouraging participation by young people in decisions-making processes. It is within this framework that opportunities can be created to increase the level of involvement of young people. But all young people must be granted the same rights to have their voices heard, even if the means, capacities and opportunities available to them may not always be the same.

The observations of some participants in the research that existing decision-making structures such as school council can be monopolised by those of a certain class and are viewed by others as ineffective, illustrates that young people are capable of acute critical analysis and are able to find ways of coping with structural inequalities without necessarily seeking to change them.

Therefore the promotion of involvement and participation by young people in decision-making structures will require a commitment on the part of those who now manage those structures to create opportunities that young people will view as relevant, and that challenge their perception that decision-making is often the reserve of particular groups or classes.

Young people are sceptical of the authenticity of existing decision-making mechanisms, but if the opportunities presented to them are seen to be genuine and clearly promote equality of outcomes, young people will participate. Such a strategy may appear quite simple, but presents major challenges in its implementation.

Genuine participation by young people in decision-making at all levels of societal systems is clearly an unrealistic aspiration, but practical steps can be implemented to promote their involvement in decision-making processes within organisations and agencies that work with young people.

To implement the shift towards youth involvement recommended by the National Children's Strategy (2000) at practice level, organisations and agencies must encourage participation by their target clients. If they are to develop services relevant to young people exposed to multiple risk factors, then they must involve those who experience these situations in their day-to-day lives.

However to create opportunities and increase participation is not enough; implementing decisions taken is also essential. The failure to provide follow-up action will only increase disillusionment and suspicion among young people towards the process.

Until organisations and agencies are willing to take the risk of actively involving socially excluded and disadvantaged young people, and subsequently implementing decisions arrived at, the development of services for young people will continue to be planned without the input of their expert knowledge.

7.9 Engagement Strategies

The fact that some young people do not access services, for whatever reason, provided a starting point for the research, and the exploration of two different engagement methods – detached and thematic – formed an integral element of the research methodology.

The effectiveness of each method in successfully engaging with young people exhibiting multiple factors of vulnerability was considered, and the advantages and disadvantages associated with both were analysed. In general the detached approach, based on principles of equality and participation, was regarded by the researchers as the more effective.

The detached approach proved effective during the research process in gathering young people's perceptions of their needs, their attitudes to current services and their ideas on the development of new services. It also enabled the researchers to gain valuable information about young people's behaviours, their social spaces, communities and peer groups. This data can inform the delivery of existing programmes and can also be used to develop new approaches to meet the needs of those most excluded from mainstream services.

The approach itself appears quite simple – walking up to young people and requesting to speak to them. However this point of contact is reached only after careful preparation, including mapping of the area, contacting local gatekeepers and service providers, and raising awareness through the local media and community organisations of the aims and methods of the project.

In developing trust, the priority for the researchers was always to ensure that their approach facilitated the young person to dictate the pace and scope of the interaction.

However as an engagement process in long-term practice, the method does not lend itself to rigid structuring, measurements of productivity or predictable outcomes. But the essential flexibility and adaptability of the approach proves compatible with the sometimes chaotic lifestyles of young people.

To describe this form of engagement as detached perhaps underestimates its inherent power to facilitate very positive outcomes. The term "connecting" suggests associations which are the very opposite of detached, and is perhaps the more appropriate for this type of engagement, as it focuses on the positive empowering nature of the process with its emphasis on inclusion and participation.

Clearly, the purposes of the engagement must be understood by all participants from the outset. As an approach for reaching and involving young people who exhibit multiple factors of vulnerability, this method can prove very effective, provided the approach is integrated into a holistic strategy for long-term practice.

7.10 Overall Conclusion

The findings and analysis illustrate that the concerns, issues and needs of young people are complex and are embedded in cultural and social contexts. Any attempt to focus on a specific area in isolation will fail to accommodate the diversity of interdependent factors that influence their lives. Therefore, for those working with young people who face multiple difficulties, the most logical and productive approach would appear to be one which seeks to integrate services, thereby creating a flexible and comprehensive response to their multiple needs.

Service providers from the statutory, social and community and voluntary sectors already co-operate in many situations through partnership and collaborative structures. This type of horizontal integration requires commitment at both management and practice levels, and a necessity that all involved have a clear understanding of agreed aims and objectives at the outset.

The development of abstract systems which rely on 'expert' knowledge to implement and maintain responses to their clients' needs is a feature of modern society. In light of this, most established services for young people would seem to have been developed on incomplete information, as traditionally, young people who after all possess the 'expert' knowledge in this field, have been excluded from decision-making in these services.

The National Children's Strategy (2000) recognises the need to consult young people in matters that affect them, and for the first time offers a statutory mechanism to vertically integrate the development of services to respond to their needs. The participation of young people in this way acknowledges the need for services to ask for and use the 'expert' knowledge that young people themselves possess regarding their own situations.

Such participation may not provide equality of opportunity, however. Even where systems already employ decision-making structures, many of their young clients often view such structures as irrelevant to their needs, because they see the opportunities they provide for involvement being appropriated by their more privileged middle-class peers.

If organisations wish to provide effective services to meet the needs of young people who already experience social exclusion and are potentially most at risk, then they must develop genuinely inclusive participatory methods that their target clients see as relevant to themselves and appropriate to their social and cultural experiences.

Such methods also need to overcome the negative attitude shared by many young people that adults frequently let them down, do not listen to them, break their promises to them and generally cannot be trusted. Young people generally regard anyone they do not trust as placing them 'at risk', and as a result, many are reluctant to collaborate with adults.

Opportunities for participation must involve the socially excluded. Otherwise, the seemingly positive proposal in the National Children's Strategy (2000) to encourage participation and inclusion by young people in decision-making structures could metamorphose into a further 'risk' for those young people who currently display multiple factors of vulnerability, and hence increase their sense of alienation.

Issues of trust and risk are intertwined, not just for young people but also for the agencies and organisations working with them. In adopting the strategy proposed in this report, agencies and organisations would be taking many risks at both management and practice level: to integrate services; to commit to a collaborative approach; to be transparent about their practice; to be flexible and responsive to other service providers. More importantly, they would have to risk becoming easily identifiable to the young people they speak to and listen to if they wish to involve them in the reciprocal risk of participating in collaborative initiatives.

Any expectation by services that young people will take the first step in coming to them is unrealistic, and focuses the responsibility for participation squarely upon the young person. To assume our responsible role as adults we must share the responsibility with these young people. The research clearly indicates that young people are willing to interact with adults positively, if approached with respect in their own environment. Therefore to reach those most 'at risk', we as adults within services are surely obliged to access young people, rather than expecting them to always access us.

The point of contact is where trust and risk are intertwined. It is here that potential gains and losses, both expressed and implied, are assessed. First impressions at the point of contact will provide the young person with an assessment of the overall approach, and influence their subsequent decisions on whether to become involved, and to what degree.

If the adult is easily associated with a specific service, the young person's response can be precipitated. Young people's attitudes to services depend largely on previous contacts and cultural labelling. They tend to view the majority of services they are aware of as anonymous and faceless, and some they view as hostile (e.g. the Justice System).

Therefore it is important that adults attempting to access young people are not identified by them with a specific organisation or service, but rather as a connector. The connector must be identifiable, flexible, and non-judgemental in approach, and needs to ensure that the young people have the free choice to connect and at what level.

Connection can be interpreted in various ways. At its most basic, it establishes on-the-street engagement. It can be used to share or relay information; it can provide links into support services; it can offer advocacy and mediation services, etc. Adults engaged in this work should understand and appreciate the complex range of connections and possible outcomes that can result from what may initially appear to be a simple approach.

Such a flexible, adaptable form of connection, with all its inherent complexity of associated linkages, seems to the researchers the most suited to engaging with young people who exhibit a wide variety of needs incorporating a range of services. However to successfully establish such a method of engagement, all organisations and agencies involved need to understand, value, commit to and support the approach at all levels of their structure. To deliver a service so dependent on connection without a fully interconnected support structure would clearly be futile, and would only serve to confirm any negative views target clients might hold regarding the risks involved in collaborating with adults.

Chapter Eight
Recommendations

8 Introduction

The information yielded through the research process has provided an insight into the social reality of young people. It confirms their competence in identifying their own needs, in articulating their perceptions of services already available to them, and in suggesting ways of developing new structures and services to better meet their needs.

Above all, this report will hopefully demonstrate to those working directly with and for adolescents the need to value and trust their clients' 'expert' knowledge of their own environment and culture, and persuade relevant organisations of the need to provide authentic opportunities for young people to participate in decision-making regarding the development of services appropriate to their needs.

The recommendations presented here follow the same order of categories as the previous chapters of this report.

8.1 Risk and Resilience

1. To respond to the needs of young people by seeking to identify the complex interrelationship of factors that define every individual situation.
2. To develop a multi-agency response through effective co-ordination of existing services to respond to the multiple needs of young people at risk
3. To utilise the wide range of resources already available to meet identified needs, and to provide new resources where gaps are seen to exist.
4. To work with young people through processes that promote their empowerment.

8.2 Health

8.2.1 Organisation

1. To collaborate with other organisations and agencies working with young people to develop a multi-agency response to the multiple needs of young people 'at risk'.
2. To develop strategies to make the Health Services more identifiable and accessible to young people.

8.2.2. Information

1. To address the lack of awareness among young people of the Health Services available to them, and to establish more effective methods of providing information on Health Services to young people.

2. To provide and promote a comprehensive and consistent programme on Relationships and Sex Education, suitable for young people in different contexts and age groups, including those who may have left the education system.

8.2.3 Support Services Identified by Young People

1. To provide appropriate supports that will assist in creating possible solutions where young people live in stressful family situations.
2. To establish a confidential walk-in Counselling and Crisis Intervention Service for young people.
3. To provide a Health Awareness Service specifically targeted at young women staffed by female personnel.
4. To set up a local confidential Telephone Helpline specifically for young people.

8.3 Education

1. To implement and promote compensatory measures in schools to break the cycle of disadvantage in the communities they serve, by ensuring equality of outcomes to all their students through positively discriminating in favour of those students suffering social exclusion.
2. To develop and promote a wider variety of meaningful and affirmative extra-curricular activities for students who tend to feel excluded from existing programmes.
3. To increase the range of opportunities available to Leaving Certificate Applied, Leaving Certificate Vocational Programme and Transition Year students for appropriate work experience, by strengthening the links from schools and VECs to employer organisations such as the Chambers of Commerce, IBEC and the Construction Industry Federation.
4. To increase students' awareness and understanding of career options and training opportunities available to them on leaving school.
5. To treat transfer of a student from mainstream schooling to an alternative service only as a final option, when all other options have been fully explored by the School Management in consultation with the student, their parents/guardians and all relevant supporting services.
6. Alternative counselling services to be provided for young people who are reluctant to approach teachers when experiencing emotional or social problems.
7. Planning for new or amalgamated schools to include consideration of the maximum student population appropriate to the social and cultural patterns of the communities in the catchment area.

8.4 Youth Services

1. Access to existing services provided by the community and voluntary sectors to be expanded, to include late night and weekend openings.
2. To establish or expand existing services' advocacy role in facilitating young people to engage with relevant adults with a view to their gaining greater access to under-utilised venues and resources in their community.
3. To investigate the possibility of redirecting the role of volunteers within youth services more towards the support and co-management of programmes.
4. To provide mobile teams of full-time youth workers who can operate in areas currently lacking youth services.
5. To incorporate into youth programmes a greater range of developmentally enhancing risk activities in controlled and supervised environments applying adequate safety and security features.

8. 5 Justice

1. To provide and promote an Information and Awareness Programme adaptable to different contexts (e.g. schools, youth and sports clubs, community groups, etc.) to be delivered by Garda personnel to build better relations between young people and the Gardai.
2. The Probation and Welfare Service to develop and train a team of "Youth Advocacy Workers" who would be available to any young person detained by the Gardai.
3. To hold a conference in 2003 to explore the implications of the Governments/NDP proposals on "Crime Prevention, Social Inclusion and Alternatives to Custody" and its relevance to young people at risk in County Wexford.

8.6 Independence

1. To develop an advocacy and mediation support service for young people experiencing persistent family conflicts.
2. To regard the peer group as the natural unit of organisation in working with young people.
3. To direct resources towards older adolescent peer groups (i.e. those over 15 years of age), as they can have a significant influence on the attitudes and behaviours of their younger counterparts.
4. To build on existing positive attributes operating within peer groups.
5. To work with young people within their own environment whenever possible.
6. To highlight and utilise the resources and resilient qualities of their communities when working with young people.
7. To develop and deliver more accurate and relevant information on appropriate employment and training opportunities for young people.

8.7 Culture

8.7.1 Technologies

1. To investigate ways of developing effective and appropriate methods of harnessing mobile telephone technologies to deliver information to young people.
2. To expand the use of video, DVD and the Internet in the education and training of young people in Schools and Training Organisations.

8.7.2 Critical Analysis

1. Through the school curriculum to promote greater critical analysis among young people of the influence of the media and marketing techniques on their culture.
2. Through schools and youth and community-based organisations to promote critical analysis among young people of existing social divisions, to enable them to explore ways of challenging prevailing values based on social class and economic power.
3. To facilitate young people through creative activities to identify, portray and record their own perspectives on their changing communities.
4. To promote anti-racist and intercultural perspectives and values when working with young people.

8.7.3 Creative Activities

1. To create alternative opportunities in their communities for young people who choose to exclude themselves from mainstream creative or sporting activities, to celebrate and develop their creative talents and interests.

8.8 Political Involvement

1. Young people from disadvantaged communities to be actively involved in the development of new services for and with youth in their area.
2. Structures to be developed and employed to provide ongoing opportunities for the authentic participation and involvement of young people in management and decision-making processes in Youth Services.
3. Recruitment of young participants to working groups and committees to offer genuine and meaningful representation to all groups, including those most disadvantaged.
4. Appropriate training and ongoing support to be provided to young participants to facilitate them in their work.

8.9 Engagement Strategies

1. To establish a Pilot Project incorporating the detached/connector method as part of an overall strategy to engage with young people exhibiting multiple factors of vulnerability.

Chapter Nine
Pilot Project

9. Introduction

The project's aim of developing models of practice to meet the needs of young people exhibiting multiple factors of vulnerability required proposals that were firmly based on the Findings and Analysis of the research. Three models are proposed here, each intended to inform practice at both management and grassroots level. These are:

1. The Youth Connector Model
2. The Mobile Unit
3. The Triune Youth Model.

9.1 The Youth Connector Model

The Youth Connector Model is an approach that uses face-to-face work with young people within their own areas. It is intended to move the interface of access away from buildings and institutions out onto the streets. A description of the model is presented under the following headings:

- Aims
- Objectives
- Ethical Considerations
- The Youth Connector Model
- Underpinning Principles of the model
- From Theory to Practice

9.1.1 Aims

The three overall aims that distinguish this model are:

1. To initiate and establish a distinct engagement process that will not be identified by its target group with any particular service;
2. To connect with young people in their own environment;
3. To ensure that young people always have the free choice to participate at whatever level they find appropriate.

1. A distinct engagement process that cannot be identified with any particular service

The research indicates that when a young person identifies an adult worker with a particular service, their interaction is influenced by the young person's perception of that service. An agenda is already established, whether their experience of the service has been positive or negative.

A structure free of any association with established services provides an opportunity for young people and workers alike to engage in an interaction without a set agenda.

2. To connect with young people within their own environment

Connection can take a variety of forms. It can offer basic on-the-street engagement or provide links into support services; it can offer advocacy or mediation; it can be used to share or relay information, etc. Different levels of connection are possible, allowing a flexible response to the various needs of different client groups.

The research demonstrates that young people from a wide variety of backgrounds will engage with adults using this approach, and it does not draw attention to their relative social disadvantage or vulnerability.

3. To ensure that young people have the free choice to participate, and at what level

The decision whether to engage with the youth connector in the first place, to identify personal needs, to seek additional information, to participate further – all these choices remain with the young person. As the relationship between the young person and youth connector is intended to promote empowerment, the lead is taken always by the young person. In this way, young people are facilitated to make their own choices.

9.1.2 Objectives

The model has four objectives:

1. To connect with young people who do not attach to existing services for whatever reason;
2. To facilitate young people to identify their own needs;
3. To facilitate young people in developing positive strategies to meet those needs;
4. To relay information between young people and service providers.

1. To connect with young people who do not attach to existing services for whatever reason

Young people do not attach to services for a variety of reasons, including lack of awareness, lack of access, exclusion, fear of not being listened to, and deliberate choice.

Many young people can feel disconnected from the wider community, leading to a sense of personal or collective isolation. A youth connector operating in their area can provide young people with an identifiable and reliable point of contact to the wider community.

2. To facilitate young people to identify their needs

The research has shown that through this model of interaction young people are both willing and able to identify many of their own needs.

3. To facilitate young people in developing positive strategies to meet those needs

By offering links into existing services or supports, the method presents young people with opportunities to become involved in further connections with organisations and systems working to meet their needs. But they remain free to refuse or to withdraw from the process at any stage.

4. To relay information between young people and service providers

Information can be sourced by the youth connector and disseminated quickly to youth in any area, and service providers can benefit from accurate and up-to-date feedback on proposals and initiatives.

9.1.3 Ethical Considerations

Ethical considerations to be discussed, agreed and ratified by the integrated team should incorporate the following issues:

- Confidentiality
- Adoption of the 'Children First' Guidelines
- Insurance
- Safety of all participants
- Regular reflection and analysis of practice

9.1.4 Structure of the Youth Connector Model

This section explains the structure of the Youth Connector Model (See: Diagram 9.1), through describing its components, the types of connections it offers (See: Table 9.2), and the roles, duties and skills of a Youth Connector Worker.

The diagram illustrates the integrated approach required in establishing the model. Organisations and agencies participating in such a project need to co-operate in developing a holistic approach to service provision, and ongoing practical support and maintenance is vital to its success.

Diagram 9.1 – Pilot Project One – Youth Connector Model

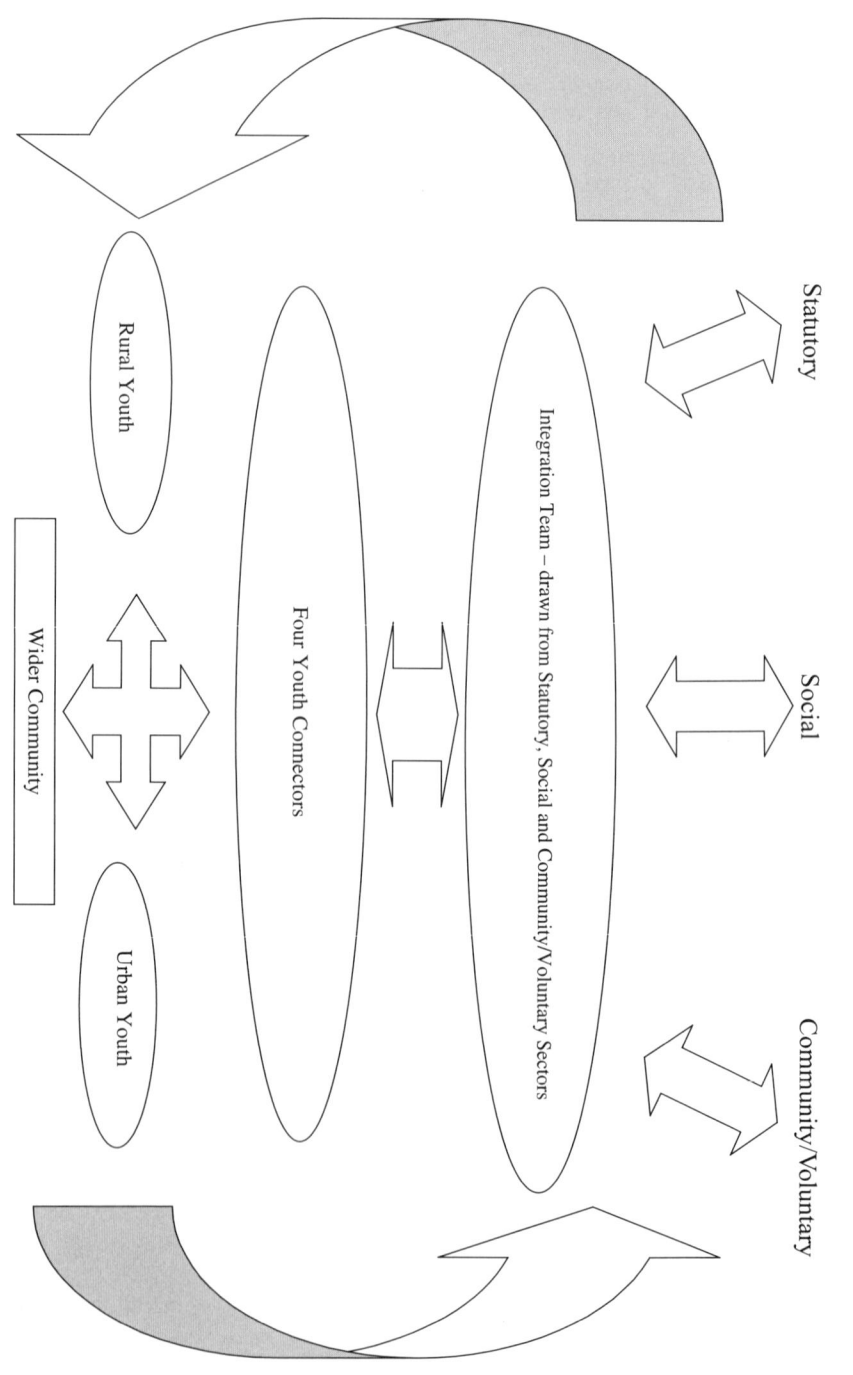

- Statutory
- Social
- Community/Voluntary

- Rural Youth
- Urban Youth
- Wider Community
- Four Youth Connectors
- Integration Team – drawn from Statutory, Social and Community/Voluntary Sectors

9.1.5 The Integration Team (Diagram 9.1)

It is envisaged that the team would consist of nine representatives, three taken from each of the sectors to ensure an adequate balance of views and interests, and an independent co-ordinator. Members of the team would be nominated and agreed by participating services.

The Independent Co-ordinator - The co-ordinator's function is to oversee the project in terms of organisation, support and co-ordination of responses. The co-ordinator's role would be:

- to organise meeting of the Integration Team as required;
- to participate in regular support meetings with youth connectors, to reflect on their practice and to ensure that the principles of the project are being adhered to;
- to facilitate the delivery of appropriate responses to young people engaged through the process who have sought support or assistance from services.

Integration Team Members - These professionals need to have in-depth knowledge of the range of services provided by the sector(s) they represent, and must also have sufficient authority to directly link with decision-making mechanisms in their organisations and agencies. Their role would be:

- to attend the regular meetings of the Integration Team;
- to help define ethical and legal safeguards for participants in the project;
- to assist the co-ordinator in delivering appropriate responses to young people engaged through the process who have sought support or assistance from services;
- to supply information regarding their sector's services, initiatives and programmes to the project;
- to participate in discussions with adults and youth in the target community with a view to developing mechanisms for their authentic participation.

Youth Connectors - To facilitate the scheduling and rotation of workers, a team of four youth connectors is envisaged, consisting of two males and two females. A total of four workers provides a gender balance and offers flexibility in arranging teams, while also being compact enough to maintain close working relationships and limited overall cost. The role of the youth connectors would be:

- to maintain a visible and ongoing presence in each target community;
- to engage with the young people of the area in a non-judgmental way that facilitates their participation in and control of the process;
- to facilitate and assist young people in accessing support and assistance from appropriate services (See: Table 9.2)

- to provide information that young people have requested, and to assist them in seeking information for themselves;
- to attend and contribute to regular meetings as arranged by the Co-ordinator.

Ongoing Duties of the Youth Connectors

1. to operate a shift system that includes evening/night and weekend work, in order to meet young people on their own terms in their own physical and social environments;
2. one male and one female to work together on each shift, on grounds both of safety and gender balance; however pairings should be regularly changed to avoid over-identification or dependency by specific groups or individuals, thereby leading to the self-exclusion of other young people;
3. to record details of each shift, including location, starting and finishing time, the number of contacts made, data regarding participants' ages, gender, peer group membership, etc., in order to build up data on the observed behaviours and social profiles of youth in the area over time;
4. to assess, monitor and report to the Integration Team on the progress of initiatives and actions developed by services in response to the identified needs of the young people in the area;
5. to attend and contribute to scheduled team meetings.

Table 9.2 – Youth Connectors - Levels of Connection

Level	Purpose	Role of Youth Connector	Method	Expected Outcome
Individuals & Peer Groups (general)	• To engage with individuals • To build trust • To identify roles and responsibilities	• To initiate contact • To maintain engagement • To record observations and data	• Street work • Direct Approach to young people in target areas	• Becoming identified and known in the area • Having roles clearly understood • Gathering information
Individuals (Assistance)	• To raise awareness of existing services • To provide an access point into appropriate services and supports if required	• To facilitate young people to identify their needs • To explore available options with them • To facilitate the development of a holistic solution with all involved • To provide access to information requested by young people	• Discussion • Development of practical strategies (informal) • Facilitating the implementation of agreed strategies • Sourcing of information and contacts	• Identifying youth needs • Developing courses of action • Implementation of agreed plans • Relevant information accessed if requested
Open Forum (Young people, adults in the community Integration Team)	• To facilitate young people in putting forward ideas to service providers • To assist in developing structures to encourage participation of young people • Ongoing reflection on practice	• To relay information and co-ordinate meetings	• Discussion • Informal workshops • Accessible, user-friendly information	• Recognition and acceptance of young people's expert knowledge by service providers • Review of practice and progress of the project • Ongoing development of practice
Wider Community	• To introduce workers to the target community • To map the area to identify resources • To include participation of the wider community • To build relationships within the community	• To Provide Information • To communicate and liaise with gatekeepers and community leaders	• Information leaflets • Personal contact • Working through gatekeepers • Engagement with local organisations and services	• Clarification of role of worker for young people • Participation by young people
Integration Team	• To develop a holistic response to identified needs • To co-ordinate the delivery of appropriate services and supports • To monitor the effectiveness of the model • To support and advise Youth Connectors in their work	• To be an advocate for individual clients • To facilitate individuals to seek assistance for themselves • To supply information to the Integration Team • To supply information to young people • To support young people to access information for themselves	• Informal Contact • Relaying information • Meetings— formal and informal	• Identifying young people who are in need of specific assistance or support • Identifying possible elements of a holistic response • Ensuring that cross sector responses are recommended and delivered to meet identified needs

Requirements for the Youth Connector

1. Skills: Communicating, Negotiating, Mediating, Strategic Planning, Administration
2. Capacities: Self management, Team work, Analysis, Empathy, Reflection, Tolerance
3. Knowledge: Youth Cultures, Youth Issues, Youth Behaviours.
4. (Optional): Special Training in Youth Work, Counselling, Mentoring, Health Education, etc.

9.1.6 Underpinning Principles

The principles of equality and participation which underpin this project are most apparent at the connection point of the model (Fig.9.1). However, to assume that young people will volunteer to participate from the beginning in other areas of the model is perhaps unrealistic.

As the research indicates, those most confident about participating in formal structures and discussions with adults are likely to be seen by other young people as privileged and arrogant ('the Posh Ones'). If committees are to accommodate confident and articulate adolescents only, then their deliberations will be seen by young people generally to be unrepresentative, and their recommendations are likely to further isolate those already experiencing exclusion.

Organisations and agencies themselves have been slow in encouraging young people to become involved in their decision making processes, and time will be required for them to create meaningful and authentic mechanisms for genuine and representative participation.

The underpinning principles of equality and participation need to be based upon realistic expectations. Providing an identifiable person or team whom young people trust and can connect with offers a positive starting point that can be built upon.

Participation and involvement requires both support and opportunities to be provided. An Open Forum, involving the Integrated Team, local community figures and young people themselves, provides such an opportunity. Practical supports such as childcare and transport costs could be offered to participants. The Youth Connectors would support the young people emotionally in encouraging them to take the risk to participate. Their interaction with members of the Integrated Team and local community figures at the forum would be felt as a positive step by young people who have traditionally felt excluded from decision-making processes.

9.1.7 From Theory to Practice

Even when models are accepted and agreed on, different organisational and personal values will influence various stakeholders' views on how a recommended approach is to be best implemented.

Clearly the purpose of the method must first be understood and accepted by all involved. Commitment by organisations and agencies to the Youth Connector Model will require them to deliver practical action and support.

The role of the Youth Connectors is to work at the interface between services and young people. They must acknowledge to their clients from the outset that they have no control over allocation of resources from organisations and agencies.

Without the ongoing commitment of service providers to the project, the Youth Connectors will be placed in a difficult position, and the success of the overall project will be jeopardised.

Any lack of clarity in this area may create false expectations among the young people involved, and lead to their further disillusionment and mistrust regarding services. Such an outcome would only serve to further alienate those already exposed to multiple risk factors and experiencing exclusion.

9.2 Mobile Youth Unit

A Mobile Youth Unit provides a way of working with young people within their own environments which is not associated with other venues or facilities available to young people, such as youth clubs, sports clubs, discos, pool halls, etc. A description of the model is presented under the following headings:

- Mobile Unit
- Meeting Identified Needs
- Aims
- Objectives
- Mobile Unit Personnel

9.2.1 Mobile Unit

The mobile unit would be a converted vehicle, (e.g. a refurbished double-decker bus, mobile health service unit or mobile library). The vehicle would arrive at each of two selected locations on separate evenings each week, and its facilities made available to young people in the area (Diagram 9.3). A mobile unit has been in use in Calgary, Canada on the EXIT street programme for some time now and is consistently used by 'at risk' youth.

Ideally the mobile unit would be divided into different 'rooms': a chill-out area, a small food preparation area, and a games area with video and music equipment, etc. It would provide footballs and basic games equipment for organised outdoor activities in the immediate area, and would be accessible to the disabled.

To facilitate the scheduling and rotation of workers, a team of four is envisaged, consisting of two males and two females. A total of four workers provides a gender balance and offers flexibility in arranging teams, while also being compact enough to maintain close working relationships and economies of scale. The wider community would be given prior information on the presence and purpose of the project in their area.

9.2.2 Meeting Identified Needs

Stereotyping of existing facilities - The Findings of the research indicate that fixed facilities can become negatively stereotyped by young people, who may then reject their services by self-excluding. The fact that this unit is mobile and therefore does not become associated with one particular group, allows it to avoid such stereotyping. Consequently it provides a method of reaching different peer groups in the same or neighbouring locations.

Transport - A moveable unit minimises the amount of travelling young people have to arrange to access the service. This is particularly important in rural areas. In urban areas, many younger adolescents prefer to socialise in their immediate locality too. So this service provides a practical focus for engaging with young people in their own environment, which makes it more acceptable to them.

Ownership and Connection - The mobile unit would provide a venue for young people to spend time in a secure space, a venue that for two evenings a week they could call their own. The facility also offers a connection point to young people where they can obtain information or gain access to further services. While specific programmes need not be organised in a formal way, the youth workers involved would facilitate young people to identify their own needs and to discuss and develop ways of meeting these needs.

Training Venue/ Erratic School Attendance - The vehicle could provide an informal setting for the provision of additional services that young people in an area requested. It could for example offer information on legal rights, on employment and training options, on sex and relationships education, etc. Young people with poor school attendance records could be facilitated to access information they may have missed out in their school.

The delivery of agreed programmes could be provided by qualified trainers from the statutory, social or community/voluntary sector. All the sectors would therefore be involved, and would have a responsibility to provide practical supports to promote and maintain such a model.

Connection Point - As a connection point, the mobile unit would allow its clients through the youth work team to access a multiplicity of services through a mechanism similar to that described in the Youth Connector model.

Dissemination of Information - The Research Findings revealed that young people's knowledge of existing services is limited, and that awareness needs to be raised across all sectors. The mobile unit could be used as an easily identifiable base for the dissemination of information at popular events such as teenage discos, sports meetings, community fairs and fetes, etc., where young people tend to gather in large numbers. Youth Information Staff could be seconded from their organisations for a day to operate such a service, therefore maximising the use of the vehicle.

Community Involvement - The local young people and adults from the wider community need to be involved in the management of the mobile unit and its operation within their area. Active and focussed participation involving young people and adults in such a project might provide the first step towards both parties collaborating in developing further facilities and venues for the young people of the area. The Research Findings identified a number of communities where facilities for young people are lacking and yet where suitable venues do exist, but are either under-utilised or closed.

Mobile Youth Unit
Diagram 9.3

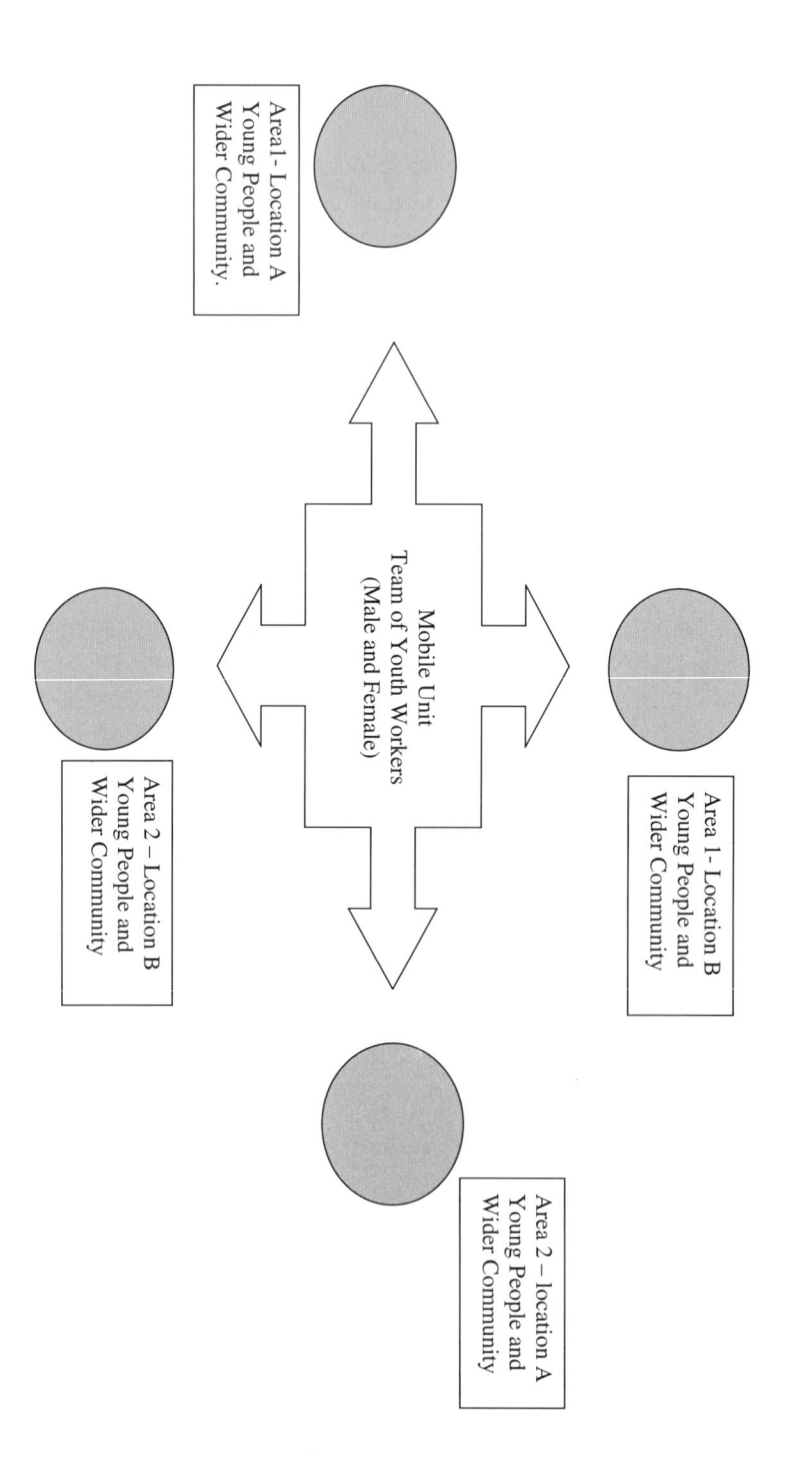

- Area 1 - Location A Young People and Wider Community.
- Area 1 - Location B Young People and Wider Community
- Area 2 – Location B Young People and Wider Community
- Area 2 – location A Young People and Wider Community

Mobile Unit
Team of Youth Workers
(Male and Female)

254

9.2.3. Aims

1. To provide a quality facility for young people within their community;
2. To develop quality supports with and for young people;
3. To provide a Connection Point for young people.

9.2.4 Objectives

1. To provide a regular service to young people;
2. To enable young people to identify their own needs;
3. To facilitate young people in discussing and developing ways of meeting those needs.

9.2.5 Local Area Management Team (Diagram 9.3)

It is likely that young people would wish to use this facility in different ways, reflecting the different social needs and preferred activities of younger and older teenagers. These can vary from engaging in sports and outdoor activities to playing music and videos, to chilling out (See: Analysis of Cultural Needs, 6.7.6).

The management team's main functions, apart from assessing and supporting the unit's work, are to liaise with the local community to ensure their acceptance of the unit, and to raise awareness among both adults and young people of its activities and services.

Ideally one adult member and one young member of each local management team would represent their area at each of two meetings per year with the integrated management team. These meetings would both provide valuable feedback to management from each location and reinforce participants' sense of ownership of the project.

9.2.6 Structure of Integration Team

This is identical to the structure described for the Youth Connector Model (See: 9.1.5).

9.2.7 Mobile Unit Youth Workers

Their role is identical to that described for Youth Connectors above (See: 9.1.5)

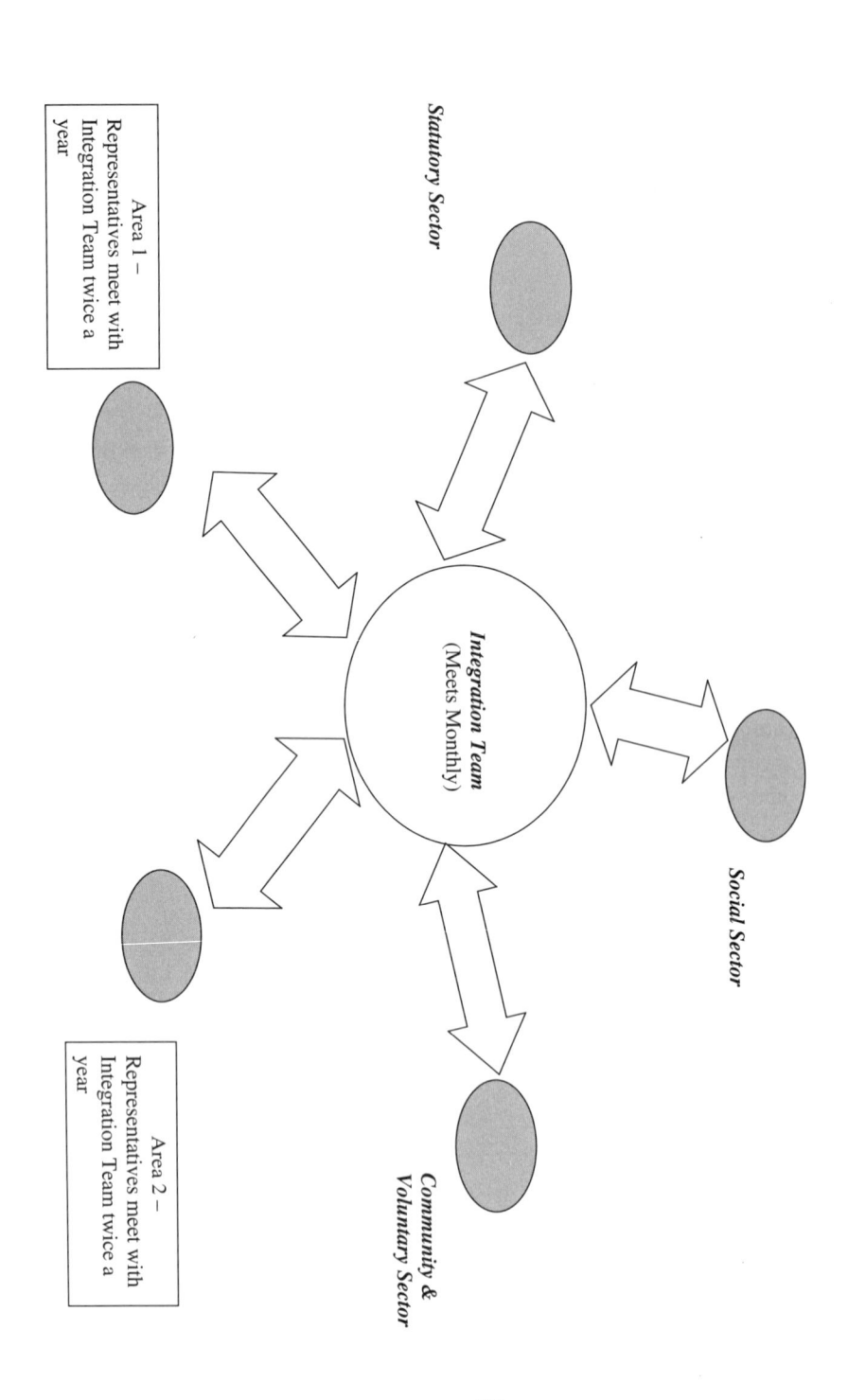

Mobile Youth Unit – Management Structure – Diagram 9.4

Statutory Sector

Integration Team
(Meets Monthly)

Social Sector

Community & Voluntary Sector

Area 1 – Representatives meet with Integration Team twice a year

Area 2 – Representatives meet with Integration Team twice a year

256

9.3 The Triune Youth Model

The Triune Youth model proposes three elements, all of which use an approach underpinned by the principles of equality and participation. Each element has specific aims and objectives, but all share a vision to promote a flexible, multi-dimensional response to identified youth needs. This model is presented under the following headings:

- The Vision
- The Approach
- The Youth Connector
- Youth Workers
- Youth Mentor
- The Team

9.3.1 The Vision

The model seeks to engage with young people within their communities to enable and empower them to identify their own needs on three levels, the individual, the family, and the community, and to encourage their active participation in bringing about positive change in their situations.

9.3.2 The Approach

The approach occurs at three levels, and involves teams of workers who possess specific skills. The group consists of three Youth Connectors, and three Youth Workers. One additional Youth Mentor will operate in a flexible role, linking with the Youth Connectors and Youth Workers as appropriate to make up each full team. A total of four workers in each team provides a gender balance and offers flexibility in arranging teams, while also being compact enough to maintain close working relationships and economies of scale.

9.3.3 The Youth Connectors (3 workers)

The Youth Connectors will establish the initial contact with young people in a targeted community. They operate in a non-judgmental way and the agenda for further work is primarily set through the ensuing interaction between them and the young people. Through discussion, they facilitate the young people to raise topics and issues that help identify their needs.

At this point the Youth Connectors can access their established connections to service providers and organisations with a view to considering appropriate responses to address these identified needs. But the role of the Youth Connector is principally to assist and enable young people to seek and access additional services for themselves. As many young people are reluctant to connect into services, having a connection to an identifiable professional representing their interests to the services may prove adequate, at least for a time. However through this process they are also acquiring information and opportunities to access and negotiate for additional services for themselves, if they so wish.

Aims

- To initiate and establish a distinctive engagement process that cannot be identified by participants with any particular service provider;
- To connect with young people within their own environment;
- To ensure that young people have the free choice to participate at a level of their own choosing.

Objectives

- To connect with young people who for whatever reason do not attach to existing services;
- To facilitate young people to identify their own needs;
- To facilitate young people to develop strategies and plans of action to meet their needs;
- To relay information between young people and service providers when required.

9.3.4 Youth Workers – Mobile Unit (3 Workers)

This response forms one part of a holistic approach to meeting the needs of young people, who through the research have consistently identified a specific need for their own secure place to meet, participate in recreational activities and socialise. It also seeks to overcome the negative perception of many young people that promised services and facilities frequently fail to materialise.

The Mobile Unit offers a response that would have an immediate positive impact on young people's perception of the Triune Youth Model, as it delivers instantly identifiable benefits. The role of Youth Workers is as described in the previous section on the Mobile Unit (See: 9.2). Once the community had agreed to the provision of this service in its area, local adults and young people would quickly gain a sense of ownership of the unit, if only for one or two evenings per week.

The youth work approach promoted by the unit needs to be underpinned by the model's principles of equality and participation, providing continuity in its overall approach. The research has identified that young people generally desire and are capable of organising themselves. Therefore meaningful participation by young people is a key element of developing programmes and activities, and continuous evaluation is essential in maintaining a youth led focus.

Aims

- To provide a quality facility for young people within their community;
- To provide a regular and reliable service to young people.

Objectives

- To enable young people to identify their own needs;
- To facilitate young people to develop appropriate programmes and activities for themselves.

9.3.5 Youth Mentor with Specific Skills (1 worker)

The role of the Youth Mentor is to support and assist specific individuals who are considered to be 'at risk', through providing them with relevant information and facilitating their access to specific services (Justice, Health, Education, etc.) when required.

The Mentor also provides ongoing support to young people who are already in contact with agents such as Probation and Welfare Officers and Social Workers, and facilitates the young person to prepare for and keep appointments.

The Research has highlighted the reluctance of many young people to enter official buildings, which can cause some to become excluded from services. The Mobile Unit offers an informal setting for delivering programmes and conducting interviews and counselling and therapy sessions. Because it is available in the client's immediate neighbourhood, it offers a method of reaching those most isolated. The mentor, operating from the Mobile Unit, can organise the delivery of supports in a familiar, secure and relaxed environment, thereby removing barriers that often prevent young people from accessing more institutional structures.

Specific supports that could be accessed by the mentor include psychological services, addiction counselling, health issues, crime diversion programmes, social welfare services, training, career guidance, etc.

Aims

- To provide accurate information to young people;
- To provide access to quality training for young people;
- To empower young people to develop and negotiate appropriate solutions to meet their needs;
- To provide support services with and for young people within their community.

Objectives

- To deliver information and training to young people in a relaxed and informal setting;
- To offer follow-up contact and support if required;
- To deliver a confidential service to young people who present a specific need (e.g. addiction, eating disorder, pregnancy, etc.)
- To empower young people to access information for themselves.

9.3.6 The Team (Diagram 9.4)

It is important that the members of the team understand their individual roles but adopt a flexible approach in order to maximise the benefits for their clients. Regular team meetings and support sessions are vital in assisting the team and ensuring that the focus of the approach is maintained.

The three elements are co-ordinated in a schedule that facilitates the presence of each team member (the Youth Connector, the Youth Worker and the Youth Mentor) in the ongoing delivery of the service. Through the combined skills and efforts of the team, operating in partnership with the young people themselves, a variety of needs can be identified and met. For young people whose needs may require skills unavailable within the team, connections into the Integration Management Team can provide access to further services and supports.

TriuneYouth Model – Diagram 9.4

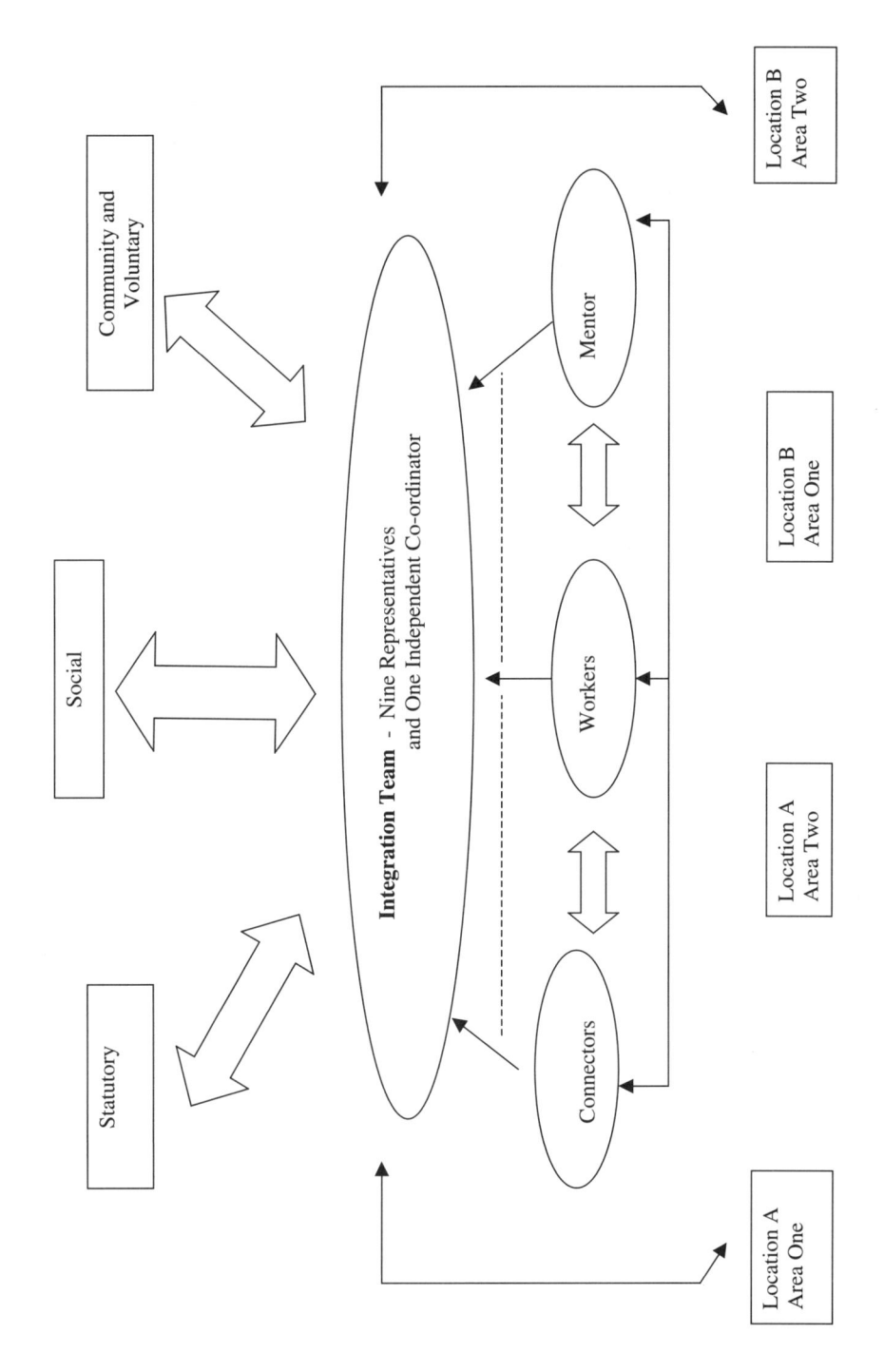

9.4 Conclusions

The three models presented here are all based on the principles of equality and participation, and offer different methods of engaging with young people exhibiting multiple factors of vulnerability.

Each of the models considers management and practice, identifying specific aims, objectives and roles for the stakeholders involved. It is essential that a common understanding is achieved among those who commit to a method. Organisations that offer their support must be willing to provide adequate resources, and to facilitate the structural changes that meaningful participation of young people demands.

With adequate resources and sufficient support, and a willingness by service providers to implement changes in their decision making processes, the models presented here offer a realistic and practical method of empowering young people exhibiting multiple factors of vulnerability to become involved in developing services and supports to meet their multiple needs.

Appendix One

Organisations represented on the COUNTY WEXFORD YOUTH AT RISK FORUM (CWYARF)

South West Wexford Community Development Project
Noreen Healy Magwa, Ramsgrange

St Vincent de Paul
Mary O'Rourke, Carne Holiday Centre

ISPCC
Aine Crawley
Abbey St, Wexford

Young Women's Project, FDYS
Catherine Cleary and Michelle Byrne, c/o Youth Info, Wexford

FAB Community Development Project
SAFE Project, FAB CDP
Annie Reynolds and Brenda Wadding Byrne, Ferndale
(Brendan Hynes, c/o Wexford County Council)

Gorey Youth Needs Group
Pat Kelly, Gorey

Enniscorthy Community Youth Project
Mairead Duffy, St Patricks Community Youth Centre

Coolcots Community Youth Project
Carolyn Cleary, Ferndale

Templeshannon Community Youth Project
Murt Flynn, Templeshannon

Traveller Youth/Community Worker

Youth Info, FDYS
Asylum Seekers Refugee Project, FDYS
Sheila Dempsey, c/o Youth Info, Wexford

Youth New Ross
Julie Somers, CBS New Ross

Wexford Area Partnership
Tom O'Donoghue, Wexford

Wexford Community Care
Thelma Blehein, Gorey and Sheila McNasser, Wexford

County Wexford Partnership
Sara Kickham, Enniscorthy

Appendix Two

Members of the WEXFORD YOUTH NEEDS PROJECT STEERING GROUP

Mr. Bernard O'Brien	Chairperson
Dr. Niall McElwee	Research Consultant
Mr. Tom O'Donoghue	Wexford Area Partnership
Ms. Sarah Kickham	County Wexford Partnership
Ms. Phyllis Barry	Welfare and Probation Service
Ms. Sheila McNassar	South Eastern Health Board
Ms. Catherine Cleary	County Wexford Youth At Risk Forum
Ms. Noirin Healy-Magwa	County Wexford Youth At Risk Forum
Ms. Sheila McArdle-Walsh	Researcher
Mr. Dave O'Grady	Researcher (Jan 02 – Sept 02)
Mr. Conor Dervan	Researcher (June 01 – Nov 01)

Key to Map

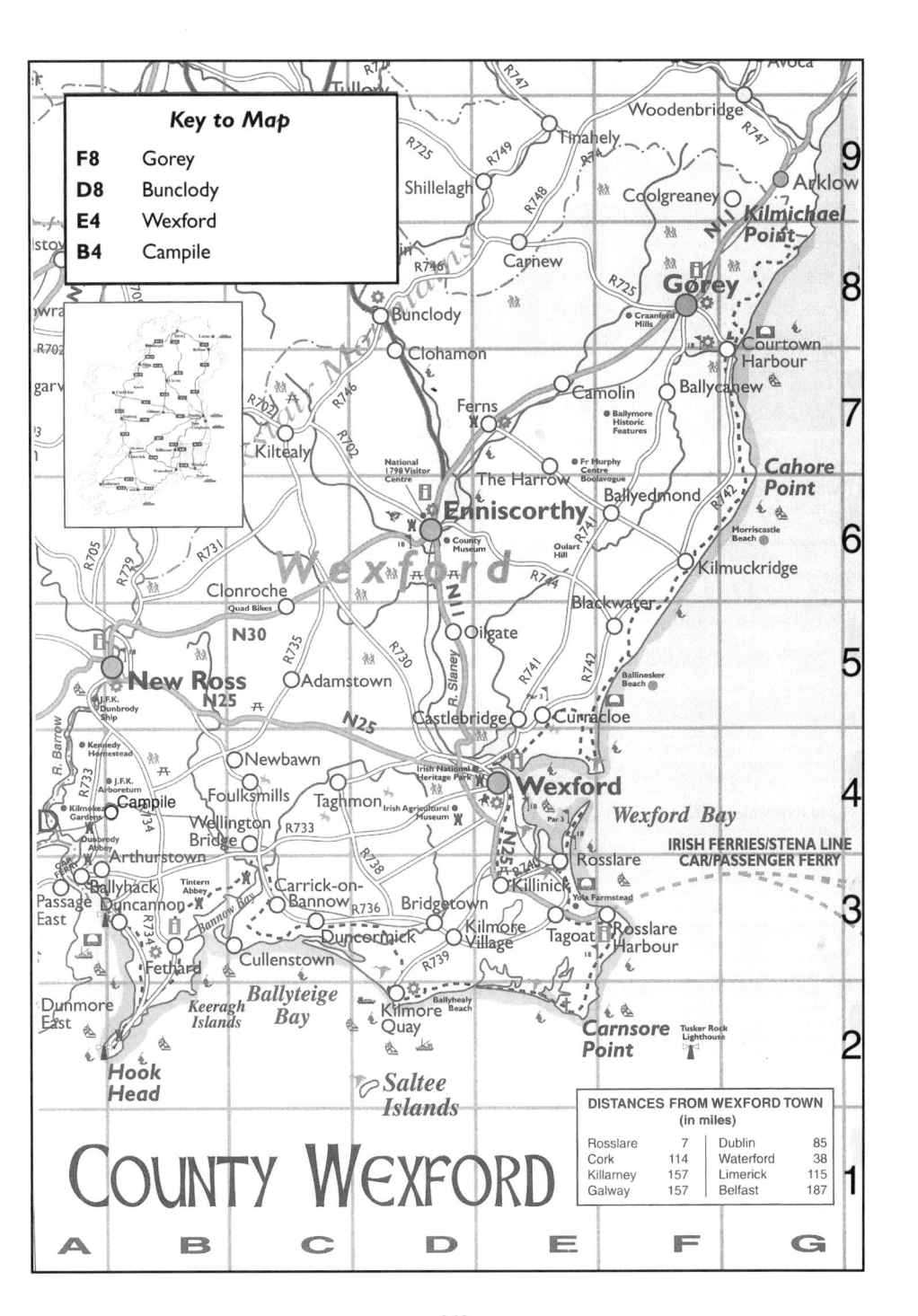

F8	Gorey
D8	Bunclody
E4	Wexford
B4	Campile

COUNTY WEXFORD

DISTANCES FROM WEXFORD TOWN
(in miles)

Rosslare	7	Dublin	85
Cork	114	Waterford	38
Killarney	157	Limerick	115
Galway	157	Belfast	187

Appendix Four

Letter of Introduction via Thematic Entry Point

Dear

We will be calling to see if you might be interested in helping us with research into what are the needs of young people in Wexford. The Researchers are trying to talk to different young people in the County about what they think of where they live, what there is to do, is there enough things for young people, is there help for you in the area if you needed it and stuff like that.

XXXXXX said to us that he thought you might be interested and we would be delighted if you could spare a bit of time to talk to us.

The research is being carried out by two people Conor Dervan* and Sheila McArdle-Walsh. We will be around at XXXXXXX so we will call to see if you are interested or you could come and meet us afterward if the that time doesn't suit and find out more of what its about.

Otherwise you could phone us and leave a message on: 053 –23994

We really would like to talk to as many different young people as possible so your help would be great.

(*Later replaced by Dave O'Grady)

Appendix Five

Extract from Field Notes

(All names and dates have been deleted, R1 and R2 are the researchers, yf means young female, and ym means young male.)

7.10   Arrived in xxxxxxx, logged in with Gardai. Walked along Main St, to the xxxxxxxxx School and back through the lane to xxxxxxxx Square. Although the night was fine and reasonably warm, there was no sign of young people on the streets.

7.50   Played a game of pool in xxxxxxxx. Two men in charge, with about eight others (aged 14-17) playing on tables. One girl (16) seemed to be the resident expert in fixing problems, and showed great authority and considerable knowl edge in freeing blocked balls by lifting tables. At this stage we were looking for specific individuals so we didn't try too hard to engage those there in conversation.

8.10   Went to xxxxxxxx for a coffee, sat in window seat. After ten minutes, saw xxxxx and xxxxxxx on street, and called them in. They refused offers of coffee or food, but seemed happy to stay for a time. xxxxxxx was quiet, had a scar on his cheek but made positive eye contact. xxxxxxx. was happy to see us and enthusiastic about the activity day. Both gave us permission to visit their homes, supplied their addresses and took copies of the information letters. We agreed arrangements about calling to their homes the following night. Then xxxxxx and xxxxxx walked by and were called in by xxxxxxx. Both seemed enthusiastic about Activity day. We chatted for some minutes more, R1 and R2 sitting at the table, the four young people standing in an awkward circle, waiting to leave but alert to the etiquette involved. Only when R1 suggested we finish, did they feel able to move off.

8.30   Went to the park and through theatre car park where xxxxxxxxx was engaged in 'chase the hat' again with two ym. She seemed to be enjoying the activity, but was clearly losing to the other two. We went with them towards xxxxxxxx St, where a larger group (6-8) of ym and yf was gathering.

8.45   Checked xxxxxxxx and xxxxxxxxx, but no-one around. Went back along xxxxxxxx St. and met the group of 8 ym and yf gathered around a bench. One ym was sitting on a litter bin, rolling it around and making a lot of noise. Others were laughing and talking loudly. This behaviour might from a distance seem unruly, even threatening, but up close the atmosphere was warm, good humoured and tolerant. To R2, the sense of solidarity was the most striking aspect of the group. The oldest ym waited talking to us as the rest moved up a side street, and groaned as they made a racket outside a particular house. He explained that the owner was regularly harassed by the group because he reacted so strongly to provocation. He excused himself to follow after the others.

9.15   Went towards xxxxxxxx and xxxxxxxx to check out the area and the surrounding estates. No sign of anyone around. Went on to xxxxxxxx.

Appendices Six to Thirteen provide an example of a complete set of Data Matrices from one Focus Group (F1) for each of the Topic headings.

Appendix Six – Risk

Risk A - F1 – Young persons' perceptions of Risk

		Alcohol Reference	
19		What would you consider to be risky or harmful to other people?	*Cross Reference with Perceptions of Risk
19	5	At the house parties you know drinking and all you know X they get to drunk. You kind of say stop like	
19		Unconscious and you don't know what's wrong with them	
19		Like that one remember she drank the naggin of Vodka or something	Reference to a case reported in the local newspaper regarding fatality of young girl from choking on vomit
		And she died	*Cross reference to cultural/social matrix
19		Risk of being caught	Aware of possible consequences of behaviour
3	3	Who'd catch you then, who would you be worried about catching you then?	
3	3	Parents	*Cross reference with resilience
3	1	My father	Drinking is seen as crossing boundaries set by Parents
4	3	I was up in the park one day and my mother walked through we had to hide in the bush	Seen as a source of amusement
		Tape One- Side B	
19	R1	What would you consider to be risky or harmful to other young people?	
		Just drugs something like if they were taking you know E's or something like that	
		Tape Two –Side A	
13	R1	What do you consider too be risky for you?	
3	3	We don't do nothing risky	
	R1	No?	
	3	Actually don't	

268

Appendices Six to Thirteen provide an example of a complete set of Data Matrices from one Focus Group (F1) for each of the Topic headings.

Appendix Seven – Health

F1 Health – Associated Behaviours

Alcohol

Pg No	Respondent Code	Quote	Comments
		Tape One – Side A	
		Tell us about alcohol?	Research question
1	3	It's nice	
1	4	We go up to our friend's house, we drink and then we go to the disco and we're drunk	Consumption of Alcohol normal activity Location identified
1	3	For a bit of excitement and	Associated with fun
1	3	None of us really get into pub so	
1	4	Yeah we only go into pubs at birthdays or new years	
		What would you drink?	
2	1	Bacardi breezers orange	General consensus among the group that
2	2	Smirnoff Ice	The consumption of alcohol is acceptable
2	3	No cider or anything like that it's sick. It would make you sick	Rejection of cider
2	3	Tequila	Preference for spirits
2	1	We wouldn't drink pints or anything	
2	3	I'd drink pints, I love them	
		Why do you like pints?	
2	3	Nicer	Preference for beers
2	1	I think they last longer	
2	3	Have our different opinions like	Respondent appears to be able to resist peer pressure Resiliency factor *
2	5	Drink down a laneway	Location identified
3	3	Yeah we used to do that before we'd go when we were younger like when a few years we used to go discos and get flagons. You know flagons of cider	Participants average age 14 – refer to previous drinking of cider illustrating started to drink at a very young age. That would make you sick quote page 1 by same respondent.
3	5	And drink that up in the park or something	Location identified
3	3	Fall over ourselves	
		How would you get the alcohol then?	

269

			Links into older peer groups
3	4	Somebody	
3	3	Somebody on the street would get it for you or like anybody you know like we'd know people who are over 18 so we could get them we'd just go up to them and they'll get it for you	
3	1	As long as you don't get caught	Concerns around getting caught
3	3	Who'd catch you then, who would you is worried about catching you then?	
3	1	Parents	Drinking is seen as crossing boundaries set by Parents
4	3	My father	
4	3	I was up in the park one day and my mother walked through we had to hide in the bush	Seen as a source of amusement
		How many of you would normally go drinking together?	
4		Loads of us, everyone like really, then sometimes if we were lucky our friend would have a free house or something we could go to then	
		Tape One – Side B	
18	5	They're starting to get stricter now alcohol cause the disco's they're going in on the buses and checking everybody	* Cross –reference (Justice Matrix) They are the Gardai
18	1	People drinking down by the river	Location identified
18	3	They caught L and all drinking already	Young people had been caught
19	3	They had to pay £30 fine and their parents had to go up (barracks)	Identification of consequences of being caught
19	5	What would you consider to be risky or harmful to other people?	*Cross Reference with Perceptions of Risk
19		At the house parties you know drinking and all you know X they get to drunk. You kind of say stop like	
19		Unconscious and you don't know what's wrong with them	
19		No that never really happened like, if they were going to get to drunk we take the drink off them and we'd say stop like	
19		We've actually done that before remember	
19		Who	
19		Ah no it was you, it was you remember? Took the drink off me, remember I was drinking up at the Tech (school)? Were you not there? A and all were there.	*Resilience factor – peers
19		Yeah, they were drinking and they wouldn't let me finish my drink	
19		Like that one remember she drank the naggin of Vodka or something	
19		And she died	Reference to a case reported in the local newspaper regarding fatality of young girl from choking on vomit
19		And they put her on her back, they should kind of get first aid like	*Cross reference to cultural/social matrix
21		Cause like if you put them on their back they're going to choke and if you put then on their belly they're going to smother like so.	Aware of possible consequences of behaviour * Resilience factor – coping skill identified

270

F1 Health – Associated Behaviours

Drugs and Solvents

Pg No	Respondent Code	Quote	Comments
17		Tape One – Side A	
17	3	Well only one group of people actually, like there's loads of groups of people in X like, but only one group of druggies. Sorry for saying that, but it is druggies that go there	* Cross reference with perceptions of services Labelled and associated with "druggies" therefore service seen as negative
17	1	It's just the people that hang around with that group go there like	Ownership of service associated with one group
17	R1	How do you know their druggies?	
17	4	We don't mix with them	Really don't mix with the group An "out group"
17	3	They don't mix with us, so like we talk to them	Rival group
17	1	We'd say hello	
17	3	If their in school with us, we'd say hello, but half of them we don't really know them…	
17	1	Communicate with them cause their all really high as kites, like	Judged as being "high"
30	R1	Tell us about substance use?	
30	1	What that mean?	
30	3	Drugs?	
30	R1	Not necessarily drugs, but you know	
30	2	Sniffing stuff	Group boundaries – not acceptable for girls in Their peer group
31	3	I've never done it and I intend never to do it	Negative risk
31		Never do it	
31		No	
31		Never taking any drugs either or tried it	
31		It's stupid	
31	2	Alcohol's a drug	Analysis
31		We mean as in	
31		We know that like	
31		Hash and stuff	
31		Sniffing and stuff	
31		And would people you know have or…?	
31		No	

31		Any of your mates use it?	
31		No	
31		Yeah, some of the lads do stuff once or twice like, I'd say they have, but they don't, like, they're not druggies	Social construction of drug taking – acceptable behaviour among their own peer groups. Honesty about use of drugs by friends –male peer group
31		They're not druggies	Group response
31		Or anything, they have smoked a bit of hash a few times	Minimise the behaviour – that would be labelled negatively if occurring in other rival peer group
31		Once every four months	
31		That's about it like	
32		But not popping pills or not E's or all that	A boundary set between hash and pills
32		But there is other young people in X that do drugs and their all big druggies there just not our crowd	Creation of in and out group
32	R1	How do you know their big druggies?	
32		For dealing did they, oh in school?	
32		For selling drugs, like	
32		Cause two of them got suspended from school	
32	3	They go around with their big stoned heads on 'hem	Viewed negatively by the group
33		And they were caught up the back pitches was it?	
33		Tell us a bit about them then, what happened?	General question to the group
33		Ball Alley	Response from members
33		Oh the Ball Alley and they	
33		Searched (by the Gardai)	
33		They gave your one (some girl in school) the drugs and she told	
33		And they've in court and all loads of times	
33	3	This one here was there	Pinpoint member of the focus group that was present in the Ball Alley during the search
34		So tell us about it then, if you want to. If you don't its OK.	
34	2	It's not going to get said back or anything like?	Questioning confidentiality of the group/research
34	R1	Clarified the procedure regarding the tape and subsequent report	Reassuring respondent
34	2	No	
34	2	Can we change it now? (referring to the topic card)	Respondent previously member of druggie peer group. Became uncomfortable around the subject. Requested to move onto other topic.

F1 Health – Associated Behaviours

Sexual Health

Pg No	Respondent Code	Quote	Comments
22	2	But you really wouldn't go to a man doctor if you had problems – if you know what I mean	Initial embarrassment
22	5	No because like when, if you go to a male doctor, when you have something wrong the nurse has to come in, so like for safety for him, like so. You're got two in at you then like...	Aware of ethical considerations
23	2	I get embarrassed saying stuff to the doctor	
23	1	So do I	
23	3	I won't go to the doctor just wait for the problem to pass	
24	R1	Would any of your friends have a baby?	
24	3	Yeah our friend from school has a baby. She's in my year, she's sixteen	Early parenthood
24	4	She was fifteen when she had, it's now sixteen	
24	4	I wouldn't like a baby now	
24	2	I'd love a baby	
24	3	Enjoy life, you don't want to be stuck with a baby	
26	3	Cause imagine like you'd have to, imagine having a baby at 21 you wouldn't be able to go out with your friends	
36	3	And you go out and there's another certain lad there, and your there I want you, but I have a fella at the same time.	
36	3	It wouldn't stop you either (everyone laughs)	
36	2	At house parties	
45	1	When I'm21 with my baby and hopefully find a man	
	Tape Two	Side A	
7	R1	What do you feel about sexual health?	
7	2	Like thrush and all and AIDS and all?	
8	3	Always use a condom	
8	5	We got PD in school, but when you go about these things the teachers go about talking about us being friends and all	*Cross Reference with Education
8	3	They talk about friends and all they don't talk about boyfriends or sex or anything	
9	5	Mrs S she talks about all that, she has videos and everything and she uses condom	

F1 Health – Other Health Issues

Pg No	Respondent Code	Quote	Comments
9	5	Demonstrations and practical	
10	5	They should like you know the first years, how to put them on your knickers, you know the yokes like and stuff like, sanitary towels	
10	5	I think you should start education like in 5th & 6th class, you know when the girls are getting their periods because some of them don't what that is like	
10	2	And they're afraid to say it to their family or whatever	
10	1	I think they should learn about when they're older 16 0r 17	
10	5	No but then if you show them younger like	
10	3	Yeah but there's more people to bet pregnant like	Difference of opinion about sex education
11	1	And your going to hear about it anyway on the street, like no matter what age you are like to know properly like	
11	4	Instead of just picking up bits here and there	
12	5	Like the lads are saying oh you'll be all right with me, like and so on, so forth, and yet they don't know what they're doing themselves like	
12	1	"..but you hear about young people that are riding and like some of them are queer young"	
12	R1	And do you think they are sexually active?	
12	5	Yeah some of them	Aware not just a female issue
12		"… girl that lives near us and she was pregnant at 14 …"	

Mental Health

Pg No	Respondent Code	Quote	Comments
12	R1	What does healthy living mean to you?	
12	1	Eating healthy	
13	3	Happy	
13	3	To be out on the street and enjoy yourself	Social interaction important to feeling healthy
13	3	Were people persons	
14		Tape 1 side 2	
14		He's actually mentally sick like	
14		He was in a centre and he got out like	Recognised that person with mental health issue
15		No he's just an alco like, he'd be always, his always drunk that makes him	Send to centre rather jail

		do all that like
		Tape 2 side 1
5		What do you think would help a young person feeling down or suicidal?
6		Friends
6		Family
6		If your out with your friends the whole time you're having a laugh you'll think
7		I actually don't know you'd have to be in a situation to know what you were going to do first

Eating Disorders

Pg No	Respondent Code	Quote	Comments
43	5	Like for a project in school if you.. about health and all you'd go to .. sure in the chemist like there's loads of leaflets	Identified location of health information
44	5	Anorexia you don't eat, and bulimic is when you eat and throw it back up	*Cross Reference to Culture/Media
44	5	Like in home and away the little one was doing it	Hidden feature of eating disorders
44	5	There's nothing really you could say cause you wouldn't know about it	
46	3	Yeah go to their parents, but if you told the parents that could start an argument between you and the friend like so.	Trust among friends vs. parents – Importance of loyalty to the group
46	1	Better than to start an argument than lying wouldn't it	Values different – priority health of friend

275

Appendices Six to Thirteen provide an example of a complete set of Data Matrices from one Focus Group (F1) for each of the Topic headings.

Appendix Eight – Education

F1 – Education

Pg No	Respondent Code	Quote	Comments
17	3	Tape One Side A	
17	3	If their in school with use we'd say hello, but half of them we don't really know them we don't really	
17	1	Communicate with them cause their all really high as kite	
26	2	I want to finish school, go to college then I want to tour the world	
26	3	When I'm finished school I'm doing hairdressing course right ….its easier to get your visa	Career opportunities discussed through having children
27	5	Work in a clothes shop 9 to 5	
27	3	I want to go to six year, do my leaving, repeat it for the second time …	
27	4	And I'm going for leisure management	
27	1	I want to be a vet	
32		Cause two them got suspended from school	
		For selling drugs	*Cross reference with Health Section (Drugs)
28		Tape Two	
28		Mixed responses of hate and love school (not quote)	Initial Response to school
		5th Year	
		Yeah and I mean I hate it	
28	3	And my mocks are in February	
		The think I like about school is you meet all the friend and all and you go for lunch and all but the horrible thing is the teachers on your back saying study study study	
28	5	Yeah and you've to do all this homework	
28	2	If you didn't have to do homework I wouldn't mind	
29	3	About our school though	
29	3	You can mitch so easy	Truancy
29	2	Its so big	
29	1	I hate getting up early in the morning that's the only thing	
29	3	And we go in late than and marked absent	Behaviour of early school leaver

276

29	5		Some people go Wexford for the whole day	
29	4		Walk the corridors	
29	R1		Just walk the corridors in school seriously?	
29	4		Or sit in the toilets	
29	4		The teacher meets you and where you suppose to be now, Oh I'm going to get my book out of my locker	
29	3		That is and then you just hope you don't meet them again	
30	R1		Is there any services that they offer in school apart from teaching?	Identification of other services
30	All		Sport, young entrepreneurs, student council, school bank	Listed by different responses
31	2		They're all posh like	Social Analysis of School System
31	3		They don't associate with anyone else	
31	5		You only go on a trip if your good like so like this Y this is going on and you have to be good and you have to be in with all these student counsellors to go these trips like so its kind of...	Have conform to being "good" standards set by the posh ones on the student council
32	3		They kind of think their too good for us like so.	Different peer groups in the school
32	4		Its too big	Identity within school
32	3		But we manage all right though I think	Identify their own way of coping
32	1		We do manage	
32	4		Like from our primary school like all the teachers knew your name, you knew everybody nearly in it ..like	Sense of identity in primary school
33	4		But when you go into this school there's so many teachers, you don't, you don't know the teachers names	Loss of identity you don't know all the teachers
33	5		When you go in like you would think cause a lot of people know first years… with their plastered make-up, eyeliners, mascara and all that sure the lads and all think that its so funny looking	
33	4		The first year's when you get in first year you don't know what to do because when you're in primary school, its just girls and then you're with the boy…	Not known what is expected
36	3		They want it, they ask for it, they don't get though	Reference to student council
36	3		I've to be in at 10 on school nights	Link between school and home
48	3		Me mammy told me cause my report was bad	
48	5		Like at the end of the day like the posh ones are going to end up thick like cause were working, were trying to work for something we don't have, like and they got it and they don't care like	Work ethic
48	1		End up thick	
48	5		And their like I still got money, but there's going to be a time when they're not going to have it	
48	3		Hey I don't need to work for money	
48	5		They won't understand the concept of working for money like	Contradicting pervious statement of participant

		Tape Two	
1	5	I use to have to go in at 11 O'clock like they didn't mind as long as I was not doing nothing bold and all, school reports bad, I've to be in at ten now on school nights	
1	3	But that's just pointless because your not going to come in at 10 o'clock and study anyway	Negative reaction
1	1	But I'm queer glad you've to come in at 10 o'clock cause you can walk up with me.	
8		Different quotes regarding Personal Development Class	
8	5	There was one teacher I had that talked about anything you wanted	*Cross reference Health
8	1	JK	
8	5	No and you know the new one that came to school she....	
8	1	Oh Yeah	
8	1	Mrs H	Identification of "nice" teachers
8	5	Mrs S	

278

Appendices Six to Thirteen provide an example of a complete set of Data Matrices from one Focus Group (F1) for each of the Topic headings.

Appendix Nine – Youth Services

F1 – Development of Youth Services

Pg No	Respondent Code	Quote	Comments
15		Tape One – Side A	
15	R1	If you were developing a service for young people what would be important?	
15	3	Shed	
15	R1	She's still at this	
15	3	No I don't mean a shed right just listen to me. You know like the way we'd be freezing cold like walking up along the streets.	
15	R1	Hmmm	
15	3	With nowhere to go like especially in the winter and not even a shed, like, just a room or a house even that we can go into and sit down…..instead of walking around the streets, sitting in the car park	Identification of service
15	4	Like a sports hall or something	Multi-purpose use
15	1	Cause if we go home like you go home like you can't bring four or five girls like and then lads as well into your house, you want a place were all your friends can go as well like.	
15	5	A place that you don't need to worry about fucking ornaments (laugh) …	
15	R1	No. It's all right don't worry go on, it makes no difference say what ever	
15	5	getting broken and all that	
15	R1	So a centre with no ornaments in it	Purpose build for youth needs
15	ALL	Yeah	
15	1	And no windows	
16	3	Anything like	
16	R1	And how would that be run then? How would that centre be run, who would run it?	
16	3	I'd run it	
16	1	And I'd help	
16	3	Like we'd all have the key like you know like let ourselves in	
16	3	If you are feeling generous now you could give us like a telly or pool table or something and some one could have the key and run it every night	The centre would have to be open every night

279

F1 – Perceptions of Youth Services

Pg No	Respondent Code	Quote	Comments
16	R1	So who would have to be there, would anybody	
16	1	All of us would be at it every night anyway it wouldn't make a difference.	
17	4	Yeah well that's just us. What about the other groups like	
17	3	But they have their drop in centre and everything like	
18	R1	So none of you have actually ever used the drop-in?	
18	2	I was in it, I use to be in it	
18	R1	What did you think of it, when you were in it?	
18	2	It's stupid all they do is play pool, sit around and smoke	
18	3	It's better than staying out on the town	
18	2	Yeah, but I use to go up after school and it closes at six, two hours	In appropriate timing of services
18	3	At six?	
18	1	Yeah It closes at six	
18	3	All we want is, when we come out of the X (snooker hall) at nine o'clock, we have to sit in the car park freezing cold, all that want is a room to sit in…	
18	5	You know like, all them old houses no one in them, sure we could have them sure	
19	All	Yeah	
19	3	You know, like the same Sarah McCoy kind drop-in centre on home and away, we could do it up like that	*Cross reference to Culture Section/Media
19	1	Cause like we – we would do it up and all if we got a place wouldn't we like?	
19	All	Yeah	
19	3	Cause that would give us something to do, as well	
19	1	Yeah like umm we'd have something to keep us busy for a while then	
19	5	Parties and all like that	
19	2	We wouldn't have parties at it	
19	3	No 5, stop, we're suppose to be trying to promote this	
19	5	No, but you know what I mean like	
19	4	Something like a proper sports hall, like	Sharing of facility
			*Cross reference to perceptions of youth services

Pg No	Respondent Code	Quote	Comments
6	R1	Tape One – Side A What services are available to you? What do you think about these services?	
6	3	There's none and that's just it	

280

6	R1	None at all?	
6	All	There is none	
7	4	Well there is one, was Irish Dancing, like we did do it	Identification of service
7	1	But we're not into that now	
7	3	We're too old for that now	
7	4	There is sport I play sport	Identification of service
7	1	Yeah there is sport	Identification of service
7	3	Some, most people don't play it (sport) the only thing we have to do is go down to the X (Snooker Hall) it closes at 9.00. then we go up and sit in the car park or sit around the streets for the night, cause we don't want to go home it's boring so	Activity – "on the street"
7	1	And everyone like mouthing about us	Think people talk about them negatively for hanging around
8	3	They (adults) don't let us, we sit in the car park and the guards come up and give out to us for sitting there, but we've nowhere else to go	
8	R1	Right	
8	5	In the summer it was alright because it was warm like, but now it's getting freezing cold like and we've just nowhere else to go	
8	1	And we're not allowed sit anywhere like	
9	3	And we didn't have permission to play football in the hall like so we had to get out	*Cross Reference Relationships Try to initiate activities themselves, but adults intervene Gardai move them on
9	5	Yeah and we bring down a football and lads play football and we sit there watching them and then they come down (Gardai) and say they don't have permission so we've to get out (Car park)	
9	2	I don't know what there talking about providing a service for us, cause they don't.	
17	3	But they have their drop-in centre and everything	Identification of service – not accessed barrier
17	1	We don't go there like	*Cross reference with education and health
17	R1	What about the drop-in? Why don't you go there?	
17	3	Well only one group of people actually, like there's loads of groups of people in the town like, but only one group of druggies. Sorry for saying that but it is the druggies that go there	Service associated with peer group – access barrier
18	R1	So none of you have actually ever used the drop-in?	
18	2	I was in it, I use to be in it	
18	R1	What did you think of it, when you were in it?	
18	2	It's stupid all they do is play pool, sit around and smoke	
18	3	It's better than staying out on the town	
18	2	Yeah, but I use to go up after school and it closes at six, two hours	In appropriate timing of services

18	3	At six?	
18	1	Yeah It closes at six	
18	3	All we want is, when we come out of the X (snooker hall) at nine o'clock, we have to sit in the car park freezing cold, all that want is a room to sit in…	
19	5	Well we had a cinema for like a week, but like	
19	2	That wasn't even a cinema, that was all the old pictures	
20	3	No one actually went because ever time you went in it was broke	
20	1	That's in C you can't walk	
20	5	It's still like you have to pay money for a taxi and all that. Can't afford cabs there and cabs back like	Cost of accessing services -barrier
20	1	Then to get in and out like	
21	3	We've only been to the cinema like twice in the last year, all of us like, you get a taxi down it's about £30.00	Cost of accessing services- barrier
		Tape Two – Side A	
3	3	Well at least, we had the summer fair, but every time the summer fair is on it's raining.	(Possibly time of the foot and mouth)
3	1	They stopped that	
3	R1	How come, did they say why?	
3	1	No	
3	3	No cause they're just thick	
3	3	Sure that was another thing we had that, that was kind of the only thing we did actually look forward for in the summer	Lack of facilities
4	3	That the only thing we did have to look forward to in the summer you know like. That another you know like the cinema. The activities that's another one and they've taken that away now as well	Supply of activities by the community
4	R1	And what about the theatre in town..?	Removal of existing services
4	3	We're going to see X	
4	R1	Would you ever get a chance to act in any of them?	Identification of service
4	All	No	
4	R1	Would you be interested?	
4	4	Same people are in them all	
4	2	You kind of have to know how to sing and all, musicals	
4	3	Posh Ones	
4	5	You kind of have to be able to sing and dance	
4	2	You know you'd have to be a posh knob to be able …	
5	1	I can sing lads, I've only	Perceived barrier
5	2	Sure I can dance	

5	3	2 you can dance now all right	Referring to 2 currently on crutches
5	4	Like people who go to dance school and singing school they get in before…	Analysis of why some people are chosen
5	3	Anyone else	
5	R1	Anyone else?	
5	3	They've an advantage upon us	
5	R1	And how do you feel about that?	
5	All	Don't care	
5	R1	Really don't care?	
5	3	I wouldn't be able to remember the lines	
5	1	Either would I	
5	5	I wouldn't either. I wouldn't be bothered	Rationalise by providing reasons why they couldn't take part. Self perpetuation of exclusion?

Appendices Six to Thirteen provide an example of a complete set of Data Matrices from one Focus Group (F1) for each of the Topic headings.

Appendix Ten – Justice

F1 Justice – Illegal Behaviours

Pg No	Respondent Code	Quote	Comments
5		Alcohol	*See Health section
5	3	Drugs	*See Health section
5	1	Sexual activity	*See Health section
5	4	Tape 1 – Side A	
5	3	We all got barred cause we were fighting (disco)	Girl against Girls from different areas
5	1	I never got barred	
5	4	Me and No3 got kicked out and they followed us	Physical fighting led to being barred
5	3	We've never got on like, we always fight with them no matter what. (Girls from neighbouring area)	
29		They can go around with no seatbelts… and give other people tickets, but they don't do it.	Reference regarding seatbelts
30	1	.. this lad came in handcuffs after being up in court, he was kind of cool looking… guard went down to the chipper and brought him up curry and ….	
30	1	It was cool looking, the garda went to the chipper for him like	
		Tape One –Side B	
4	2	I think it was just the people, you know you hang around with people you get in trouble..	*Cross Reference Peer Group Analysis by young people of peer group influence
4	1	He got in trouble with them, then he started to hang around with us and he actually didn't get in trouble like.	
5	3	"and then like they put him away and when he goes away like he's just going to come back out and his going to be worst again like	Person they knew had been in trouble with the law
5	3	If he keeps getting put away and keeps getting in trouble his going to be like that for the rest of his life	
5	3	But his family like have been in as well so its not just him	*Cross Reference with family
6	1	"I think it's just boredom	
6	1	You'd be doing so many things you wouldn't be thinking of doing mischief like	Ways of preventing boredom – cause of boredom –crime
6		What would you consider mischief?	
7	R1	Like breaking windows, banging doors, nick knocking, that kind of stuff	(Knocking on peoples doors and running away)

284

7	1	Were not bold anyway but	
7	R1	No, I 'm not saying that you are. I'm just saying what would you think, is what about shoplifting and stuff like that?	
7	1	Don't do it	
7	3	Yeah we use to	
8	3	Will I tell you a good example?	
8	R1	Yeah tell us a good example	
8	3	It's really really funny	Petty larceny seen as "fun". Told story and was quite funny.
9	4	No but like we use to … you know like when we were younger, younger we use to go down on the street and get make-up and sweets	
9	4	Or go into Y and you know the pick and mix like go around and eat them	
9	3	I think everyone goes through stages of shop lifting then they'll get over it	Normal activity
9	4	Not really, they'll get caught	Recognition of possible consequences
9	1	I never robbed lads	(Peer pressure – from looks from participants)
9	1	Oh yeah I did	
9	1	Umbrella and a taz bar	
9	3	Nothing really valuable you'd rob like	x
10	R1	You never broke into anyone's house or anything like that?	Social construction of acceptable theft
11	All	No	
11	2	Might get caught	Again fear of being caught
11	3	You used to be able to do that go down the street and leave your door open or whatever like	
11	1	A house was robbed up in my estate the other night	
11	1	The back door was left like unlocked ard someone went in and raided the house	
13	3	"… he sells drugs, deals drugs to everyone, he keeps drugs in the house with his kids and everything like …"	
14	5	Yeah (P) four months for robbing a stereo and then this big druggie gets four months for dealing drugs	
14	3	… that's just unfair like…	
14	3	I think he is actually mental	Robbery
15	5	His more of a threat to society than P is and P get 18 months for sweet fuck all like	
16	1	The car park or whatever. No that's not fair, cause we don't be doing anything	
16	4	And there's nothing there to damage	
16	3	… like if we walk up the street we're only annoying people who live on the street or whatever. When we're sitting there (car park) like we're not	Space that is open not near houses so they don't annoy people.

18	4	annoying anybody like	
18	4	One garda was on patrol and he came in and he was going mad and the other squad car came in	Reference to drinking in public
18	4	X (Garda in other car) just laughed at us and said go on	
19	4	They had to pay £30 find and their parents had to go up	Fine of other young people
22	3	Just say his father would be out and we get the car and go up the country	Under age driving of motor car
22	1	It wouldn't be like the whole time	Rationalising the activity
22	3	But his able to drive, he doesn't be driving into bushes or anything like his able to drive	
22	3	That's all really driving we do	
22	1	We don't be getting people racing each other nothing like that	

Appendices Six to Thirteen provide an example of a complete set of Data Matrices from one Focus Group (F1) for each of the Topic headings.

Appendix Eleven – Independence

F1 – Family

Pg No	Respondent Code	Quote	Comments
3	R1	Who'd catch you then, who would you be worried about catching you then?	Cross Health Section/Alcohol
3	3	Parents	Drinking is seen as crossing boundaries set by Parents
3	1	My father	
4	3	I was up in the park one day and my mother walked through we had to hide in the bush	Seen as a source of amusement
5	3	But his family like have been in as well so its not just him	*Cross Reference justice
43	3	Hmm I'd go to my mammy	Regarding information
43	5	So would I	
43	1	I'd go to me dad his brilliant	Resilience Factors
		Tape One –Side B	
24	R1	So what do you all do for money then?	*Cross Reference Employment
24	3	Scrounge	
24	1	Scrounge off my mammy	Family supply monetary support
24	4	Baby-sit once now and again	Source of income –baby sitting
42		I wouldn't be able to afford to live on my own like	Realistic about the cost of living outside of the home
43		I can't cook you'll starve	
43		I'd love to live on my own	
43		I wouldn't I wouldn't be able	
43	R1	Why would you love to live on your own?	
43		I don't know when, I'll have my baby, I'll move out	*Shift in morals –
43	4	You don't realise how easy you've got it, cause everything is done for you	Appreciates family support
43	3	I know we go mad, oh I've to wash up or whatever like	
43	5	But, if were out in the house on our own, like, if we didn't have them there (referring to family) we'd have to make our own dinner, we'd have to wash up after it, dry up what ever	
43	R1	…. Young people we've met on the streets, their parents would be separated… do you think that makes a difference to young people	

287

43	No	No	Separated families are acceptable
43	All	No, not me anyway	
43		Not me either	
43	2	No not as long as you've got someone there to nag	
43		When I'm 16 I'm moving out	
43		What did you say you're going to do when you're sixteen	
43	2	Move out	
43	2	I'm going to move in with my daddy	
43	3	No number two	
43	2	Why?	
43	3	Cause	
43	2	Its nearer to the town though lads	
43	2	Stay out all night	
43	3	So	
43	3	It's better having to be told what to do	
43	2	Sure he'll tell me what to do	
43	3	What	
43	2	He makes me clean up the whole place	Role given as carer by father to daughter
43	R1	Why is it better to be told what to do?	
43	3	I don't know cause like, if you, if you were allowed to do whatever you wanted you'd be a little terror, you be doing like	Setting Boundaries
43	2	No you wouldn't	
43	3	You could be in trouble	
43	4	If you were brought up being allowed	
43	3	Do whatever you want	
47	All	We all live in a council housing estate	(Singing)
47	5	But then again there's all the posh knobs and everything, but we were, I don't care like we were brought up in the council houses. But we were brought up better because their all to posh and spoilt to know right from wrong like, but we do cause we were brought up like that.	Assumed posh one don't know right from wrong. The group's perception of right from wrong
		Tape Two – Side A	
1	3	I came in at 10.15 I wasn't allowed out, then another night I came in at 10.15 and I gave out, or then I shouted at my father, and he says "your grounded for a week" "I'm what for a week"	Setting Boundaries
1		She was going to run away and everything	
3		And I was cracking up in my house, cause I'm not use to sitting in all the time	

288

F1 – Peer Groups

Pg No	Respondent Code	Quote	Comments
		Tape One – Side A	
5	3	We all got barred, cause we were fighting	Aggressive behaviour
5	1	I never got barred	
5	4	Me and No.3 got kicked out and they followed.	Indicated rest of focus group participants Illustrating strengthen of peer group
5	3	They don't like us and we don't like them	Stereotyping other girls from different area
36	3	No but wait we hang around with the lads were with so	*Cross Reference Relationships
36	1	Naturally enough if you're going with them	
36	3	No like we hung around with them before we got with them anyway so.	*Cross Reference Relationships
18	2	I was in it, I use to be in it	*Cross Reference Youth Service
18	R1	What did you think of it, when you were in it?	
18	2	It's stupid all they do is play pool, sit around and smoke	Previously focus group had identified a similar service for themselves. Person changing peer groups to illustrate dislike for previous peer group and the service associated with this group.
18	3	It's better than staying out on the town	
4	2	I think it was just the people, you know you hang around with people you get in trouble...	*Cross Reference Peer Group Analysis by young people of peer group influence
4	1	He got in trouble with them, then he started to hang around with us and he actually didn't get in trouble like.	

F1 – Relationships

Pg No	Respondent Code	Quote	Comments
		Tape One –Side A	
10	R1	Sexuality, attitude about gay and lesbian people?	Individual Personal Relationships
10	2	I don't like gay people	Mixed reaction –some more tolerant than others
10	3	I don't know any so I don't care	Some think it is ok
10	1	Remember at the X in the summer a while ago and there were two lesbians there from a foreign country there	
10	2	That was disgusting	
10	5	I don't care whatever they want themselves	
11	1	…As long as they didn't try kissing me they'd be all right	
12	2	Well its disgusting seen two lads kissing each other	
34	1	…Sexuality does it matter if you have a partner? (girlfriend or boyfriend)	
34	All	No	
34	R1	Doesn't matter?	
34	3	No because were young, better off not	
34	1	Well you would say that and you're the one with a boyfriend	
34	2	It doesn't matter and she's the one with the boyfriend	
35	3	You've a boyfriend too	Heterosexual Relationships
35	2	Yeah I know but…	
35	4	Everyone of us do, 5 she's nearly getting there with her man	

290

35	3	Give her a week! Give her a week	
35	1	But it wouldn't matter if we didn't have a boyfriend	
35	2	But it would sometimes	
35	3	But if we broke up with them now, we'd be all sad, but then we'd got over it like	
35	5	Yeah, but sometimes you want to be with other people like and you can't	Moral boundary
34	3	No. 5 that's only you	
34	1	That's only you	To have more than one partner
36	5	And you go out and there's another certain lad there, and you're there, I want you, but I have a fella at the same time	
36	2	But sure that wouldn't stop you 5	
36	3	It wouldn't stop you either	Laughter among the group
36	3	You've done it enough times	
36	2	Once, twice, three times	
36	3	How is it three?	
36	2	The house party, the surprise party and X's party	
36	2	Yeah, but its only two lads	
36	3	Same two lads	
36	4	Oh you're so committed	
36	3	No but wait we hang around with the lads were with so	
36	1	Naturally enough if you're going with them	
36	3	No like we hung around with them before we got with them anyway so.	*Cross Reference Peer Group
39	R1	What happens if you didn't have your phones? How would you keep in contact? What would happen to You?	

291

Pg No	Respondent Code	Quote	Comments
39	3	I'd cry	
39	1	You wouldn't get a lad really as much wouldn't you not	
39	5	We never leave down our phone	
39	1	You wouldn't cause that's how you get with them, by texting them	Establish relationships
40	5	But if you forget to erase text messages that proves that's bad things like can happen, some people could write something like and not want other people to see it, but then they will see it like	
40	3	Or they can find out stuff like, if you have a fella and his texting a one like you can find out like if his doing the dirt from the messages like	Checking relationships – monitoring behaviour
			Adult Relationships outside of the family
7	1	And everyone like mouthing about us	Think people talk about them negatively for hanging around
8	3	They (adults) don't let us, we sit in the car park and the Gardai come up and give out to us for sitting there, but we've nowhere else to go	Garda viewed negatively
9	3	And we didn't have permission to play football in the hall like so we had to get out	*Cross Reference Youth Services Try to initiate activities themselves, but adults intervene
9	5	Yeah and we bring down a football and lads play football and we sit there watching them and then they come down (Gardai) and say they don't have permission so we've to get out (Car park)	Gardas move them on
		Tape Two – Side A	
10	5	And they're afraid to say to their family or whatever	*Cross Reference Health Section

F1 – Employment

Pg No	Respondent Code	Quote	Comments
		Tape one –side A	
26	2	I want to finish school, go to college then I want to tour the world	*Cross reference Education Section
26	3	When I'm finished school I'm doing hairdressing course right….its easier to get your visa	Career opportunities discussed through having children
27	5	Work in a clothes shop 9 to 5	
27	3	I want to go to six year, do my leaving, repeat it for the second time ….	
27	4	And I'm going for leisure management	
27	1	I want to be a vet	
42	5	If I was looking for a job or something like	

42	5	Go to the unemployment centre	
2		Tape One – Side B	
2	2	I don't like foreigners	*Cross reference with cultural and social needs Response related to ethnic backgrounds
2	R1	You can't get a job?	
2	2	Cause they've taken over all the jobs, you can't get a job then	
2	5	No..the only reason their getting a job is because you can pay them cheap, because you can't pay us like	Evidence of Social analysis
2	1	Two for one package	
2	4	They pay them less than the minimum wage	
23	R1	What about employment for you as a young person?	
23	3	There is none	
23	2	Can't get a job with the foreigners	Racist remark
23	1	I'm too young	Aware of employment legislation
23	R1	Your to young right, and you can't get one	
23	2	Cause all the foreigners have taken	Same respondent as before at page 2 Racists remark
24	3	Mainly the jobs are for they want someone for the school hours… they want people for the week and weekends	
24	4	They want people want people part time they want them to do Sunday nights and they've got school the next day, so it hard to.	*Link to school not stated in school matrix
24	3	And some people want people with experience. But how are you suppose to get experience if they won't give you a job	
24	R1	So what do you all do for money then?	
24	3	Scrounge	
24	1	Scrounge off my mammy	Family supply monetary support
24	4	Baby-sit once now and again	Source of income –baby sitting
24	3	We might get £20 for ourselves. 20 Euro for ourselves	
25	4	Other than that we don't (Referring to job)	
25	3	I had a job for the summer	
25	R1	In the famous chipper	
25	2	I worked there as well	
26	4	Yeah the BS shop	
26	5	Waitressing	*currently working
26	5	I didn't like the chef	
26	5	She was an old bitch	
26	5	She expected me to do everything and I there working a day	

Appendices Six to Thirteen provide an example of a complete set of Data Matrices from one Focus Group (F1) for each of the Topic headings.

Appendix Twelve – Culture

F1 – Culture and Social Needs

Pg No	Respondent Code	Quote	Comments
12	4	Tape One – Side A	
19	3	Ibiza uncovered and all	
	3	You know like the same Sarah McCoy kind drop-in centre on home and away, …..	Media Referencing
	3	We've only been to the cinema like twice in the last year, all of us like, you get a taxi down it's about £30.00	
29	3	Miss Congeniality	
44	3	Like in Home and Away the little one was doing it	Reference to media
39	R1	Use of ICT's	
39	All	This texting the messages I find it's brilliant cause you text each other all the time.	
39	R1	Yeah	
39	3	What happens if you didn't have your phones? How would you keep in contact? What would happen to You?	
39	1	I'd cry	
39	5	You wouldn't get a lad really as much wouldn't you not	
39	1	We never leave down our phone	
40	5	You wouldn't cause that's how you get with them, by texting them	Establish relationships
40		But if you forget to erase text messages that proves that's bad things like can happen, some people could write something like and not want other people to see it, but then they will see it like	*Cross Reference - Relationships
40	3	Or they can find out stuff like, if you have a fella and his texting a one like you can find out like if his doing the dirt from the messages like	Checking relationships – monitoring behaviour
40	1	Proof as well this is good evidence	
41	3	Just ring and see are you X or Y	
41	4	Yeah, where are you in X, right down in a minute	Self-organisation
41	5	Or if you have no money, keep your phone charged and you play the games on it like	

294

			Tape One – Side B	
			Different Backgrounds	
1	1	R1	Tell us about an experience with someone from a different background?	
1	2		Don't like them Dubliners	
1	3		Because they come down in the summer as if they own X like, and then the move here, they mouth about us like, bogger land	
1	4		The way we dance	
1	1		They think they own the place like	
1	2		And people don't like different religions	
1	5		We don't care like but we know the lads and all, your protestant and all like	
2	3		Your orange, orange or whatever like	
2	2		I don't like foreigners	*Cross reference to employment section Racist remarks
2	R1		You can't get a job?	
2	2		Cause they've taken over all the jobs, you can't get a job then	
2	5		No..the only reason their getting a job is because you can pay them cheap, because you can't pay us like	Analysis offered to the group
2	1		Two for one package	
2	4		They pay them less than the minimum wage	
2	3		I don't mind anyone else, it's just Dubliners the way they think they own the place	
2	1		I don't mind anybody	
2			Change in Community	
2	4		Cause X was tiny like, you knew all the streets exactly, where you were going, but now	
2	2		You can't find the place	
2	3		We use to know every street in X like whatever we knew, nearly everyone in X we walked up and down the street and say hello to everyone you see cause we knew them all. Now there's loads of streets I haven't even heard of like	Urban Expansion of the area
2	4		We'd be walking up the road like and we'd be oh God there's more houses there like and all	
2	3		Everyone we see like, we barely know anyone like	
3	R1		How does that make you feel?	
3	4		Bad like, really we can't…	
3	3		We don't know everyone ourselves like	
3	1		You don't know who's in you own town like	
3	4		It's not a community like it more like….	
3	3		They don't mix either it's the same people that where here all the time are still mixing and then	Not integrated as a community

3	4	R1	Use to be like you know, just a small little town, like everyone knew everyone, but now it's bigger and nobody knows anybody and whatever like.	
47	3		Cause like all of us, you know like, we live in a council house right, all up there	Locate themselves with an area
47	All	All	We all live in a council housing estate	
47	5		But then again there are all the posh knobs and everything, but we were, I don't care like we were brought up in the council houses. But we were brought up better because their all to posh and spoilt to know right from wrong like, but we do cause we were brought up like that.	(Singing) Assumed posh one don't know right from wrong The group's perception of right from wrong *Cross Reference Family/Community/Peer Group
4	R1		The Arts	
4	3		And what about the theatre in town..?	
4	R1		We're going to see X	
4	All		Would you ever get a chance to act in any of them?	
4	R1		No	
4	4		Would you be interested?	
4	2		Same people are in them all	
4	3		You kind of have to know how to sing and all, musicals	
4	5		Posh Ones	
4	2		You kind of have to be able to sing and dance	
4	1		You know you'd have to be a posh knob to be able ...	
5	2		I can sing lads, I've only	
5	3		Sure I can dance	
5	4		2 you can dance now all right	Referring to 2 currently on crutches
5	3		Like people who go to dance school and singing school they get in before...	Analysis of why some people are chosen
5	R1		Anyone else	
5	**R1**		**Anyone else?**	
5	3		They've an advantage upon us	
5	**R1**		**And how do you feel about that?**	
5	All		Don't care	
5	R1		Really don't care?	
5	3		I wouldn't be able to remember the lines	
5	1		Either would I	
5	5		I wouldn't either. I wouldn't be bothered	Rationalise by providing reasons why they couldn't take part. Self perpetuation of exclusion?

296

Appendices Six to Thirteen provide an example of a complete set of Data Matrices from one Focus Group (F1) for each of the Topic headings.

Appendix Thirteen – Political Involvement

F1 Political Involvement – Participation Decision Making

		Involvement of young people	
36	3	They want it, they ask for it, they don't get though	Reference to student council
37	R1	...We have the idea of you house, right, and adults wanted to set up the house, right, should young people be involved in setting it up?	Leading on from young peoples ideas
37	All	Yeah	
37	4	If it going to be for us like, we have to you know help our or something as well	
37	3	No, we don't even need that fancy or anything like, we're not asking for that much, just an old room, even just an old shed or something with a bench even anything like	Ownership appears more important that the quality of the facility
37		And if we wanted to decorate it, do it ourselves like, you know	
37	1	If we wanted to	
38	5	Like we could go around to houses and say, oh are you throwing out any old furniture and get that stuff like	Strategy to obtain equipment
38	3	Even a big bench	
38	5	So many people throw out good...	
38	1	The lad would do that, or something the lads would	Identified male roles
39	R1	...Do you think it's important that young people should be involved in developing services?	
39	2	No	
40	3	The old ones should kind of you know from their experience tell us before we go up	
40	1	We never heard much about it to get involved	Never been asked to participate before -
40	R1	Ok Ok	
40	3	So we wouldn't be bothered	
40	R1	....someone came along to you and said we're setting up anew service in the health board and we want young people to come up, would you go up? (referring to clinic)	
40	2	What would the service by like?	
40	R1	Well it all depends	

297

40	4	We'd go up to see what it is	
40	3	Well it would only be a doctor or something wouldn't it not?	Service associated with doctors can identify a role for themselves
40	3	We'd go up and be nosy and see what's happening	
40	3	Go up and be nosy and see what's happening	
40	3	And then if we interested we'd get involved	
		Tape Two –Side A	
10		I think you should start education like in 5th & 6th class, you know when the girls are getting their periods because some of them don't what that is like	
10		And they're afraid to say it to their family or whatever	
10		I think they should learn about when they're older 16 0r 17	
15	R1	Is there anything that you think people like myself and R" could be doing to encourage young people to take part in research?	Research method
15		Not really	
15		Ask them	
15		Just get talking to and..	
15		So if someone came around later on and started talking to you again, what would you think??	
15		No, we'd actually talk	
15		I think it's cool	
15	R1	We don't mind it really	
15		Hmmm	
15		Yeah, actually it is cool	

*Cross Reference Health Section /Sexual Health

Appendix Fourteen
Focus Group Interviews - Open-Ended Questions

These questions were standard questions used on cards that were turned upside down on a table. Participants chose the cards randomly so there was no specific order in the way questions were put to the focus groups. The interaction in the group led to the participants asking their questions of each other and providing insights into their perceptions of issues.

Tell us about alcohol

Tell us about substance use

Tell us about drugs

What do you consider as a young person, to risky or possibly harmful to you?

What would you consider to be risky or harmful to other young people?

What does healthy living mean to you?

What about employment for you as a young person?

What do you think would help a young person feeling down or suicidal?

What do you think about school?

Sexuality – Attitudes about gay/lesbian/bi-sexual people?

A) What services are available to you? B) What do you think of these services?

Culture/Ethnic Background –Tell us about an experience with someone from a different background?

Can you list health services that are available to you?

Have you as a young person, been asked for opinion about service before?

People have different types of families. What does your family mean to you?

What do you know about sexual health?

Sexuality- does it matter if you have a partner?

If you were developing a service for young people, what would be important?

What do you know about the justice system?

If you as a young person needed information about something where would you go?

Bibliography

Author's Surname	First Name	Title of Publication	Publishers	Country	Year
Adams, Montemayor & Gullotta	Gerald, Raymond & Thomas	Psychosocial Development During Adolescence-Progress in Developmental Contextualism	Sage Publications London	UK	1996
Aluffi-Pentini & Lorenz	Anna & Walter	Anti-racist Work with Young People European Experiences and Approaches	Russell House Publications	UK	1996
Ansbacher, H. and Ansbacher R. (eds.)	H & R	The Individual Psychology of Alfred Adler	Harper and Row New York	USA	1964
Arts Council, The		1999-2001 The Arts Plan	The Arts Council	Ireland	1999
Bacon & Associates	Peter	County Wexford: A Strategy for Economic Development	Wexford County Council	Ireland	1999
Bacon & Associates	Peter	County Wexford – A Rural Development Strategy	Wexford County Council	Ireland	2001
Barry	J	Healthcare of Irish Travellers Irish Doctor Journal January 1991		Ireland	1991
Beck, (trans. Ritter)	Ulrich	Risk Society - Towards a new Modernity	Sage Publications London		1992 (1986)
Bell & Bell	Nancy J & Robert W.	Adolescent Risk Taking	Sage Publications London	UK	1993
Benson	Jarlath	Working More Creatively With Groups	Routledge	UK	1997
Beresford & Croft	Peter & Suzy	Citizen Involvement A Practical Guide for Change	The Macmillian Press London	UK	1993
Blaxter, Hughes & Tight	L.,C. and M	How to Research	Open University Press	UK	1997
Bowers	Fergal	Suicide in Ireland	Irish Medical Organisation Dublin	Ireland	1994

Brendtro, Brokenleg & van Bockern	Larry & Martin & Steve	Reclaiming Youth at Risk Our Hope for the Future	National Education Service	USA	1990
Brown, (ed.)	L	The New Shorter Oxford Dictionary	Oxford University Press Oxford	UK	1993
Buckley, Skehill and O'Sullivan		Child Protection Practices in Ireland	Oak Tree Press, Dublin	Ireland	1997
Burgess	Paul	Youth and Community Work: Course Reader	University College Cork	Ireland	1996
Central Statistics Office			www.cso.ie		2001
Central Statistics Office		National Childcare Census Report for Wexford	www.cso.ie		2001
Co. Wexford Community Based Drugs Initiative		Responding to Substance Misuse in our Communities	Co. Wexford Community Based Drugs Initiative (CDBI), Wexford	Ireland	2002
Combat Poverty Agency		Child Poverty in Ireland	Combat Poverty Agency, Dublin		1999
Commission for the Status of People with Disabilities			www.wexfordcdb.ie		1996
Community Workers' Co-operative		Strengthening our Voice	CWC Galway	Ireland	2001
Community Workers Co-operative		Strategies for Social Partnership	CWC Galway	Ireland	2000
County Wexford Partnership		County Wexford Partnership Action Plan 2001-2006	Wexford	Ireland	2000
Dalrymple & Burke	Jane & Beverley	Anti-oppressive Practice Social Care and the Law	Open University Press Buckinghamshire	UK	1998
Department of Education and Science		Statistical Report 1998/99	Stationary Office, Government Publications Dublin	Ireland	2000

Department of Social, Community and Family Affairs	Strengthening Families for Life - Final Report of Family Commission	Stationary Office, Government Publications, Dublin	Ireland	1998
Department of Education & Science	Bruton Report A Policy for Youth and Sport	The Stationery Office - Government Publications	Ireland	1977
Department of Education and Science	Department of Education and Science Annual Report 1998/9	www.wexfordcdb.ie/education training .html	Ireland	1998/9
Department of Education and Science	Guidelines on Traveller Education in Primary Schools	The Stationery Office Government Publications Dublin	Ireland	2002
Department of Health and Children	Youth as a Resource Promoting the health of young people at risk	Stationary Office, Government Publications Dublin	Ireland	1999
Department of Health and Children	Children First National Guidelines for the Protection and Welfare of Children	The Stationery Office Government Publications Dublin	Ireland	1999
Department of Health and Children	The Child Care Act	Stationary Office, Government Publications Dublin	Ireland	1991
Department of Health and Children	Youth Homeless Strategy	Stationary Office, Government Publications Dublin	Ireland	2001
Department of Health and Children	Youth Homelessness Strategy	Stationary Office, Government Publications Dublin	Ireland	2001
Department of Justice	Garda Commissioners Report	Stationary Office, Government Publications Dublin	Ireland	2000
Department of Justice	Probation and Welfare Service Report 2001	Stationary Office, Government Publications Dublin	Ireland	2001
Department of Social, Community and Family Affairs		www.wexfordcdb.ie		2000

Department of Social, Community and Family Affairs		Pensions Services Office	www.solo.ie/info/309 9.html		2000
Department of Social, Community and Family Affairs		National Anti-poverty Strategy (Green Paper)	Stationary Office, Government Publications Dublin	Ireland	1997
Department of Social, Community and Family Affairs		Annual Statistics Report	Stationary Office, Government Publications Dublin	Ireland	2001
Department of the Environment		Annual Housing Statistic Bulletin	The Stationery Office Government Publications Dublin	Ireland	2001
Department of Tourism, Sport and Recreation		Building on Experience National Drugs Strategy 2001 - 2006	The Stationery Office Government Publications Dublin	Ireland	2001
Drucker	Peter	The Next Society – A Survey of the Near Future	The Economist (Nov 3rd- 9th, 2001) London	UK	2001
Drudy & Lynch	Sheelagh & Kathleen	Schools and Society in Ireland	Gill & Macmillan Ltd	Ireland	1993
E.F.A.		Assessment Country Reports- Ireland	www.2unesco.org/wef/countryreports/ireland/contents/html		2000
EMCDDA		Annual Report on the State of Drugs Problem in the E.U.	www.emcdda.org/infopoint/publications/annreps.html		1998
Erikson	Erik	Childhood and Society	Penguin, Middlesex		1963 (1950)
Erikson	Erik	Identity: Youth and Crisis	Norton, New York	USA	1968
ESRI for Department of Health and Children		Smoking and Drinking among Young People in Ireland	Stationary Office, Government Publications Dublin	Ireland	1996

Eurostat		Statistics in Focus : Population and Social Conditions	Eurostat, Luxembourg	EU	1997
Falk and Falk	G & G	Ageism, the Aged and Aging in America : On Being Old in an Aging Society	Charles Thomas, Illinois	USA	1995
Ferns Diocesan Youth Service		Rural Youth Work in Co. Wexford	Co. Wexford Youth Forum	Ireland	1999
Forkan	Cormac	Rural Youth Work in County Wexford	Ferns Diocesan Youth Service in collaboration with Foroige and Macra na Feirme	Ireland	1999
Forkan	Cormac	Needs, Concerns and Social Exclusion The Millennium and Beyond. The results of a survey of needs of young people aged 10-18 in the New Ross Area	New Ross Youth and Community Forum in association with the Centre for Social care Research Waterford Institute of Technology	Ireland	2001
Fromm	Erich	The Fear of Freedom	Routledge and Kegan Paul, London	UK	1960
Galbraith	J.K.	The Culture of Contentment	Houghton Mifflin, New York	USA	1992
Garratt, Roche & Tucker	Daren, Jeremy & Stanley	Changing Experiences of Youth	Sage Publications in association with The Open University	UK	1997
Gay HIV Strategies and Nexus Research Co-operative		Education Lesbian and Gay Students- Developing Equal Opportunities	Gay HIV Strategies	Ireland	1996
Gay	Peter, (ed.)	The Freud Reader	Random House, London	UK	1995
Gibbs	Anita	Focus Groups Social Research Update Issue Nineteen March 1997	Department of Social Medicine Bristol University	UK	1997

Giddens	Anthony	The Consequences of Modernity	Stanford University Press, California	USA	1990
Gilligan, R. in Horwarth J. (ed.) *The Child's World* Reader		Promoting Positive Outcomes for Children in Need : the Assessment of Protective Factors	University of Sheffield	UK	2001
Gordon	Jack	Ecological Perspectives in Assessing Children and Families in in The Child's World Reader Horwarth J. (ed.)	University of Sheffield	UK	2001
Hall & Jefferson	Stuart & Tony	Resistance through Rituals Youth Subcultures in Post-War Britain	Routledge	UK	1991
Hill	J.P.	Some Perspectives on Adolescence in American Society	U.S. Dept of Health, Education and Welfare		1973
Hogan & Gilligan	Diane & Robbie	Researching Children's Experiences: Qualitative Approaches- Proceedings of Conference,27th May 1997	The Children's Research Centre, University Dublin, Trinity College	Ireland	1997
Hollin	Cormac	Just a Phase? Essays of Adolescence	Youth Clubs UK Publications Leicester	UK	1988
Howard and Johnson	Sue & Bruce	Tracking Student Resilience *(AARE Conference, Adelaide)*	University of South Australia	Australia	1998
Hurley & Treacy	Louise & David	Models of Youth Work - A Sociological Framework	Irish Youth Work Centre	Ireland	1993
Irish Government		Irish Social Service Inspectorate Report	Stationery Office Government Publications Dublin	Ireland	2001
Irish Government		Ireland's National Drugs Strategy 2001 - 2008	The Stationery Office - Government Publications	Ireland	2001
Irish Government		The National Children's Strategy - Our Children - Their Lives	The Stationery Office - Government Publications	Ireland	2000

Irish Government		O'Sullivan Committee (1980) The Development of Youth Work Services in Ireland.	The Stationery Office - Government Publications	Ireland	1980
Irish Government		Costello Committee Report The National Youth Policy Committee Final Report	The Stationery Office - Government Publications	Ireland	1980
Jeffs & Smith	Tony & Mark	Youth Work	Macmillan Press Ltd	UK	1987
Jenkinson	Hilary	History of Youth Work in Youth and Community Course Reader Burgess P (ed)	University College Cork	Ireland	1996
Jenkinson	Hilary	"Youth Work in Ireland: The Struggle for Identity" Journal of Applied Social Studies Vol 2 2000 in McElwee N (ed)		Ireland	2000
Kelleher & Cahill		Trends in Treated Drug Mis-Use in the S.E.H.B. area 1996-2000 (Occasional Paper drug mis-use Research Division Health Research Board)	South East Health Board Kilkenny	Ireland	2000
Kellmer Pringle	Mia	The Needs of Children (3rd Edition)	Routledge	UK	1993
Lutz	F	Focus Group Research in American Politics	www.pollingreport.com/focus.html		1994
Mac Giolla Bhain	Phil	The Flight of the Earls -Why more and more young Irishmen are killing themselves	Magill Magazine November 2001	Ireland	2001
Mark	Raymond	Research Made Simple A Handbook for Social Workers	Sage Publications Londong		1996
Mayock	Paula	Chooser or Losers? Influences on Young People's Choices about Drugs in Inner-City Dublin	The Children's Research Centre, University Dublin, Trinity College	Ireland	2000
McElwee	C.N.	Children At Risk	StreetSmart Press, Waterford	Ireland	1996

McElwee	C.N.	Removing the label of 'at risk' and moving towards an understanding of high –promise children and youth in a resiliency context	Paper to International Forum for Child Welfare, Limerick	Ireland	31st August 2001
McGee, Garavan, de Barra, Byrne, Conroy		The SAVI Report - Sexual Abuse and Violence in Ireland	The Dublin Rape Crisis Centre/The Liffey Press		2002
McMahon, Mortell & Jenkinson	Sinead, Phil & Hilary	Responding to Early School Leaving in the Wexford Area	Wexford Area Partnership Wexford	Ireland	1998
Miles & Huberman	Matthew B & A. Michael	Qualitative Data Analysis (2nd Edition)	Sage Publications	UK	1994
Monaghan, Bloor, Dobash and Dobash		Drug-Taking, 'Risk Boundaries' and Social Identity: Bodybuilders Talk about Ephidrine and Nubain	Sociological Research online,		2000
Muncie & McLaughlin	John & Eugene	The Problem of Crime	Sage Publications in association with The Open University	UK	1996
Murphy	Brian	Support for the Educationally and Socially Disadvantaged - An Introductory Guide to Government Funded Initiatives in Ireland	Education Department, University College Cork	Ireland	2000
National Anti-Poverty Strategy		Sharing in Progress	Stationary Office, Government Publications Dublin	Ireland	1997
National Conjoint Child Health Committee		Get Connected – Developing an Adolescent Friendly Health Service	National Conjoint Child Health Committee	Ireland	2000
National Economic and Social Council		Early School Leavers and Youth Unemployment	Stationary Office, Government Publications Dublin	Ireland	1997
National Economic and Social Forum		Rural Renewal – Combating Social Exclusion	Stationary Office, Government Publications Dublin	Ireland	1997
National Economic and Social Forum		Early School Leavers Forum Report No. 24	Stationary Office, Government Publications Dublin		2002

National Roads Authority		Young Drivers Accident 2000 Report	Stationary Office, Dublin		2001
National Traveller Accommodation Consultative Committee Report			www.paveepoint.ie/fs-distribution.html		1999
National Youth Council of Ireland		The Plunder Years	National Youth Council of Ireland	Ireland	2001
Nexus Research Co-operative		Report on Travellers' Needs in the Wexford Area	Wexford Area Partnership	Ireland	1997
Nolan		Child Poverty In Ireland	Combat Poverty Agency in association with Oak Tree Press Dublin	Ireland	2000
NUI Galway for Dept. of Health and Children		Health Behaviour of School Children	Stationary Office, Dublin		1999
O'Leary	Eileen	Taking The Initiative – Promoting Young People's Involvement in Public Decision Making in Ireland	National Youth Council of Ireland, Dublin in association with The Carnegie United Kingdom Trust	Ireland	2001
O'Dwyer	Anne	"In From the Cold" Towards a Strategy for Rural Youth Work in Kerry Diocese	Kerry Diocesan Youth Service	Ireland	2001
Padgett	Deborah	Qualitative Methods in Social Work Research	Sage Publications London		1998
Prendiville	Patricia	Developing Facilitation Skills – A Handbook for Group Facilitators	Combat Poverty Agency Islandbridge Dublin 8	Ireland	1995
Rak & Patterson	Carl F & Lewis E	Promoting Resilience in At-Risk Children - Journal of Counselling and Development March-April 1996 Vole 74 Issue 4	EBSCO Publishing		1996
Research Council of Norway		The National Committee for research ethics in the social sciences and the humanities	http://www.etikkom.no/NESH/eretn.html		

Roche & Tucker (ed)	Jeremy & Stanley	Youth in Society	Sage Publications in association with The Open University	UK	1997
Rogers	Alan	Starting Out in Detached Work	Youth Clubs UK Publications	UK	1981
Senderowitz,	J	Involving Youth in Reproductive Health Projects	Focus on Young Adults, Washington	USA	1998
Shanahan	Catherine	Irish Teen Birth Rate Tenth Highest Irish Examiner May 31st 2002	Irish Examiner Cork	Ireland	2002
Sheridan, K		Punch Drunk - Fear on the Streets 6th April 2002	Irish Times Dublin		2002
SIPTU		Submission to Southern and Eastern Regional Assembly "Sub-regional Disparities" – the Needs and Problems of Specific Areas	SIPTU		2001
South Eastern Health Board		Addiction Service 2000 (Statistics)	www.wexfordcdb.ie		2000
South Eastern Health Board		South Eastern Health Board Annual Report 1999	SEHB Kilkenny	Ireland	1999
South Eastern Health Board		South Eastern Health Board Annual Report 2000	SEHB Kilkenny	Ireland	2000
South Eastern Health Board		Annual Review of Child Care and Family Support Services	SEHB Kilkenny	Ireland	1998
South Eastern Health Board		Our Children's Health	SEHB, Kilkenny	Ireland	1998
Staunton	Dennis	Models of Youth Work in Burgess	University College Cork	Ireland	1996

Strasburger	Victor C	Adolescents and the Media - Medical and Psychological Impact	Sage Publications	UK	1995
Task Force on the Traveller Community		Task Force Report on the Traveller Community	Brunswick Press Dublin	Ireland	1995
Thomas and O'Kane	Nigel and Claire	The Ethics of Participatory Research with Children Children and Society Volume 12 1998 International Centre for Childhood Studies University of Wales Swansea	John Wileys & Sons New York	USA	1998
United Nations		Convention on the Rights of The Child	UN, New York	USA	1990
van der Ploeg & Scholte	Jan & Evert	Homeless Youth	Sage Publications London	UK	1997
Walberg, Reyes & Weissberg (eds)	Herbert J., Olga and Roger P.	Children and Youth Interdisciplinary Perspectives	Sage Publications London	UK	1997
Wales Youth Agency		Guidelines and Information Pack on Detached and Outreach Youth Work	http://way.newi.ac.uk/ENGLISH/Publicatons/04wemg/html		
Wexford Area Partnership		Responding to Early School Leaving in the Wexford Area	Wexford Area Partnership Wexford	Ireland	1998
Wexford Area Partnership		Social Inclusion Plan for Wexford Area 2000- 2004	Wexford Area Partnership Wexford	Ireland	2000
Wexford Area Partnership		Traveller Accommodation Programme	Wexford Area Partnership Wexford	Ireland	2000
Wexford Community Development Board		Wexford Community Development Board Quality of life task group discussion paper -health	www.wexfordcdb.ie/quality_life_report.html		2000
Yawney,	David	Resiliency – A Strategy for Survival of Childhood Trauma BCIFV Newsletter	British Columbia Canada	Canada	1999